D0948911

BRADFORD
COLLEGE
LIBRARY

The American Connection

This book is dedicated to

Nadia,
Yalena and Stephan

The American Connection

The Influence of United States
Business on South Africa

Vic Razis

St. Martin's Press, New York

338. 88
R278a

© Vic Razis 1986

All rights reserved. For information, write:
Scholarly & Reference Division,
St. Martin's Press, Inc., 175 Fifth Avenue, New York, NY 10010

First published in the United States of America in 1986

Printed in Great Britain

ISBN 0–312–02203–4

Library of Congress Cataloguing-in-Publication Data

Razis, Vincent Victor
    The American Connection.

    Bibliography: p.
    Includes index.

    1. Corporations, American——South Africa
    2. Investments, American——South Africa. 3. South Africa——
    Foreign relations——United States. 4. United States——Foreign
    relations——South Africa. I. Title.
    HD2922.R39   1986   338.8'8973'068   85-25026
    ISBN 0–312–02203–4

BRADFORD COLLEGE

JAN 1 8 1988
Samson   31.50
LIBRARY

OCLC 12665879

Contents

List of figures and tables

Figures

Tables

1 Introduction

The key questions

How does American business in South Africa affect business, the economy and the larger polity? This is the core question tackled in this book. Although the central concern is business, it is immediately apparent that business matters cannot be examined adequately in isolation from larger questions of economics and politics. So, of the myriad of networks (from state treaties and trade, to tourism and landing rights) that connect the two abstract notions of 'America' and 'South Africa', this work is concerned primarily with the effects of the American multinational corporations on South Africa; but it is also concerned with related issues such as American policy towards South Africa, trade, bank loans, and the racial and cultural impact of the American presence. When some of the major strands in the web making up the relationship between the two countries are analysed together, an answer may begin to be formulated to the larger question: what does the American connection mean for South Africa?

A number of important points about this book need to be made in this introductory chapter. Firstly, the fact that the argument favours increased foreign investment and general economic involvement rather than disinvestment and economic sanctions, certainly does not imply acceptance of the apartheid state. On the contrary, it is argued that greater economic involvement by South Africa's major trading partners is the best way to break the shackles of apartheid and build a better post–apartheid society, through sustained economic growth. Nevertheless, it is true that privileged elites, like the Whites in South Africa, rarely give up their privileges without some pressure, so the threat and actuality of economic sanctions may be productive up to a point. Beyond that point, which of course is exceptionally difficult to determine, the implementation of sanctions may result in the halting of real development in Southern Africa for decades to come, so that whatever political victories are gained will be hollow.

This book, then, is less concerned with, for example, media events about South Africa in the world, sensational headlines about this or that sanctions bill, or the posturings of politicians on the South African issue, and more concerned with the larger picture and the long term. Although current political, financial, and other factors affecting South Africa may fluctuate alarmingly, the arguments in this book in favour of continued foreign economic involvement in South Africa are definitely valid over the long run. The powerful need for future economic development remains, whatever else happens politically and socially to the troubled society of South Africa.

The long–term problems

It cannot be overstressed that even when apartheid is removed, the real and massive problems of economic development and the elimination of poverty will remain. And for tackling these under-lying problems economic disengagement is a crazy strategy to pursue. Any worthwhile future political system, established at great human cost through, for example, internal unrest and economic sanctions, may face the additional tragedy of foundering in the quicksands of a ruined economic base. South Africa might then be nominally politically 'free', and forgotten by the pro-ponents of disinvestment who will have won an easy 'moral' victory, but the country might become yet another poor, stagnant state on the African continent. The real challenges which all South Africans face in the next fifty years are high population growth, redistribution of income, housing, feeding, schooling (of the kind which will equip the burgeoning population to be productive and compete effectively with the growing high–tech economies), medical care, jobs, infrastructure, agriculture, adequate water supplies and so forth — and to tackle these effectively the country needs the diametric opposite of disinvestment.

Those individuals and groups who do not want to win a superficial, symbolic victory, but wish to help solve the real long–term problems of South Africa and the surrounding regions should pour billions of dollars into the economy, not necessarily as aid, but as *investment* in economic growth through trade, loans, technol-ogy, know–how and direct investment. This approach would result in the speedier demise of apartheid, through the positive exigencies of massive modernization and economic growth, than would be achieved through negative sanctions, and would, moreover, put something of real value in its place: a peaceful and prosperous South Africa in which the Blacks have the concrete means (education, skills, income) to achieve social and political equality in fact, and not just in name.

South Africa's people are suffering the agonies of a fragmented society without consensus, a society living with the spectre of civil war. So in truth, the move away from a social–engineering, ideologically–driven, authoritarian state, and away from the apartheid economy, towards a real democracy and liberal economy needs to be swift, or Brecht's words in the play St. Joan will become increasingly and tragically applicable to South Africa:

> For there is a gulf between top and bottom, wider
> Than between Mount Himalaya and the sea
> And what goes on above
> is not found out below
> Or what happens below, above
> And there are two languages, above and below
> And two standards for measuring
> And that which wears a human face no longer knows itself.
>
> But those who are down below are kept below
> So that the ones above may stay up there
> And the lowness of those above is measureless
> And even if they improve that would be
> No help, because the system they have made
> Is unique: exploitation
> And disorder, bestial and therefore
> Incomprehensible.
>
> Only force helps where force rules,
> And only men help where men are.

This book suggests that, far better than fostering the bitterness which sees *force* as the only solution, would be the encouragement of hope engendered by rapid evolution towards equal citizenship in a just society in South Africa — but that evolution requires enormous investment in South Africa to pay for the structural changes which are required. Yet the pro–sanctions lobby is strong and one needs to confront the case of those advocating economic pressures on South Africa. Before doing so brief definitions of terms like 'disinvestment' and 'divestment' are necessary.

These terms are generally used somewhat loosely in the press and by politicians, and by proponents and opponents of economic disengagement from South Africa. Sometimes the same word is used with different meanings. For the purposes of this book, however, *disinvestment* will be defined as the act of removing from South Africa direct investment (e.g. factories, machinery), or non-direct investment (e.g. shares in South African companies), or bank loans, or preventing further such investment or loans. *Divestment* will be defined as shedding stocks and shares, or otherwise refusing to do business with any American firm which itself does business with South Africa in any way whatsoever (e.g. through trade, loans, know–how). Disinvestment might be characterized as primary economic sanctions, whereas divestment might be described as a secondary — though no less powerful, probably even more so — form of economic boycott.

The proponents of economic pressure

There are at least three discernible strands of thought among the advocates of economic pressure.

In the first place, there are those who view actual physical disinvestment as a useful tactic, somewhat analogous to a strike tactic. According to this view, disinvestment, though admittedly a dangerous policy to advocate over the long term, may in the short term force concessions from the government, at which point there can be a return to more normal business practices — in the same way that a strike forces concessions from management, and then the business carries on with its normal functions. Although the democratic 'bona fides' of some advocates of this course on both sides of the Atlantic are not in question, the use of this powerful weapon is perilous, not only because of its immediate consequences on growth, employment, productivity and business confidence, but also because of the unintended consequences. The economic consequences are undoubtedly bad, and may or may not lead to a determinate outcome as envisaged, i.e. democratic concessions by the White ruling elite. The unintended consequences may be worse, not only throwing the country into a downward economic spiral, but also into social and political turmoil. Proponents of disinvestment who hold these views are generally anti–apartheid and abhor discrimination on grounds of race so it is possible that they would withdraw economic pressure in the event of the abolition of racial discrimination. There would be no need for sanctions against a democratic, non–racial, class–differentiated society which approximated to the structure of some Western democracies.

The second strand of thinking behind the advocacy of disinvestment does not view it as a powerful (albeit dangerous and distasteful) tactic to bring about democratic concessions, but as a weapon with which to attack both South African and international capitalism, the ultimate aim being the establishment of socialist or communist states wherever possible. A liberal democratic South Africa, with a capitalist or even welfare capitalist economy would not satisfy these proponents of disinvestment: only a post–revolutionary, Afro–Marxist Azania would do that. Clearly, this pro–disinvestment group would not be satisfied with the removal of apartheid and the establishment of some sort of democratic free enterprise state.

A third strand of thinking seems to be that the very threat of disinvestment and divestment, and the heated debates which the threat engenders, serves a sufficient purpose in highlighting the iniquities of the apartheid state, in making people think about South Africa, and in gaining wide publicity for anti–apartheid coalitions. This tactic, if tactic it is, has had considerable success in publicizing the South African issue in the United States. Calls for disinvestment, Bishop Tutu's Nobel Prize (and his high–profile advocacy of economic pressure), publicity–gaining arrests at South African embassies in American cities, the serious Black uprising in South Africa, the State of Emergency, the exceptional world–wide media coverage of unrest events and the financial problems of South Africa, all have contributed to a marked increase in awareness of South Africa amongst a wider public in a relatively short space of time. Again, this approach (sanctions threats) to pressurizing official South Africa is subject to the laws of un-intended consequences.

This third group comprises a number of thoughtful individuals in both South Africa and the United States who seem to want the pressure for change that comes from the disinvestment campaign, but *without* the disinvestment itself. Despite the dangers, that is, the possible unintended consequences of this course of action, the continuing unrest in South Africa has enormously strengthened the case of these advocates of economic pressure. This third group, too, might well be willing to relinquish economic pressure if apartheid were removed and there was a genuine and sustained effort to bring about common South African citizenship in a more just, equal opportunity society.

This analysis suggests that South Africa *could* satisfy at least two of the three groups, that is, the democratic and anti-racial proponents of disinvestment/divestment (and become an accepted member of the Western community of nations), through the removal of statutory, legislated barriers between South African citizens. These groups probably form the majority of decent, ordinary Americans who are currently advocating economic pressure. There is another group, probably a smaller one, which would not be satisfied with a democratic, free enterprise South Africa, but only with an Afrosocialist state.

The inference is that South Africa could and should meet the requirements of the first (democratic capitalist) grouping — *not* to appease foreign pressure but because it is right for South Africa itself (and Western acceptance, trade and investment is an important bonus), while understanding that there are some groupings which will never be satisfied by anything less than revolutionary upheaval and the emergence from the ashes of a pure Marxist phoenix. The proponents of this latter approach have yet to make a convincing case that South Africa will be a better society for all its citizens after such a revolution. Indeed, the history of the twentieth century makes such a case difficult to construct.

The nub of the issue is whether all South Africans should endure further economic privation and probably social and political upheaval, because of a strategy which is based on the assumption that the apartheid state is amenable to change through economic pressure and ultimate isolation. Many analysts agree that disinvestment and divestment are amongst the most serious issues facing South Africa in the immediate future. This book examines some of the evidence on the value of foreign business involvement in South Africa, using American business as an example, and therefore makes it easier to adopt a considered viewpoint on economic sanctions. Admittedly, this book is informed by a strong feeling for the fragility of human freedom; and coloured by the vision of the apparently irretrievable poverty of many parts of Africa, with rapidly rising populations, large inefficient states and little industrial or agricultural productivity. With the burden of these perceptions though, it seems inhumane folly and morally questionable to advocate any course of action which either increases violence or damages the productive capacity of the economy. A victory won by political violence, and resulting in a destroyed economy ruled over — in all probability — by a new entrenched elite would be a sad, Pyrrhic victory for South Africa.

The role of business

The role of business is crucial to the discussion in this book. Foreign multinationals are an integral and important part of the local South African business community, so they are included in arguments about the functions of business in the future of the country. Business activity in South Africa, including that which results from foreign trade, bank loans, portfolio and direct investment does have a primary and utterly important responsibility — and that is to use the scarce resources of a developing country efficiently, and to maximize economic growth to pay for all the structural changes that have become urgent. However, because the ground rules governing the political economy have not yet been established to everyone's satisfaction (as in, say, the United States), business in South Africa might have to go beyond its immediate concerns, at least *temporarily*, to help establish the future rules of the game in which it wishes to continue to play. South African businessmen, for example, are talking to the banned African National Congress about South Africa's future, an activity which does not fall within the ambit of normal business concerns — but which makes some sense in terms of all South Africans establishing ground rules for the future. In September 1985 ten American companies involved in South Africa formed the US Corporate Council on South Africa to lobby Pretoria to move more rapidly towards reform.

This book suggests that South Africa's commercial, industrial and agricultural productivity should be encouraged and increased for the benefit of all South Africans — and perhaps one day for the benefit of sub–Saharan Africa. Although South Africa generates most of its capital requirements internally, foreign investment is an essential addition because so much capital is needed to develop the country, particularly now that gold is no longer providing economic windfalls to counter–balance political disasters. Foreign investment should be encouraged, because economic development is as important to Buthelezi's South Africa and to Mandela's South Africa as to Botha's South Africa. South Africa needs now to be *developed* towards democracy by the world community, not isolated and destroyed by civil war.

If American business remains fully involved in South Africa, what further can it do positively? South Africa presents American business with a paradox: in order to make South Africa safe for business in the future, American corporations have to play a role that seems out of character and that would not be required of business in the United States itself. And that role is one of social and political responsibility which goes well beyond the bounds of normal business considerations. The nub of the argument is that unusual situations call for unusual responses: the business community, in which the foreign multinationals play an important part, is probably best–placed to break the apartheid controls on the South African political economy, and to free the nation's potential. Business has achieved much already, though this is not conceded by its critics; but admittedly there is a long way to go.

Apart from the all–important effects of economic growth, to which business makes the greatest contribution, what has business done directly? A quarter of a century ago, during the state of emergency after Sharpeville, the major business organizations, the Associated Chambers of Commerce, the Afrikaanse Handelsinstituut, the Chamber of Mines, the Federated Chamber of Industries, the Steel and Engineering Industries Federation and prominent businessmen argued that Blacks had genuine grievances which should be addressed, preferably by consultation; that urban Blacks should be given certain rights and that barriers should be removed so that they could make the maximum contribution to a single unified economy; that the pass laws and influx control be reviewed; that business confidence was being undermined; and that the country's future depended to some extent on economic links with other countries. Individually and collectively, they petitioned the government of the day. Critics of business argue correctly that as memories of Sharpeville faded, so too did the urgency with which business had lobbied government during the emergency.

Sixteen years later during the crisis at Soweto, the same arguments were repeated. This time some sections of business took more concrete steps themselves, such as eliminating racial discrimination in their own firms and establishing the Urban Foundation, as well as lobbying the government. Within a couple of years events had taken place which would have been unthinkable under Prime Minister Vorster: the new Prime Minister met with business at the Carlton, labour reforms were initiated that brought Blacks into the mainstream for the first time in a century, and there were moves to free the economy from the constraints of the ideological blueprint of apartheid.

Business pressure led to the removal of job reservation, to stepped-up training and education, to the 99-year leasehold for Blacks, to increased access by Blacks to business activities, to the review of the pass laws and influx control, and to greater efforts towards Black housing. Clearly, these measures make sense from a business point of view and might owe as much to enlightened self-interest as to altruism — but that is a perfectly acceptable reason for doing the correct thing. Undoubtedly, they do not go far enough, and this book argues strongly that business has both the power and the responsibility to change South Africa away from apartheid before there is another major rebellion in the country. After all, history suggests that both the frequency and the amplitude of Black rebellion will increase in future unless fundamental grievances are removed and consensus achieved. The time between Sharpeville 1960 and Soweto was sixteen years. The time span between Soweto 1976 and the start of the 1984–5 troubles was eight years. Extrapolating from this, it seems that business must act decisively now if there is not to be another major Black uprising in about 1990.

Business is well placed to transform society away from apartheid. For example, through internal training, education and promotion policies, business firms can help to overcome the sociological and psychological effects on Blacks and Whites of a generation of apartheid amongst their employees. As business leaders point out, the historical segragationist culture cannot be changed overnight, but the biggest employer of people — the business community — can lead the way in operating harmonious multiracial organizations. Business has strongly supported common South African citizenship for all, the removal of influx control and group areas, and the opening up of central business districts to everyone who wants to do business there. The larger businesses, at least, have shown a remarkable degree of corporate social and political responsibility, driven partly by business reasons — such as the need for skilled manpower and managers in the country — and partly by the perception that the stability and peace on which business thrives requires an active input from business itself if it is ever to come about.

In all of this foreign multinationals have played an important part. In the research done for this book, almost all South African firms accepted that the American companies, and the application of the Sullivan code by many of them, at least helped to create a climate in which both business and government reforms could take place; some indigenous firms admit that the foreign codes led them to establish their internal, South African, company codes, and to organize and improve their own company policies. The American companies, particularly, have been leaders in the educational area. American Sullivan signatory companies have spent over $100 million on health, education, community development, training and housing since 1978. They are working on projects which aim at achieving long term results in these fields. Black entrepreneurship is being encouraged.

What are the likely consequences if American firms are forced to pull out of South Africa? The problem is that American dis-investment might have consequences which are unforeseeable and potentially far-reaching (such as acting as encouragement to violent uprising in South Africa or causing other foreign investors to withdraw), as well as more obvious and limited ones. The foreseeable ones are that South Africa would lose even more of the $15 billion that was invested (in bank loans, American-owned shares on the Johannesburg Stock Exchange and direct invest-ment), which would undoubtedly affect economic growth and employment, and damage business confidence in the country. In the short run, South Africa would lose the finance, managerial skills, technology and expertise of the American companies, as well as their social responsibility approach and the worthwhile projects which they are undertaking.

These are all serious effects, but it is doubtful whether they could, by themselves, cause the overthrow of apartheid. Since the numbers of people employed and the proportion of GNP generated by American firms is relatively small, the loss could probably be absorbed. South African capital could take over American sub-sidiaries: the process of local buying of shares in American companies has been going on for a while. Most of the management is South African. In addition, the Europeans, Japanese, Koreans, Taiwanese and others might be willing to take over former American investments which might again in the future yield high returns by world standards, if there is real reform and consequent stability in South Africa.

Business cannot avoid becoming politicized in South Africa. Inevitably, the Reverend Sullivan, for example, has reached the point of asking that American corporations should support political change: but the underlying reality is that it is the South African situation that requires it, not the dictates of one man's conscience or the manifold and mounting pressures for economic disengagement.

Business, both domestic and foreign, is now working on changing the system in two ways. One is direct, both by lobbying for the repeal of the laws that prevent the realization of a genuine liberal economy and by having exemplary labour relations, arranging training and education schemes, providing housing and transportation for their own workforce. The other way is indirectly, by contributing as much as possible to the economic growth that is essential to lift the country's poor majority into a position which enables them to aspire to social and political equality. The way to pay for the requisite investment in human capital is to allow business to build a successful economy in South Africa, unfettered by uneconomic ideological blueprints.

In addition to the concrete contributions of foreign business that would be lost in the event of disinvestment, South Africa would lose its strongest links to the world's largest democracy, and to the values which are upheld by that society. It is in the United States that the ideas of human freedom and economic freedom working together come to their greatest fruition, so the American connection is psychologically important for South Africa.

This book suggests that the domestic and foreign business sector is able to play the most important role in both the immediate task — the removal of apartheid — and also the long-term task, that of developing South Africa, but American and other foreign businesses cannot assist if they are not physically present. South African business and the foreign corporations have the power and, it is argued here, the responsibility to attempt tasks which are not normally required of business in First World countries and which business executives may not like performing. Nevertheless, they are tasks well–worth tackling, both for the long–term self–interest of business itself, and for the welfare of the country.

American and other foreign business links

Although this book tends to focus on those highly visible symbols of American business involvement, the multinational corporations which invest directly, there are of course other — and enormously important — business links between the two countries. The most vital link is trade : South Africa is 50–60 per cent an open economy. When more than half of the nation's GNP is earned each year through trade with our major partners in the world, it is clear that South Africa is very vulnerable to trade boycotts. Like Japan, South Africa has to export to grow and prosper. Another big link is bank loans : indeed, it was the refusal of American banks to roll over short–term debts that precipitated the South African moratorium on capital repayments between September and December 1985, to allow time for rescheduling. Americans have also been the biggest foreign buyers of shares (particularly gold shares) on the Johannesburg Stock Exchange. Some American companies have only minority holdings in South African operations, while other American companies do business through licencees, franchisees, sales representatives, distributors and professional partnerships. All of these business links, taken together, form the main substance of the American connection between the United States and South Africa.

It is important to state in this chapter that all the arguments which are made using American — South African business links as concrete examples, apply equally strongly to British, German, French, Japanese or any other international business links with South Africa. Whatever happens to American economic links in particular, the arguments in this book still hold good generally for example, for British economic ties with South Africa — even more so, perhaps, since Britain has a much greater economic stake, relatively and absolutely, in South Africa than does the United States. Indeed, the case made here may have a much wider applicability to the question of Western economic involvement in other developing countries in Africa and elsewhere.

The situation in 1985

I. South Africa

During talks held on the subject of investment in South Africa with businessmen, bankers and officials in New York, Washington and London in the summer of 1985, the most commonly-heard refrain was: 'it is what happens *in* South Africa which will largely determine what actions are taken here'. What is happening within South Africa? The current crisis is of greater magnitude than those of 1960 or 1976. A State of Emergency is in force in many magisterial districts. The Black uprising against apartheid seems more widespread and better organized than previous ones. But it is not that simple : just about any division between human beings that one cares to think of — between Black and White and Coloured and Indian, and tribe and tribe, and capitalist, liberal, communist, between right-wing Whites and the Government, between the Government and the ANC, between the Zulu Inkatha and the hotchpotch United Democratic Front and the ANC, between 'puppet' leaders and 'real' leaders, between the poor and the rich, between Church and State, those for and against the 'system' — all have surfaced in bitterness and violent dispute. A situation of low-level civil war and sporadic violence lends itself to brutality on all sides, and the world has watched on television and read about Blacks burning a Black woman, police and army (allegedly) beating up demonstrators with unnecessary force, townships burning, Zulus killing Indians, Coloureds attacking a White suburb to be repulsed by gunfire, the State closing down schools and reacting to threats everywhere with further suppression — in a spiralling circle of violent confrontation.

And yet there is another South Africa, one in which life perforce goes on, in which there is goodwill and in which honest and courageous people on all sides and of all types are trying to build bridges to each other and to secure the future. Slabbert and Buthelezi, Relly and Tambo, State and Church, are talking to find some way out of the mess.

From the Nationalist Government's point of view, there have been reforms in the past few years. Black trade unionism has been recognized and is in operation. All colour discrimination has been removed from industrial legislation (in relation, for example, to job reservation and minimum differential wages) and from tax legislation. The political constitution now includes Coloureds and Indians to the extent that there is a multiracial coalition government. Sexual relations and marriage are permitted across 'colour' lines; and so is the activity of individual political parties. Central business districts have been opened to all. There is no political interference in sport. Ninety–nine–year property leaseholds for Blacks are now available throughout the country, freehold rights have been promised. Blacks have had a foothold in government since 1983 in the form of their own town councils with the same powers as their White counterparts, and the government has pledged, through the agency of cabinet committees and a negotiating forum, to extend this process. The State President has supported the idea of common citizenship in a United South Africa and a 'universal franchise' — but it is not clear what structures are envisaged to give these ideas concrete form. Blacks are being included in the President's Council. Forced removals have been suspended and the dismantling of the pass law system promised. More reforms, according to the Government, are on the way.

The leader of the opposition has said that the announcement on Black citizenship, particularly, signalled the end of the apartheid dream. Many critics, both inside and outside the country, dismiss these changes as cosmetic. Certainly it is not yet clear whether the citizenship move has real political significance in the sense of paving the way for negotiation on Black political rights, and at least one minister has denied such political significance.

No one really knows the strength of the right–wing Whites, nor how well represented they are in the bureaucracy, army and police, nor to what extent they can stall reform. No one is entirely sure who the real Black leaders are. But Percy Qoboza, the editor of the Black newspaper *City Press*, said in an interview that they included the leaders of the banned African National Congress (ANC), banned Pan Africanist Congress (PAC), Inkatha, the United Democratic Front (UDF), and the Azanian People's Organization (Azapo). They would also include church leaders, like Bishop Desmond Tutu and Dr Allan Boesak, and labour leaders like Mr Cyril Ramaphosa, of South Africa's largest trade union, the National Union of Mineworkers, which claims about 130,000 signed–up members. One of the key figures is Mr Nelson Mandela, the ANC leader, now aged 67, who was jailed for life in 1964. His wife, Mrs Winnie Mandela, who is banned and restricted to Brandfort, is a political leader in her own right. The leader of the exiled wing of the ANC, Mr Oliver Tambo, aged 68 years, a former legal partner of Mr Mandela, is another key figure. The smaller PAC is not generally regarded as being as significant as the ANC, but recently Mr Johnson Mlambo, aged 45, who was jailed on Robben Island in 1963 for twenty years and who left South Africa last year to join the central committee of the PAC, was elected the new leader. Inkatha, which claims more than a million members, is the largest Black political organization in South Africa. Its leader, Chief Mangosutho Buthelezi, who is 57 years old, is also the Chief Minister of the KwaZulu homeland. In contrast to the ANC and PAC, Inkatha has opted to work within the system to destroy apartheid. This strategy is often criticized by other Black political organizations, but as Mr Qoboza implied, it cannot be dismissed because of this, particularly because of its popular support. Chief Buthelezi is often portrayed in the White-orientated press as a person with whom the Government could strike a deal. But after Mr Botha refused to negotiate with him about the constitutional future of Black people, he said: 'I am probably more estranged from the State President than I have been at any other time during his term of office'. The UDF consists of some 660 different affiliated organizations and is more an alliance against apartheid than a political party. Its leadership is straddled between these different bodies but, says Mr Qoboza, two significant figures within it are Mr Popo Molefe, its general secretary, and Mr Patrick 'Terror' Lekhota. Mr Molefe and Mr Lekhota are in jail and have been refused bail, although this decision is being appealed. They are facing high treason charges following the unrest in the Vaal Triangle near Johannesburg in September of 1984. Within the Black consciousness camp, the Azapo president, Mr Ishmael Mkhabela, and Mr Saths Cooper, a leading figure in National Forum, a Black consciousness grouping, could be included among the 'real' leaders. There have been no free elections in South Africa to choose the 'real' leaders but, as public opinion surveys have shown, people such as these do have popular support.

A recent survey of Indians, Coloureds and Blacks has revealed dramatic changes in their attitudes towards political groups and their leaders. While the United Democratic Front was found to have the most declared support among Blacks and Indians, the survey also showed a doubling of support for the House of Delegates and the House of Representatives among Indians and Coloureds.

Support for the National Indian Congress, an affiliate of the UDF, dropped by half among Blacks and Indians. Among the Blacks surveyed, backing for Chief Mangosuthu Buthelezi, KwaZulu's Chief Minister and Inkatha president, was shown to have declined considerably and support for the jailed African National Congress leader, Mr Nelson Mandela, to have increased significantly. The random sample survey was conducted by the University of Natal's Institute for Black Research in eleven of Durban's Black surburbs, including KwaMashu, Inanda, Phoenix, Chatsworth, Reservoir Hills, Wentworth, Newlands East and Greenwood Park.

Meanwhile, many Whites in South Africa are worried about the Government's management of the economy as well as its handling of the political unrest, fearing that the Government is somewhat unsophisticated and out of its depth in dealing with the exceptionally complex and acute problems which South Africa is facing both at home and abroad. Whites are also very reluctant to surrender power wihout guarantees for their own security — and all they are told is the 'the people' will decide when they take power. The White Community feels threatened, rightly or wrongly, because it perceives much of the opposition, such as the UDF, ANC, AZAPO, (and most of the countries in the world) as requiring unconditional surrender of power. The UDF, for example, rejects the convention alliance movement as a worthwhile negotiating instrument. At the same time, Whites across the spectrum of society seem to have accepted that substantial inroads will have to be made on White economic privilege in order to bring about an equalization of development in South Africa.

Despite current upsets, South Africa still has a basically sound economy, and, to some extent, foreign disinvestment or lack of investment can be replaced by local savings. Savings could be increased through removal of the apartheid apparatus and by reduction in both Government spending and general consumption. Conventional wisdom suggests that South Africa can finance about 90 per cent of investment from local resources. However, the additional 10 per cent of foreign investment makes all the difference between a 2 per cent and a 5 per cent growth rate. The long–term potential growth of GDP, given constant terms of trade and no change in technological advances, is around 3.5 per cent a year. Without foreign capital, a higher growth rate — which South Africa needs for its burgeoning Black population — will be very difficult to achieve.

Unemployment and underemployment are problems of massive proportions in South Africa. The latest figures from the Central Statistical Services in Pretoria indicate that the number of unemployed may be fast approaching the 750,000 mark. The figures show that there were more than 56,000 Whites, Coloureds and Indians registered as unemployed in April 1985 — but the number is now likely to be higher. In March 1985, the CSS said there were about 513,000 Blacks registered as unemployed, and in June the Bureau for Economic Research at the University of Stellenbosch estimated that there were about 606,000 jobless Blacks. Unemployment made the headlines again recently with the news that some 6,000 White pupils were receiving supplementary feeding in some schools because of poverty. Black unemployment rose monthly last year, topping 8 per cent of the workforce. Observers — including the Bureau for Economic Research in Stellenbosch — say all communities are now feeling the effects of long–term structural changes in the labour market as well as the results of the economic downturn. But according to the Department of Manpower, there is still a shortage of skilled workers and artisans. The training and education programmes of the business sector and the foreign multinationals are helping to fulfil an urgent need in the country.

When Chase Manhattan — and other big New York banks — precipitated a foreign debt crisis, which was followed by a four month capital repayment freeze on the part of South Africa, the country's international credit rating dropped (from B-plus to C-minus). At the time South Africa's total debt of about $21.5 billion was high by historical standards, but not by those of the world at large. The United States carried only one third of the burden — $7 billion — and Europe the rest. Interest costs of about $2 billion were dwarfed by total export receipts. So there was no question that South Africa could afford to service the debt. The decline of the rand was a major complication. South Africa needed more rands to service and repay its debt. If a rand was still worth a dollar, total foreign debt would have been only 20 per cent of gross domestic product, compared with Brazil's 47 per cent and sub-Saharan Africa's 36 per cent. With the rand around 40 US cents, foreign debt was 58 per cent of gross domestic product of about R100 billion.

South Africa now has to rebuild what was a previously untarnished record of international economic dealings. In order to achieve the long–term *economic* growth potential of the country, however, it is abundantly clear that political pressures must be reduced by the achievement of a much greater degree of *political consensus* within South Africa. This in turn requires states-manship on the part of all the contending leaders coupled with a great deal of tolerance and self–sacrifice on the part of all groups. But without a broadly acceptable social and political framework, the prospects for long–term development seem dim.

Any number of plausible alternative scenarios for the future can be postulated; some form of modified White minority rule; a period of worsening violence followed by Black majority rule and a one-party oligarchy; a fragmentation into warring factions, none of which can unite the country which continues to lurch from one bout of violence to another; a military clamp–down that imposes an uneasy peace, and so on. This book examines a brighter alternative, that is a Westernized development of society based on economic growth, with concomitant amelioration of the social and political position of the Blacks, paid for by real and continued increases in the country's wealth year by year.

II. The United States and other countries

Although many Americans would associate South Africa with gold, few are aware that the American connection with gold mining goes back a century, to when the Witwatersrand main reef was discovered in 1886. As Enid de Waal has pointed out in an interesting study, the gold in this region was embedded in hard quartz rock, which, unlike the alluvial gold found in the Eastern Transvaal, could be mined only after the investment of vast sums of money and using mining techniques that were then relatively new and, indeed, unknown to most British mining engineers. American mining engineers who had already had extensive experience in mines similar to those on the Witwatersrand were therefore soon offered princely salaries to come to Johannesburg and other centres on the Rand.

Before 1886 few Americans had been attracted to the Transvaal Republic but by 1899, when the Anglo–Boer War broke out, there were almost 3,000 American citizens living and working on the Witwatersrand. British citizens formed the largest group of 'uitlanders', but the second largest group of foreigners in the Republic consisted of American citizens. The presence of so many

Americans in the Transvaal Republic could not fail to exert a profound influence upon developments there, and their impact upon social and political life was considerable. At that time, too, missionaries from the United States began their work of evangelization in the region.

But it was in the field of mining that these Americans made their most lasting impact, and had it not been for their remarkable technological contribution, the gold mining industry in South Africa would not have progressed so rapidly and so successfully. When Johannesburg was declared a public diggings in 1886 there were European capitalists on hand to supply the necessary financial backing: men such as Alfred Beit, Cecil John Rhodes, Hermann Eckstein, Samuel Marks, Barney Barnato and Sigismund Neumann. But men possessing the special technical skills needed to extract the gold were not so readily available. Diamond mining and gold mining require totally different techniques, so that whatever experience men had gained in Kimberley was virtually useless on the Witwatersrand. Most of the British engineers then in South Africa had gained their experience in coal mines and this too was of little value to them when it came to tackling the hard quartz rock of the main Witwatersrand reef. One pioneer admitted that 'not until practical miners arrived on the Rand from the United States did we begin to learn the art of reef gold mining'. He was not referring to men using picks and shovels, but to mining engineers possessing not only university training but also extensive experience in the complicated processes necessary to extract gold from quartz. Most men then possessing such qualifications were Americans, and it was these men who came to the Transvaal and initiated scientific gold mining on the Witwatersrand.

Many of the American mining engineers in South Africa left the country at the beginning of the Anglo–Boer War, never to return. After the war, in the early twentieth century, the gold mining industry was re-established and substantial American capital began to be invested in South Africa. This book, in a sense, is the story of that American investment, and what it means for South Africa.

During 1985 some American companies considered disinvestment in South Africa. According to various sources, during the 1984-5 unrest, eighteen American companies stopped all or part of their South African operations, and American business reduced its employment of South Africans from 90,000 to 70,000. Some companies sold out controlling interests to South Africans, while others gradually reduced their presence. Many more American companies might have been considering pulling out in one way or another, while others were adamant that they would remain. For example, Hewlett–Packard, a world leader in computers and calculators, had resolved to stay in South Africa after looking at its position there under pressures from the disinvestment movement. Among those whose position was not clear was the Revlon organization. Another United States company with international interests, American Cyanamide, which produces chemicals, sent a vice–president to South Africa to review the situation. The Pepsi–Cola Corporation announced in 1984 that it had sold its interests in South Africa, but it made it clear that this was part of a major restructuring exercise which in no way reflected on South Africa or its policies. International Harvester is another major international company that has pulled out of South Africa, though it insisted that this had nothing to do with politics. The reason given for the firm's withdrawal was that it was cutting back on its agricultural marketing production. Apple, the world's second–largest manufacturer of personal computers, shut down its operations in South Africa and though this was ostensibly for political reasons, competing companies believed Apple was making a political virtue out of economic necessity, as its sales in that year had sagged badly. The American–based computer giant IBM had said it had no intention of following Apple's lead. Two major international airlines, Pan American World Airways (Pan Am) and Scandinavian Airlines (SAS), have pulled out of South Africa. Pan Am, the only American airline then serving South Africa, was known to be in financial trouble and a spokesman declined to say whether its withdrawal was connected with disinvestment pressures. It has been said on behalf of SAS, however, that its move was politically motivated and 'was part of the efforts to further isolate South Africa and increase international pressure on its government'. Companies which curtailed their operations in South Africa included Bluebell Inc (clothing), Perkin–Elmer (machinery) and the Singer Corporation, manufacturers of sewing machines. The American mining group Phelps Dodge had reportedly put its 44.6 per cent stake in the giant South African base metals producer, Black Mountain, on the market for about R150 million.

Rumours that the big international banks Chase Manhattan and Citibank (the world's largest) were about to close their offices in

South Africa were denied, but a number of other American banks said they were following political developments closely in this country. Banks such as Bankamerica Corporation, JP Morgan and Company Inc, Manufacturers Hanover Corp, First Interstate Bancorp and Crocker National Corporation reaffirmed their policy of not lending money to the South African Government or its agencies. Amongst manufacturers, Coca-Cola planned to sell its Johannesburg bottling plant for $36.6 million, the transfer of control to take place between 1986 and 1988. General Foods sold its 20 per cent interest in Cerebos. Smith International, a California-based mining and equipment company, sold its South African affiliate for an undisclosed amount, this sale being part of the company's plans to shift its emphasis from mining to petroleum operations. Tidwell Industries, a builder of mobile houses, sold its South African subsidiary to Murray and Roberts. Helena Rubinstein, the New York cosmetics firm, closed its South Afrxican operation. Oak Industries, a Californian maker of electric products and components, sold its manufacturing plant in South Africa. West Point-Pepperel, a textile manufacturer based in Georgia, sold its one-third interest in a South African textile firm. Ecolaire, a Pennsylvania firm whose main business is power-station development, sold its South African office to an undisclosed party. City Investing, a diversified financial and housing services company that has filed for bankruptcy, sold its office to South African investors as part of its liquidation. Despite this, most of the flagship corporations remained in South Africa, and played a more active role. How many would leave if the rand recovered is a moot point.

This process of review is not surprising as long as the risk (continuing unrest in South Africa and unrelenting pressure from anti-apartheid activists in the United States) is increasing, while the return (the poor state of the South African economy) is decreasing, from 18 per cent a few years ago to around 4-5 per cent. The limits of doing business under apartheid appear to have been reached in the perception of some American investors, and only a lasting reversal of the risk and return factors will convince them otherwise.

Officially, the United States, after trying its best to promote reform through the gentle encouragement of constructive engagement for five years, has moved over to 'active constructive engagement' – a little less carrot and a little more stick. A sentiment often heard in the United States was that Chester Crocker — and indeed the Reagan Administration — were the best friends which South Africans could have hoped for in the world, but that they were made to look ineffectual by the actions of the South African government — internally especially, and in Angola, Cabinda, Botswana, in supporting Renamo in Mozambique and so forth.

President Reagan was left with little choice — given the situation in South Africa and political pressure in the United States — but to announce limited sanctions, both in the hope of pre-empting more punitive measures by the United States Congress, and also in order to retain the initiative over the South African area of American foreign policy. The President's action was an attempt to avoid a damaging political defeat in the United States Congress which was on the point of sending him a sanctions bill which contained tougher provisions than his executive order. The president had wanted to veto the bill but his advisers warned him that his veto was certain to be overridden. The indications now are that the bill will be shelved for a while. Most of the measures announced by President Reagan are contained in the bill with some minor and technical differences. But one important measure scrapped by the president was a directive that he would order even tougher sanctions unless there was significant movement away from apartheid within twelve months. At a White House press conference in September 1985, President Reagan said:

> I respect and share the goals that have motivated many in the Congress to send a message of United States concern about apartheid. But in doing so we must not damage the economic well-being of millions of people in South Africa and Southern Africa. Therefore I am signing today an executive order that will put in place a set of measures designed and aimed against the machinery of apartheid, without indiscriminately punishing the people who are victims of that system, measures that will disassociate the United States from apartheid but associate us positively with peaceful change.

President Reagan said his policy of constructive engagement would continue but he suggested that the word 'active' be added to it. Calling for peaceful evolution toward reform, Mr Reagan repeated a frequent argument of Secretary of State George Shultz:

> We must recognize that the opponents of apartheid, using terrorism

and violence, will bring not freedom and salvation but greater suffering and more opportunities for expanded Soviet influence within South Africa, and in the entire region. What we see in South Africa is a beginning of a process of change. The changes in policy so far are inadequate. But, ironically, they have been enough to raise expectations and stimulate demands for more far-reaching, immediate change. It is the growing economic power of the black majority that has put them in a position to insist on political change.

Mr Reagan said South Africa was not a totalitarian society. 'There is a vigorous opposition Press. And every day we see examples of outspoken protest and access to the international media that would never be possible in many parts of Africa, or in the Soviet Union for that matter,' he said. Americans had influence to do good — but also had 'immense potential' to make things worse. The United States had to ask whether it was helping to change the system or punishing the Blacks whom it sought to help.

There are only vague indicators as to the real attitudes of the majority of Black South Africans towards the disinvestment campaign — and their views must be a key legitimizing factor for those who argue that economic sanctions are being imposed for the benefit of the Blacks. As a number of people have pointed out, if Blacks were in favour of disinvestment, they could simply walk away from their jobs and cause a *de facto* disinvestment themselves. Part of the problem in current South African society is that some Blacks seem to support whatever Whites oppose almost as a reflex action, even though it might be detrimental to themselves as well, though it is not clear what proportion of Blacks may behave in this way.

The American heritage was not to quit but to reach out and help. The United States was urging all South Africans of all races to seize the opportunity for peaceful accommodation before it was too late. 'The problems of South Africa were not created overnight and will not be solved overnight, but there is no time to waste,' the President said. 'To withdraw from this drama or to fan its flames will serve neither our interests nor those of the South African people.' He appealed to all Americans to go forward with a 'clear vision and an open heart working for justice, brotherhood and peace.' President Reagan said that if the Congress sent him the bill it had debated and voted on — the Anti-Apartheid Action Act of 1985 — he would have to veto it. 'That need not happen,' he said. 'I want to work with the Congress to advance bipartisan support for America's policy toward South Africa and that is why I have put forward this executive order today.'

The following are the anti–apartheid measures announced by President Reagan as an Executive Order:

- a ban on the export of nuclear goods or technology to South Africa except where they are needed to implement nuclear proliferation safeguards of the International Atomic Energy Agency or to protect health and safety;
- a prohibition on United States loans to the South African Government except those that improve economic opportunities or educational, housing and health facilities open to South Africans of all races;
- a ban on the sale of computers and computer technology to South African Government agencies that enforce apartheid;
- a possible ban on the importation of krugerrands depending on the legality of the step in terms of the General Agreement on Tariffs and Trade (the ban subsequently became effective in a matter of weeks);
- a directive that the United States Treasury report on the feasibility of a one ounce American gold coin to be minted as an alternative to the krugerrand;
- a ban on the importation into the United States of any military goods manufactured in South Africa;
- a ban on United States export assistance to any United States company employing more than twenty–five people in South Africa but failing to adhere to the Sullivan code by the end of 1985;
- the creation of an advisory committee of 'distinguished Americans' to report within twelve months on recommendations to encourage peaceful change in South Africa;
- an increase of 8 million dollars in scholarship funds for Black South Africans and an extra 1.5 million dollars to support human rights programmes, one–third to go for legal assistance;
- a directive that American agencies in South Africa buy more goods and services from Black–owned businesses.

Following President Reagan's action, nine EEC countries imposed sanctions against South Africa, but Britain did not immediately agree to all the measures proposed by its Common Market partners. The sanctions include an embargo on the import and export of arms, a refusal to embark on military co-operation, the recall of European military attachés in Pretoria and their South African counterparts in Europe, a freezing of cultural and scientific agreements, a sports boycott, an oil boycott, a freeze on the sale of sensitive equipment, and no new collaboration in the nuclear sector. Other measures approved by all ten governments will involve EEC aid to Black trade unions and support for the training and education of Black workers in South Africa.

Although the United States has been the testing-ground for the sanctions approach to pressurizing the South African Government towards reform, Britain is the country which has the most to lose. The United Kingdom has around 50 per cent of the foreign investment in South Africa, whereas the United States, at its peak investment, had about 20 per cent. More importantly, sanctions which seriously interrupt trade between Britain and South Africa could jeopardize 400,000 jobs — 250,000 of them in Britain. This is estimated by the United Kingdom — South Africa Trade Association (UKSATA), which has a membership of 300 companies. UKSATA calculates that about 350 British companies have subsidiaries in the Republic and many more trade with the country. Direct investments by British companies total £5 billion. In addition, Britain has indirect investments totalling about £6 billion in South Africa through insurance, banking, tourism and other interests. The association says South Africa rates as Britain's twelfth largest trading partner. Britain sent £1.2 billion in 'visible' exports to South Africa last year, and 'invisible' earnings were worth £1.3 billion. A further £350 million was collected from re-exports. The trade balance between the two countries is largely in Britain's favour, with South Africa selling Britain goods worth only £720 million last year. Although Britain's trade with South Africa increased over the past five years, it has now dropped to fourth place in the league of the Republic's own trading partners behind the United States, West Germany and Japan. Nevertheless, there was a mounting feeling at the Foreign Office that the British Government had to take some pre-emptive action to prevent a situation where its international isolation over South Africa undermined Britain's long-term interests. Whitehall was also concerned that going out on a limb over South Africa and refusing to follow President Ronald Reagan's example of sanctions could lead to a foreign policy defeat. Of more immediate concern to Britain, though, was its total isolation both within the EEC and the Commonwealth. The

British government took time to consider the EEC proposals to withdraw military attachés and cut cultural links with South Africa. Both proposals ran counter to Britain's policy of positive engagement and accurate monitoring of SADF intentions and actions. But neither proposal conceded the principle of economic sanctions and some at the Foreign Office clearly believed Britain should fall in line to protect its long–term interests in the EEC (collectively a far more important trading partner than South Africa). The Foreign Secretary, Sir Geoffrey Howe, said that Britain had no intention of becoming South Africa's 'lone protector'. Accordingly Britain followed the sanctions move of its EEC partners within a month. On the economic side, Britain mainly imports minerals and foodstuffs from South Africa. Strategic metals include platinum, manganese, chrome and vanadium. But dealers say that sanctions would be ineffective because the metals trade is international and Britain would receive the metals from third parties. Yet there could be indirect shocks. London is a leading gold centre. If the United Kingdom agreed on sanctions, South Africa might sell more gold to Zurich. De Beers' international diamond marketing network, the Central Selling Organization is also based in London. So in the event of sanctions, the United Kingdom could lose invisible exports from precious metals and diamond trading. A weak rand is a disincentive for British companies to sell interests in South Africa. And regardless of political problems, fear of a further decline in the rand are likely to discourage new investment.

The British Barclays Bank PLC has reduced its shareholding in the South African Barclays National Bank from 50.4 per cent to 40.4 per cent, resulting in a return to South African control of the bank for the first time since 1925.

Apartheid is a perennial issue at Commonwealth Conferences and at the United Nations. A special United Nations panel has conducted public hearings at United Nations headquarters in an attempt to identify policies that might be adopted by the international community regarding the activities of multinational corporations with branches of affiliates in South Africa and South West Africa/Namibia. However, the 1,068 multinational corporations invited by the United Nations to take part in the hearings decided to boycott the event, which concentrated on employment practices and the role of these corporations in developing South Africa's nuclear and military facilities. Mr Peter Hanson, of Denmark, the executive director of the United Nations Centre on

Transnational Corporations, said the multinationals had indicated their conviction that 'the United Nations could never be a fair and balanced forum for such discussions'. One major investor in South Africa said that he refused to participate, after simply 'looking at the panel members'.

At the United Nations' hearings on multinational company operations in Southern Africa, the Afrikaanse Handelsinstituut, the Association of Chambers of Commerce, the National African Federation of Chambers of Commerce, the South African Federated Chamber of Industries and the Urban Foundation of South Africa said that an unstoppable transformation was under way in South Africa, driven by Black aspirations and discontent. Significantly, this demand for change is being supported by the South African business community both in its own enlightened self–interest and for reasons of broader social responsibility. In late September 1985, ninety of South Africa's top businessmen — including heads of multinational corporations operating in the country — issued a powerful statement asking for the complete abolition of apartheid and for negotiations with genuine Black leaders to share power.

There can be much interesting speculation as to why the world, and the United States in particular, is so absorbed with South African issues. Obviously, United States policy has sought to protect strategic interests, including the Cape sea route and access to important minerals, minimize Soviet influence, promote multiracial and democratic governments in Southern Africa, maintain good relations with other African states, and protect American trade and investment. But this dry explanation does not altogether explain the fervour of the concern in the United States. Undoubtedly, its own history of racial conflict, and the fact that South Africa institutionalized racialism for a generation, are partial explanations. Whatever the reasons, though, it seems right that the United States and the West should be concerned — yet not only with the obvious and immediate issue that apartheid must go — but also with what will *follow* the demise of apartheid. A bad system should be replaced with a better system, and it is here that caution and cool thinking are required on the part of the major Western countries, led by the United States. South Africa is an important country, and potentially a great country, but it needs to be helped rather than bludgeoned by its friends to achieve that potential.

This book provides some comprehensive analysis of the historical, political and economic relationships between the United States and South Africa, as a background for the formulation of current business, economic and political decisions. In the past, a study of the Treaties in force between the United States and South Africa show that many were actually signed in colonial times between the United States and the United Kingdom, the latter acting for South Africa. It emerges from this book that the colonial nexus with Britain is broken (although naturally many of the norms, values, attitudes and institutions of South African society are a legacy of the British era), and that South Africa has moved into the orbit of the United States to a significant extent. The analysis also shows that the United States cannot help South Africa fully until South Africa helps itself i.e. moves in a decidedly more democratic direction. South Africa has undoubtedly become a significant American political issue, especially for the Democrats. Figures indicate that the United States has recently become one of the top three major trading partners of South Africa. The examination of American direct investment in this book shows that it is very important in certain sectors like cars, petrochemicals, telecommunications, computers, and ethical medicines. The Sullivan initiative, as implemented by American companies, may well have acted as a more powerful catalyst for changes in the workplace than is recognized by critics of American business in South Africa. Another conclusion which emerges from this book is that the American business presence in Southern Africa, that is investment, trade, bank loans, companies' social programmes, management expertise, technology and cultural impact, together with political influence and American ideology are causing South Africa to become ever more firmly locked into the Western, American–dominated world than is immediately apparent. But, on the other hand, links with the Western economies are being weakened through continuing unrest, reports of police repression, and the failure to implement far–reaching political reforms.

This book also considers the general merits of multinationals before looking at specifically American business in South Africa. Alternative socio–economic systems are discussed in some detail. Acceptance of the relative efficiency of markets in allocating scarce resources is explicit in the democratic free–enterprise model of political economy which is used in this book, with qualifications being made where necessary.

Some qualifications need to be made at the outset. Clearly, resources were not allocated in South Africa historically solely by the workings of a free market, but also by military conquest followed by massive political intervention on behalf of the Whites. Thus land, wealth, education, opportunity and skills accrued disproportionately to the Whites. A free enterprise system implies that everyone has the same right to everything in society: but even if entirely free and open economic competition were introduced now in South Africa, how does society undo a century of state bias against Blacks as embodied in the Land Act, Group Areas, unequal education and so on? Though the problems resulting from the historial backlog would remain for a time after the introduction of free enterprise — and would require considerable investment in the country's human capital to solve — in this work it is argued that genuine free enterprise can address the problems more effectively and with less damage to society than any of the alternatives. One of the most difficult tasks facing a country like South Africa in the years ahead is to maintain some sort of balance between the need for productivity and economic growth, which are well–served by the energy released by capitalism, and the distribution of the benefits of such growth for the greater equalization of life–chances (income, health, education, protection for the poor, weak, elderly), without killing the incentive which makes economic amelioration of society possible in the first place. An ingenious mix of economic policies may be necessary as a forerunner to a more straightforward free economy (little government intervention, plenty of competition) in South Africa at some point in the future. But although measures to redress economic and social inequity might need to be taken in the interim, it should not be forgotten that the freer a market, the more accurate is the computation of the value of goods traded in that market likely to be, and resources are consequently more likely to be allocated efficiently in a free market than they would be by simple bureaucratic fiat.

Whatever route is followed by South Africa in the future, there are so many pitfalls to each one that prediction of outcomes is unwise. Nevertheless, it is essential to bear some sort of ideal political economy in mind so that both thought and action may be guided and measured in relation to the ideal. This critical choice, which will determine the future of society, and of business, in the country until well into the twenty–first century, faces South Africa now.

2 The United States and South Africa

Introduction

One of the more picturesque historical contacts between the United States and South Africa came about as the result of visits to Cape Town by the Confederate steamer, the *Alabama* in the early 1860's. The American Civil War still echoes at the Cape through the song 'Daar Kom die Alabama'.

> In the song of the Cape Malays who saw her entering Table Bay from their homes high on the slopes of Signal Hill the *Alabama* will forever be coming, coming from far over the sea.
> The origin of the song is obscure. Hadji Abduraghiem Johnston who was born in 1852 remembered seeing the ship in Table Bay and hearing the Malays singing the song as they composed it. An old Malay in Paarl maintained that his father was in the group that began singing as the ship came in; and a clump of trees in Fresnaye was called the Alabama Bosch because the Malays used to congregate and sing the song there. The words of the song seem to indicate logically that it was composed when the *Alabama* returned from the East, that she was recognised from her previous much publicised visit, and that the words were spontaneously uttered by someone who saw the ship coming towards Cape Town, from one of those whitewashed houses on Signal Hill, which offer such a sweeping view of the bay.
> . . . If the ship had been called *Jefferson Davis* or *Fort Sumter* would the song still have escaped involuntarily from the lips of those watchers high on the hills? The State of Alabama and its politics was unknown to them, but the name had a euphonious, lilting sound, and the ship was endowed with the vital quality of adventure. By what strange quirk of history did the descendants of a slave people perpetuate the memory of a ship belonging to a nation striving to maintain slavery!
> What attracted the unknown composer will never be known. Sufficient that the lively, pulsating beat still kindles the imagination and recaptures that lost long ago, when the *Alabama* proudly sailed

into Table Bay and brought a breath of the great outside to a struggling people. [Bradlow and Bradlow, 1958.]

The business environment in South Africa is affected by history, politics, racial issues, international relations, and many other factors that present both opportunities and constraints. The business community generally in turn affects the larger environment, so the interaction is dynamic. It is in this context that American corporations do business in South Africa. In this chapter, the importance of history and politics, the current trends and the importance of American business itself are analysed against this background.

The importance of history and politics

Whereas in Britain there is a general awareness of South Africa, because of the historical connections between the two countries, this is not true in the United States. The British settlers, the Anglo–Boer War, the entire colonial legacy of institutions, language, education and so forth have left a historical bond between South Africa and Britain. The business relationship between the two countries is also significant for both nations.

Although South Africa's economic relationship with the United States is of long–standing and important to South Africa, it is relatively less important to the United States; and there is historically little direct connection between the American and the South African states. Even the heightened activity of recent years and months was the result of specific groups of Americans with special interests and concerns — the State Department, churches, universities, business, Black Americans — whereas for most Americans South Africa remained an unknown country. They might have heard of Soweto and apartheid and gold, yet be vague about the precise geographical, political, and other details. William Clark, the National Security Adviser, admitted in the confirmation hearings for his first State Department post in the incoming Reagan Administration that he did not know the names of the Prime Ministers of South Africa and Zimbabwe.

More recently though, and primarily because of the serious unrest in South Africa as well as the activities of the various groups lobbying for disinvestment, South Africa has received very much more attention in the United States, and there are other significant factors which have contributed to South Africa's higher profile in the United States.

The United States and South Africa have sufficient common past experience for there to be a residue of shared values, despite the dramatic differences between the two nations. Indeed, some Americans' Obsession with South Africa is out of all proportion to South Africa's actual importance to the United States. This obsession is difficult to explain.

The offer of land to Afrikaner farmers by Arkansas, Colorado, and Wyoming in 1900 reflected an admiration by rugged, individualistic American frontiersmen of what they saw as their counterparts in South Africa, suffering under the yoke of a British imperialism which they themselves had shaken off to become a democratic republic. As this century has progressed the number of values shared by most Americans and most White South Africans has diminished; as American sympathy for South African Blacks has increased, and as White South Africans have moved in opposite directions to the United States on civil liberties and citizen rights, the two Republics have been driven further apart. However, there should be a certain empathy between the two nations as the result of some similarities in their histories: for example, 'it would be impossible', Thomas Jefferson wrote in 1784 in his *Notes on Virginia*, to 'incorporate Blacks into the State', because 'deep-rooted prejudices entertained by the Whites', the bitterness of Blacks against their former masters, and 'the real distinctions that nature has made' would lead to race war and 'the extermination of one or the other race'. These views are echoed in the official ideology of the rulers of the South African state exactly two centuries later.

Why has the race history of the two nations diverged increasingly over time? A possible explanation for this divergent pattern of race relations, and one which is insufficiently emphasized in the literature, is that White South Africans may be another historical example of ordinary people being ruthless in what they perceive to be extraordinary circumstances which threaten their existence; whereas White Americans may be an example of ordinary people being relatively benign in what they perceive to be a more ordinary situation which does not threaten their existence.

When Americans have perceived themselves to be threatened, they too have reacted ruthlessly. In the months after Pearl Harbour, more than 110,000 'persons of Japanese ancestry' (those with one–sixteenth Japanese blood or more) were forcibly relocated from the West Coast to inland internment camps in desolate areas of Wyoming, Arkansas, California, Colorado, Idaho, Utah, and Arizona. Most were American citizens, while one–third were resident aliens born in Japan and therefore, under the laws of the time, ineligible for citizenship. No act of espionage or sabotage was attributed to a Japanese American during the Second World War. They were summarily imprisoned and their constitutional rights suspended solely because of their race. Of the total property loss to the internees, estimated to be $400 million in 1942, the United States Government eventually repaid $38.5 million.

Historically, there tend to be recurring American patterns of attitude and action towards South Africa. After Sharpeville, Soweto, Biko, there was a flight of capital or slowdown of investment, coupled with official moral opprobrium, but in all cases the substantive connections of trade and investment were resumed fairly swiftly, though the disapproval lingered.

The exact emphasis of American policy towards South Africa depends on their hierarchy of concerns, and these, too, have well–established parameters. If the administration is concerned chiefly with the global rivalry of the United States with the Soviet Union, then smaller countries will be seen as pawns or knights in an elaborate and deadly international chess game — the fact that some of the pawns might have distasteful internal policies is a subsidiary consideration, perhaps even a luxury to think about, when there is an undeclared global war to win.

If the administration believes that a limited adversary relationship with the Soviet Union is possible, and that the United States and its allies are basically safe, then attention shifts to less urgent and more delicate issues like North – South relations, the upliftment of developing countries, the ending of racial discrimination and undemocratic practices wherever they might be found. As a result of the former perception, South Africa is viewed principally as an ally against communism: as a result of the latter, as an undemocratic state with which it is difficult to deal in open partnership.

The important point is that, within these broad parameters, the basic policies of all administrations do not vary enormously, and indeed, beneath the rhetoric, there is considerable continuity: no American administration can condone racial discrimination; and it is also unlikely that an American administration would want to force American business out of South Africa altogether, or engage in a naval blockade or military action aimed to bring down apartheid (though the United States might be more willing to intervene *after* significant destabilization in the region had already taken place). The basic tenet of American policy towards South Africa seems to be that if the Republic moves towards becoming a democratic country as that term is understood in the United States, the United States would happily co-operate with South Africa in all matters from strategic defence to exchange of technology as an open and willing partner, unafraid of its own conscience or the countervailing power of South Africa's opponents.

What also becomes apparent is that American policy towards South Africa acts within constraints. The United States in Africa faces the possibility of Soviet expansionism, and this is usually the principal challenge for American policy makers. American policy towards South Africa, however, must also take into account domestic American constraints, the legitimate aspirations of South African Blacks unrelated to the Soviet threat, the concerns of the Whites, who are potential allies, American financial and business interests in South Africa, and the views of the rest of Africa. It requires considerable skill and ingenuity to fashion a foreign policy which balances all these requirements.

Early on in the first Reagan Administration, an analyst noted that:

> although the Reagan and white South African worldwide views have much in common, and although there are significant forces within the Administration for more or less unconditional rapprochement with South Africa on the basis of an East – West interpretation of events in the region, a number of significant factors on the domestic American front and in the international environment militate against lasting rapprochment as long as the policies which produced South Africa's pariah status in the first place remain essentially unchanged. It must not be forgotten that even the very powerful are not all-powerful. The United States, a mighty super-power, still faces internal and external constraints on its policy choices and must live with the consequences of its actions, consequences over which it hardly exercises full control. A proper awareness of these constraints cannot be encouraging to those who formulate South Africa's domestic and foreign policies. [Abernethy, 1981, p.43.]

The constraints can be listed as follows:

(a) Even a basically pro–South African President does not have either unlimited tenure or a power base that cannot be eroded.

(b) It cannot be assumed that American multinationals are entirely in favour even of constructive engagement with White South Africa, when this might imperil their economic interests in other Black states. The multinationals have made mutually agreeable arrangements with socialist governments — the FRIA consortium in Guinea, Gulf Oil in Angola, Union Carbide in Zimbabwe.

> If correct, my analysis suggests that a Marxist view, according to which public policy in a Capitalist state is a reflection of private corporate interests, is not accurate. Certainly on Angola it is Washington that adopts a hard anti–Communist line, not the more pragmatic capitalists of Wall Street. [Abernethy, 1981, p.34.]

(c) The President may have less public support on foreign policy that on domestic policy issues.

(d) The exigencies of power make it difficult to see all issues in terms of, say, East – West conflict alone, so there is a tempering of views and policies as an administration matures in power.

(e) The importance of the pro–South African views of right–wing congressmen is probably exaggerated in South Africa. Other conservatives, such as Senator Nancy Kassebaum have asserted that 'Pretoria offends everything conservatives stand for', such as integrity of the family and minimal government regulation of individual behaviour. Not all republicans, and certainly not all conservatives, are automatic supporters of South Africa. After all, it was Republican President Lincoln who freed the slaves and Republican Chief Justice Warren who presided over desegregation from 1954 onwards.

(f) There are likely to be enough anti–apartheid Congressmen, Republicans as well as Democrats, in the House of Representatives at any time effectively to restrain even the most pro–South African President.

(g) Black Americans in American politics and foreign policy-making exercise a restraining role.

(h) Concern over financial loans and investment in South Africa has been institutionalized, following successful protest in the late 1970s by student and church groups, so the issue of South Africa appears on the agendas of investment meetings regularly, and influences decisions. Recent developments have widened the base and increased the scope of anti–apartheid activities, as discussed later.

(i)   South Africa's ability to win friends in the West depends largely on the plausibility of its case for geostrategic indispensability. The less plausible that case, in light of the overall strategic concerns of the United States and other Western powers, the less likely that South Africa will be able to extricate itself from the diplomatic isolation in which its racial policies have placed it.

As American Ambassador Nickel puts it:

> Policies always reflect perceptions of interests. We don't accept the narrow view that tangible interests, like strategic minerals or the Cape Route, can be insulated from our broader interest in the political stability of this part of the world. We feel that this stability cannot be based on the *status quo*. It must be based on orderly change — change towards a system that rests on the foundation of the consent of the governed. Therefore it is in our American interest to encourage as much as possible the forces of peaceful change — peaceful change within South Africa itself, and in relations between South Africa and its neighbours. [Nickel in *Leadership S.A.*, vol.1, no. 3, 1982, p.23.]

(j)   If South Africa interprets an American constructive engagement policy as a mandate to stall on reform and persist in racial policies, it could cut short the very American experiment in more positive relations which it so welcomed when President Reagan took power.

(k)   Constructive engagement is a high-risk policy for an American administration to pursue, particularly as regards its relations with the rest of Africa and other countries opposed to South Africa's racial policies, and its internal political opponents.

All of these constraints suggest that there is a limited amount that the United States can do for South Africa without significant changes in a democratic direction within South Africa itself. In other words, the potential of the world's most powerful state to help South Africa develop and prosper in every way is restricted by the policies of the Republic, internal politics in the United States and international opinion. South African Whites and Blacks have to weigh the perceived benefits of pursuing their own policies without caring about American favour or disfavour, against the perceived benefits of doing what is necessary to ensure that the United States is a supporter in the world.

Official South Africa, and the Whites generally, do want to be regarded as part of the Western world, and this wish does give some leverage to the West's most powerful democracy, the United States. The strength of this leverage should not be exaggerated, however. As Chester Crocker pointed out some years ago, the sticks which the United States can use on South Africa turn out, on closer examination, to be twigs, and the carrots more like turnips.

Current trends in American – South African relationships

Business relationships between the United States and South Africa are no longer governed by business considerations alone: and the time conceivably could come when American corporations in South Africa are controlled by political interest groups in the United States. Already by late 1985, limited sanctions had been imposed, and more were expected to follow in the absence of sustained and meaningful reform in South Africa.

A major reason for this change is that until recently, policy towards South Africa by United States policymakers was something of a 'free–play area': because there was no politically significant constituency to which policymakers were answerable, the preferences of a policymaking elite could be decisive. Now, however, South Africa has been placed firmly on the political agenda of sizeable groups such as Black Americans, and business consequently has become a political football. An ever–increasing number of American states, cities and churches, for example, are questioning investment in 'tainted' stock of corporations which do business in South Africa, and investment firms are developing 'South Africa free' portfolios. Between April and September 1985 at least twenty–four American universities jettisoned their South Africa–related stock, and many more, including the prestigious Ivy League colleges, are reassessing their position as regards 'tainted' stock.

During the 1984 election period, all the leading figures in the

Democratic Party advocated embargoes and disinvestment in South Africa. Towards the end of that election year, President Reagan met South African Bishop Desmond Tutu in the White House. Bishop Tutu was about to be given the 1984 Nobel peace prize, and he acted as a catalyst and focal point for protests in the United States about the treatment of Blacks in South Africa. President Reagan spoke out more strongly than ever before on International Human Rights day (10 December 1984) about the costs of apartheid and the need for South Africa to move towards a more just society. There are continuing protests and arrests at South African diplomatic missions. Dr Crocker, who has made indefatigable efforts to bring about peaceful change in South Africa and stabilize the region, criticized the SABC for wilfully distorting United States policy towards South Africa. The 1985 Black uprising and the State of Emergency have brought South Africa world-wide publicity on the television screen. These recent trends indicate, not only that South Africa has become more of a high-profile media issue, but that there are well-organized forces against apartheid in the United States. There are about forty national and regional organizations, seventeen religious organizations and more than sixty campus organizations working for the end of apartheid. The most effective lobbying organizations in the United States are Transafrica, the American Committee on Africa, and the Washington Office on Africa. Ironically, the sheer size of President Reagan's 1984 victory has left disillusioned Democrats, and the Blacks who supported them, looking for a rallying cause — and Tutu's Nobel prize, the arrest of Black trade unionists in South Africa, and, most damaging of all, the continuing unrest coupled with the fact that South Africa has not made enough progress in a democratic direction in the view of most Americans, combined to make South Africa a perfectly exploitable issue. The Free South Africa Movement orchestrated the arrests and picketing at South African embassies, and suddenly Americans were exposed to a flood of critical newspaper articles, television features and debates about South Africa, all of which intensified because of violent events in South Africa in 1985.

The South African President reacted to the American President's 1984 speech and 1985 sanctions by denouncing American meddling. The political and economic indications suggest, however, that if official South Africa values the constructive engagement policy, it will have to deliver a quid pro quo in the form of significant and sustained progress in a democratic direction.

Whether the various constituencies constraining the action of American business and American policy makers towards South Africa will gain their ends — in most cases the demise of apartheid — is debatable, and this debate forms some of the substance of this study.

The importance of the American business presence

Later chapters present theoretical and empirical evidence which suggests that American business can help to develop the South African economy, irrespective of changes in political dispensation. Here we are concerned with the context in which American corporations do business in South Africa. It is important to note that, in the equation which decides whether business should be done in South Africa, the 'hassle factor' has become far weightier. Some concerned shareholders and President Reagan's sanctions are pressurizing American companies to sign the Sullivan principles in the hope of easing the pressure; others are pressurizing American corporations in South Africa to go further and to take up cudgels against the South African government to force it to ease its apartheid policies as far as possible. In December 1984, 119 American companies which are signatories to the Sullivan principles endorsed additions to the code which would expand their role in the challenge to apartheid, principally by lobbying for social change in public and in meetings with South African officials. Dr Sullivan acknowledges that some American companies have entered the South African political arena and are pushing for an end to apartheid. This latter course had been advocated strongly by, amongst others, Bishop Tutu. However, the implementation and advocacy of such a course of action by business has serious implications for the principles and practice of corporate social responsibility and these implications will be discussed later. What is becoming clearer at this juncture is the ever-increasing politicization of business issues.

From the business point of view, what is really at stake for the United States and for South Africa? The following *Time* paragraphs express the popularly-held view:

More than 350 American corporations and US banks hold investments and loans in South Africa. Activist stockholders and their supporters have tried, generally unsuccessfully, to persuade such firms to quit doing business there. Where that has failed, the move has pushed a tactic termed divestment. This involves pressurising public and private institutions to sell their stock in firms that invest in South Africa.

From South Africa's viewpoint, US holdings loom large. American companies control nearly 70 per cent of the nation's computer industry and one–half of its petroleum business. Yet from the US perspective, the activity is relatively small. Although bank loans amount to $3.88 billion and stock holdings in South African companies to $7.6 billion, direct investment of US corporations was only $2.3 billion at the end of last year. That is a mere 1 per cent of all US corporate investment abroad.

Between 1976 and 1982, thirty–six US Universities removed more than $143 million in investments from firms dealing with South Africa. At least thirteen cities, including New York, Philadelphia, Boston and Washington, have passed ordinances restricting pension–fund investments in companies operating there. So have five states: Connecticut, Maryland, Massachusetts, Michigan and Nebraska.

Corporate investors in South Africa include most of the US blue–chip giants. Among those singled out by protesters: Citicorp, which has in the past lent money to the Pretoria government; Mobil Oil, which has invested about $426 million and sells its products to the government's procurement office; and IBM, whose computers are used by the country's bureaucracy. Business spokesmen argue that US firms provide jobs for blacks in South Africa, work quietly to break down racial barriers and would be replaced by companies with a lower social consciousness if they pulled out. Indeed, many US corporations, including General Motors, IBM and Mobil, have helped foster economic equity in South Africa by adopting a set of guidelines that include maintaining an integrated work–place, adhering to nondiscriminatory pay scales and increasing the number of nonwhites in management positions. [*Time*, 17 December 1984, p. 45.]

The American Chamber of Commerce in South Africa in a 1984 letter to Honourable Howard Wolpe, United States House of Representatives, stated that 'Americans have certain values, hopes, and beliefs and we did not leave them behind when we came to South Africa'.

Although the direct impact of the United States on the level of state–to–state interaction is currently circumscribed by American domestic and foreign policy considerations, and most of all by the policies of the South African government, the United States does have an important influence on South Africa. This is not through any of the usual political mechanisms, but through American financial interests and the American multinational corporations which operate in the Republic. One of the major themes running through this study is that, irrespective of American policy under different administrations and despite whatever direction domestic South African politics might take, the presence of American business in South Africa is good for all its citizens, Black and White.

American business is the means most likely to heal the breach between the United States and South Africa and to contribute at least indirectly to solutions to the problems which caused the breach in the first place. Officially, the United States, after all, probably employs as few as seven people to look after Southern Africa; whereas American business has considerable resources committed to Southern Africa. The United States government is supporting a hundred or so Black South African students each year to study in America, contributing half a million dollars apiece to self–help schemes and human rights concerns, and spending around two million dollars a year on teaching teachers in South Africa — all of which are worthwhile, yet limited projects. If the presence of American business, however, acts as some sort of catalyst facilitating changes in the larger South African economy, it will have more overall impact on South African society than does official American policy.

However, two possible effects of pressure on American business in South Africa and on the United States itself are worthy of consideration. The first is that an anti-South Africa-at-all-costs lobby will give American business and United States geopolitical strategy, if they succumb to the pressure, the appearance and reality of amateurish operations, and cut across the free enterprise principles of America.

More subtly and perhaps more seriously, forcing American business to withdraw from South Africa will be giving satisfaction to those who believe that the ends (e.g. the end of apartheid) justify the means (e.g. disinvestment). Although disinvestment, as mentioned in Chapter 1, may be viewed by some as a useful tactic (similar to a strike) to force democratic concessions from the White South Africans, it can have unintended consequences. However, it is certain that many South Africans would suffer greater economic privation as a result of a political manoeuvre which is based on the questionable assumption that the South African government is amenable to change through economic pressure.

The pro–disinvestment argument is that Blacks are already suffering, and that a little more suffering might be worthwhile if thereby Blacks gain their liberation soon and become South African citizens with full rights. The opposing argument is that disinvestment will reduce the South African economic growth rate still further, increase massive unemployment even more, and cause great hardship to, inevitably, the poorer section of the community. The whole regional economy will be affected, since economic relations between South Africa and Black Africa include:

> such diverse aspects of the regional economy as infrastructure, technology, trade, transport, finance and productive resources. South Africa lies at the centre of this economic system and it is no secret that the economic interdependence in southern Africa is disproportionate, with many of South Africa's regional trade partners in the position of client states, who are themselves vulnerable to economic sanctions applied on South Africa in two different yet related ways. International sanctions, given existing trade links, cannot simply stop at the borders of South Africa but are bound to spill over into neighbouring states. At the same time South Africa is obviously in a position to retaliate against its neighbours...
> [Cooper, *South African Journal of Economics*, Vol. 52, no. 3, September 1984, pp.266 – 7.]

Giliomee argues plausibly that far from inducing Whites to negotiate a political statement with Blacks, disinvestment will strengthen the hardliners on both sides. The government would use all its credit to support the dropping living standards of its White constituency. The destabilizing effect of disinvestment might result in violence, uncertainty and over–reaction by both Blacks and Whites. Giliomee affirms that disinvestment is one of the most serious issues facing South Africa in the mid–1980s, and that part of what is required is a thorough and sober debate.

What needs to be noted here is that because disinvestment is a tactic which would inevitably cause hardship and suffering to many people, and perhaps far worse, it is a tactic which would negate the fundamental ethical stance, which is in the nature of a Kantian categorical imperative, of regarding people as ends, not means. An official policy of disinvestment would weaken the moral position of the United States. It is obviously naïve to think that the United States, in common with all dominant powers throughout history, does not sometimes go beyond the requirements of power politics, or that self-interest and expediency rather than ethics are not sometimes the guiding principles for American actions. But, in the final analysis the strength of American influence in South Africa, and in the world at large depends not only on its vast economy, capacity to innovate, enthusiasm, and military power, but also on moral force and the sense that there should be an ethical base for a nation's actions. And it is this vision of a justly-based society, as elucidated in the Declaration of Independence, which is quite possibly the most important single contribution (although an intangible one) which the American presence can offer South Africa as an ideal to strive for in its own evolution to a more stable, just, and democratic society.

The debate on American involvement in South Africa spans at least two decades, but the context in which American corporations do business in South Africa has changed rapidly in the 1980s, and especially so since the election of President Reagan to a second term in office. South African issues are very swiftly reaching a much wider audience in America, for reasons including Bishop Tutu's Nobel Prize, the continuing arrests at South African embassies in the United States, and the CBS 'Nightline' programme televised from Johannesburg to an audience of several millions in the United States for five consecutive nights — the latter coinciding with serious unrest in South Africa. Continuing troubles kept South Africa in the headlines throughout 1985 — not only a spiral of political violence, but a financial crisis which caused the country to suspend repayment of capital to international creditors between September and December 1985. Increasing numbers of Americans, brought up with a deep-seated belief in the principles embodied in the American Constitution, want to act against apartheid, but are not aware of the potential consequences of disinvestment and divestment. If American economic disengagement from South Africa takes place, it will be difficult to reintroduce the economic links. And although the South African economy is probably too sophisticated and diverse to succumb to an American withdrawal, it certainly would create increased hardship in South Africa, and may have a number of other unforeseeable and unpleasant consequences, which are examined further in the ensuing chapters of this work.

The final point here is that developments have led to a new climate in which, for example, President Reagan has had to impose pre-emptive sanctions — despite the fact that sanctions bills go against both his Administration's policy and probably his personal instincts on the issue of South Africa.

3 Multinational corporations: the theoretical issues

Introduction

In deciding whether or not to go international, a firm must evaluate many factors. First and foremost is its basic mission. Precisely what business is it in? If the management decides the international arena is within its sphere of operations, it can begin analysing the possible advantages and disadvantages associated with such an undertaking. On the positive side are profit, stability, and the possibility of a foothold in an economic union, of which the European Common Market is a famous example. On the negative side are financial setbacks, unfamiliar customs and cultures, delicate company-government relations, risk, expropriation, and the possibility of having to bring in foreign partners, which, for many businesses, constitutes the biggest drawback. If a company decides to go ahead with a foreign operation, it must find an appropriate organization structure. The next question is one of control . . . most firms opt for intermediate. [Richard Hodgetts *Management*, p. 472.]

It has been our constant desire to grow, and to grow by being present in every feasible market, that has led IBM to where it is today. Wanting growth has nothing to do with imperialistic motives. Rather, it is one of the conditions necessary to remain dynamic, to remain young, and to maintain a sound level of excellence. Through time, I am sure, we will have substantial changes in the structure of our company, but one thing that will remain is our desire to grow, our desire to develop the non–United States markets, and to be present, as much as we can, in all the countries of the world. [Jacques Maisonrouge, IBM Chairman.]

The essential nature of the multinational enterprise lies in the fact that its managerial headquarters are located in one country (the home country), while the enterprise carries out operations in a number of other countries as well (host countries). The degree of centralized control will vary among enterprises according to such factors as the types of economic activity in which they are engaged, the policies and practices of their managements, the particular issues on which central decisions are required, and national regulations ... [ILO, 1973, pp. 3 – 4.]

Of the hundred largest economic units in the world, fifty are nation states and fifty multinational companies. Sales of the major multinational enterprises have been growing at 10 per cent per annum, while real gross national product over the world has, on average, been increasing at only half that rate. This growth has been achieved through economies of scale, especially in R&D and marketing; by relative immunity to difficulties of price fluctuations, supply of raw materials, financial reserves, transportation, and so on that result from international operations; by on-the-spot production eliminating export problems; and by the capacity to exploit local national advantages.

These advantages give the multinational a life of its own and this autonomy gives rise to concern that vital decisions may be taken by enterprises which are outside the national community and which do not come under national regulations for example, decisions concerning the continued existence of the local branch, its expansion, activity, employment, orientation, exports, and so on. There is concern that national interests in the economic and social fields might be subordinated to the interests of the enterprise itself or of the country of origin.

Many charges are levelled at multinationals: that they are instruments of imperialism, that they exploit the countries in which they operate; for example, by repatriating earnings; that R & D, crucial seminal activities in any society, are concentrated in the country of origin; transfer pricing; insensitivity to local needs. On the other hand, multinational investment in a country often involves an inflow of foreign capital without imposing interest payments; transfer of technical and managerial expertise that upgrades local talent and standards; and despite repatriation of earnings there is an increase in business activity, tax payments and so on.

Aharoni (1977, p. 222) identifies four main responses to multinationals: laissez–faire; that their activities are essentially predatory, especially in developing countries; that the companies themselves should set up and abide by a code of conduct for responsible behaviour and good industrial citizenship; and that there is need for international surveillance. The last view led to the establishment by the United Nations in 1975 of a Centre on

Transnational Corporations. A crucial facet of the debate is that of accountability.

This chapter examines the theoretical issues surrounding the subject of multinational corporations, with reference to multinationals in South Africa wherever this is appropriate. The theoretical issues discussed are of primaty importance, since, for example, American firms in South Africa are judged partly on corporate social responsibility criteria. The debate on the effects of economic growth on apartheid is critically important, because if growth can indeed break the shackles of apartheid on the economy, and if multinationals are shown to be contributing to economic growth, then at least indirectly if not directly, they are contributing to the peaceful evolution of South Africa towards the ideal-type political economy espoused in this book.

Accountability and corporate social responsibility

Given their sheer size and importance in the world, it is not surprising that the question of the accountability of multinationals has become such a tendentious issue, and in all probability a variety of controls, ranging from self-imposed ones to stricter legal constraints will be tried in the coming decade.

One American scholar, Lindblom, shows how the dominant position of business might pose a threat to democratic institutions: the answer, to adapt Churchill, is that the free enterprise economic system is the worst for democracy, except for all the others. Lindblom does not take account sufficiently of the fact that there is always a sanction over business, namely the sanction of the free market-place, which deals severely with ineptitude and corruption over a period of time. The possibility of market failure is a better regulator than any number of bureaucratically promulgated laws, and self-interest a better motivator to work well and produce good quality goods and services over the long term than producing to order.

However, Lindblom does address the question of politics and markets, of the accountability of business to society and the tension between business and democracy, with a view to suggesting solutions:

In all market-orientated polyarchies there remains a fundamental structural problem posed by the privileges that businessmen need as a condition of their performance. It is in some part to business privilege that many contemporary problems can be traced, among them monopoly, inflation, unemployment, environmental decay, and obstruction to polyarchy ... through a skewed pattern of mutual adjustments. It is possible to reconcile the minimum privileges required by business with a withdrawal of business privilege, including privileges to veto, that might help solve these problems?

This is an old, fundamental, continuing, inescapable problem in public policy making from which no market-oriented system can escape for a year, month, day or hour. It is not a problem to be solved, as many critics of the corporation would tell us, simply by curbing the giant corporations and giving them their marching orders, without regard to their consequent performance. Nor is it a simple problem, as friends of the corporation would tell us, of protecting through no more than the most delicate of regulations their productive virtuosity. Nor is it a relatively uncomplicated problem that can be solved by a compromise between these two views, requiring simply that we give the corporations half of what they want. Half of what they want may be too much to give them in a world in which corporate discretion even thus reduced remains an insufficiently controlled source of the new chemically produced diseases of progress. And, yet, on the other hand, only half of what they want may be insufficient to induce them to produce. [Lindblom, 1977, pp. 348 – 9.]

One can take issue with Lindblom over a number of points: for example, the creation of inflation is almost entirely the province of governments, not of business. However, his main point is that hybrid forms of market and polyarchal controls might develop in which the strategy is to pay businessmen to waive some of their privileges; business would work closely with government, selling some of their privileges in return for shared risk and guaranteed market. This type of regulation may be worth exploring for some developing countries and foreign multinationals. However, a simpler solution may be to incorporate the cost of a company's negative externalities into the price of their product, thereby forcing them to clear up their own mess as efficiently as possible or face the market consequences — the key lies in information, so that the sanction would be applied by society itself in not buying the products of firms known to be engaging in anti-social activities. This might by pass the monotonous tendency of the twentieth century to set up regulations and bureaucracies to oversee and enforce them (which not only takes people out of productive employment, but wastes the time of those actively producing goods and services). In a genuine democracy, there would be no secrets, governmental or commercial, and the country's populace would vote according to its judgment of each institution's performance for the good of society with ballot papers and dollars respectively. Even Lindblom's suggested solution is elitist, proposing a more intimate relationship between big business and big government. Many of the critics of business appear to think that governments are somehow more honestly interested in the well-being of the people than are business corporations. It is, at the least, a debatable assumption, but may be truer the more democratically accountable the government. In South Africa the government already plays a large role, and it is in the interests of democracy, as well as of business, to have less interference and regulation in the Republic. In both the commercial and political arenas, more decision-making powers, and, most importantly, the information on which to base their decisions, ought to be given to ordinary citizens.

Moreover, in the 1980s, corporate social responsibility is acknowledged to be an integral part of doing business around the world. It is enlightened self-interest which dictates a responsible approach to the communities on which, after all, the company is dependent for its long term survival and growth. The advantage of this motivation for social responsibility is that it may be more realistically based than a system dependent on either altruism or coercion.

Modern corporations typically seek to achieve multiple goals, and not only an adequate return on investment. 'Grudgingly . . . driven by protests, lawsuits and fear of government action as well as by more laudable motives, managers are beginning to adapt to new conditions of production and are accepting the idea that the corporation has multiple purposes' (Toffler, 1981, p. 250). Toffler says that once the need for multiple goals is accepted, companies will be compelled to invent new measures for performance, in other words, a social audit. Instead of the single 'bottom line' on which most executives have been brought up, the future corporation will require attention to multiple bottom lines — social, environmental, informational, political and ethical bottom lines — all of which are interconnected. A Price–Waterhouse spokesman said that 'managers are being asked to account for corporate behaviour in areas where no real standards of accountability have been established — where even the language of accountability has yet to be developed' (Toffler, 1981, pp. 253 – 4).

The striving for social accountability amongst contemporary firms is apparent in this statement. It is echoed by the Dean of the Graduate School of Management in Delft, Holland, who foresees business values changing, in keeping with those of the larger society in which business operates, from an 'economic – production orientation' to a 'total well–being orientation'. The Professor of Management at American University says that 'just as the feudal manor was replaced by the business corporation when agrarian societies were transformed into industrial societies, so too should the older model of the firm be replaced by a new form of economic institution' (Toffler, 1981, pp. 253 – 4). The new institution will combine economic and trans–economic objectives.

Multinationals, different economic systems and development: some theoretical arguments.

The multinationals, with their unique position in the world economic structure, may well be in the forefront of the changes that will occur. Toffler says that 10,000 firms based in the non-communist high–technology nations have affiliates outside their own countries. Of 382 major industrial firms with sales of over $1,000 million, fully 242 have 25 per cent or more 'foreign content' measured in terms of sales, assets, exports, earnings or employment. On a given day in 1971 they held $268,000 million in short-term liquid assets. This, according to the International Trade Subcommittee of the United States Senate, was 'more than twice the total of all international monetary institutions in the world on the same day'. The total annual United Nations budget, by comparison, represented less than 0.0037 of that amount. By the early 1970s General Motors' annual sales revenue was larger than the gross national product of Belgium or Switzerland. Exxon alone has a tanker fleet 50 per cent larger than that of the Soviet Union.

Indeed, there are some fifty or so socialist multinationals which operate in the COMECON countries, laying pipelines, making chemicals and ball–bearings, extracting potash and asbestos, and running shipping lines. Moreover socialist banks and financial institutions — ranging from the Moscow Narodny Bank to the Black Sea and Baltic General Insurance Company — do business in

Zurich, Vienna, London, Frankfurt and Paris. Of the 500 Western-based, privately owned multinationals whose sales in 1973 exceeded $500 million fully 140 had 'significant commercial dealings' with one or more of the COMECON countries.

Multinational corporations are no longer based solely in the wealthy nations. The twenty-five countries in the Latin American Economic System recently moved to create multinationals of their own in the fields of agriculture, low-cost housing and capital goods. Philippine-based companies are developing deepwater ports in the Persian Gulf, and Indian multinationals are building electronics plants in Yugoslavia, steel mills in Libya, and a machine tool industry in Algeria.

Recent developments in the penetration of the Soviet bloc and China by multinationals have involved contractual arrangements about production and co-production, management, performance of all kinds of services, technology transfers, and so forth. The host countries are owners of the enterprises, and the presence of the multinationals is limited in time; contracts can be renegotiated after a certain period. It amounts to replacing ownership relations with contractual relations, with the remuneration of the multinational company taking the form of a fee instead of dividends and accumulation of assets. This is a profound change of approach by comparison with the classical direct investment, and a salutary reminder that change is occuring so quickly in global economic organization that the advantages and disadvantages of a particular form today are history tomorrow.

In the 1980s and 1990s it might be that Western multinationals will prefer to deal with socialist countries than with many of those in the capitalist world — particularly the underdeveloped part of it. From the investment point of view, socialist countries may be safer and more stable: there is virtually no risk of expropriation; there are practically no strikes or labour unrest; there is little exchange risk since payment is made in cash or kind; and they offer greater political stability than developing countries and even some developed capitalist countries; all of which adds up to a good investment climate. The position of the multinationals will grow stronger, as they will have the power to withold or relocate investments in the socialist economies as well. International capitalist enterprises have evolved a long way since Lenin wrote 'Imperialism, the Highest Stage of Capitalism', in 1916.

The co-operation between multinationals and the Soviet bloc

may simply underline the fact that, economically at least, it is not East – West but North – South which counts. It is in that heterogeneous mass of countries which are called 'the Third World' for convenience (when in fact 'Third World' and 'financially poor states' are no longer interchangeable) that the effects of the multinationals will be most important for vast numbers of people. The common approach is that

> underdeveloped countries, and not least African ones, need the markets, assistance and capital of the centre countries. At the same time, they must gradually dissociate themselves from those countries and their agencies, notably the multinational corporations. Only be associating with each other and relying more on themselves can development be achieved. This holds true for the extractive sector, where producer associations are needed, and for the processing one, where there is an urgent need for a conscious strategy of industrialisation and co-operation on planning, research and development, market sharing etc., between underdeveloped countries. [Hveem in Widstrand, 1975, p. 80.]

This approach may be good politics, but it is not clear that it is good economics — and it is good economics which is needed to alleviate the world's poverty.

Multinational corporations seem to be well-suited to the task of global development. Unlike governments and development agencies, corporations have to operate with economic efficiency: it is for the most efficient allocation of scarce resources around the world that multinationals should be held accountable to the international community.

The caveat which needs to be made here is that bribery cuts across all the principles which make international business an efficient economic unit: the significant advantages of competitive enterprise across national borders are negated if success for firms is brought about, not by superior management, but by corrupt collusion with government officials. In the absence of such gross interference with the market, everyone should gain from multinational business corporations around the world; in the presence of bribery, ordinary citizens everywhere lose.

All these developments have altered the role of the nation–state, and led to a new economic interdependence in the world. One economist has observed that 'for the past few centuries, the world has been neatly divided into a set of independent, sovereign nation–states. . . . With the emergence of literally hundreds of multinational or global corporations, this organisation of the world into mutually exclusive political entities is now being overlaid by a network of economic institutions' (Brown, President of the Worldwatch Institute). Sometimes co–operating with their home nation, sometimes exploiting it, sometimes executing its policies, sometimes using it to execute their own, the multinationals are neither all good nor all bad. However, with their ability to shunt billions back and forth instantly across national boundaries, their power to deploy technology and to move relatively quickly, they have often outflanked and outrun national governments.

Another commentator has affirmed that 'it is not just, or even mainly, a question of whether international companies can circumvent particular regional laws and regulations, it is that our whole framework of thought and reaction is founded in the concept of the sovereign nation state while international corporations are rendering this notion invalid'. Raymond Vernon suggests that the host state, and sometimes the home state, are at odds with the multinationals because the state strives to maximize national benefits whereas the multinational strives to maximize global objectives. At times the two objectives are compatible but there are always instances of incompatibility, which usually place a strain on national objectives. The answer, one would suggest, is not the negative approach of keeping out the multinationals, but for national governments to learn to practise an international policy in such matters as anti–trust legislation, taxation, company law, patent law, interest and credit policy.

In *North – South: a Programme for Survival*, the report of the Independent Commission on International Development Issues under the Chairmanship of Willy Brandt (usually known as the Brandt report), the following recommendations are made regarding multinational corporations, investment and the sharing of technology: effective national laws and international codes of conduct are needed to govern the sharing of technology, to control restrictive business practices, and to provide a framework for the activities of the transnational corporations.

(a) Reciprocal obligations on the part of the host and home countries covering foreign investment, transfer of technology, and repatriation of profits, royalties and dividends.

(b) Legislation, co–ordinated in host and home countries, to regulate transnational corporation activities in matters such as ethical behaviour, disclosure of information, restrictive business practices, and labour standards.

(c) Intergovernmental co-operation in regard to tax policies and the monitering of transfer pricing.

(d) Harmonization of fiscal and other incentives among host developing countries.

The Brandt report goes on to suggest that in addition to improved access to international development finance, the bargaining capacity of developing countries vis-à-vis the transnational corporations should be strengthened with the technical assistance increasingly available from the United Nations and other agencies. It is argued that permanent sovereignty over natural resources is the right of all countries, but that nationalization be accompanied by effective and appropriate compensation, under internationally comparable principles which should be embodied in national laws. Increasing use should also be made of international mechanisms for settling disputes. Greater international, regional and national efforts are needed to support the development of technology in developing countries and the transfer of appropriate technology to them at reasonable cost. There should also be increased efforts in both rich and poor countries to develop appropriate technology in the light of changing constraints regarding energy and ecology; the flow of information about such technology should be improved. The international aid agencies should change those of their practices which inhibit the recipients' freedom to choose technology, and should make more use of local capacities in preparing projects.

Brandt's argument is not that the rich should give to the poor, but that if the rich are to maintain their standard of living in the long term it is necessary to help the poor to become larger markets for their goods. The globe is seen as an interdependent economic unit, and one can see how mutually beneficial transactions between the developed and developing countries can be mediated by the multinationals.

Part of the reason for the attack on multinationals, and particularly the American ones, is political, and takes place in the context of the clash between 'left' and 'right' in the world since the Second World War. According to G.W.H. Relly of the Anglo-American Corporation, 'you have in the transnationals the living and irritating proof that they are able to get things done in a manner which no amount of philosophizing can make up for. The multinationals are an abiding offence to socialist thinking'. (Relly, GSB/UCT, 1980).

Some of the more advanced developing countries – Ireland, Singapore, Malaysia, South Korea, Kenya, Taiwan, Brazil – provide incentives for foreign investment on the grounds that the benefits outweigh the costs, and these economies have shown growth, whereas stagnation has characterized some socialist experiments, such as those in Tanzania, Vietnam, and Mozambique, in the Third World.

It is an increasingly questionable assumption that host governments are not capable of controlling the activities of the multinationals. Governments can control local equity participation, for example, and insist that foreign corporate planning which will have local effects be co-ordinated with state planning systems. Some kind of social contract, or symbiotic relationship, can exist between multinationals and host countries so that both are better off than they would have been without each other. The inevitable tensions which arise between them from time to time can be creative, leading to better solutions. Whereas national governments often make decisions on political grounds, and sometimes on even more narrowly defined sectional interests, multinationals tend to make decisions on economic grounds, and might therefore have a stabilizing and rationalizing effect on the world order. Nations linked by trade and investment, while maintaining their national characteristics, are more likely to have common interests in maintaining international stability and prosperity.

Naturally, the role of the multinationals is not usually viewed in isolation, but as part of a specific economic system; and one's views of that system, and of the alternatives, will to some extent determine one's evaluation of the multinational corporations themselves. Much of the evaluation in current economic literature, beginning from a premise that there is a better alternative, is critical and follows the line that

> such evolutionary changes (as third world economic nationalism, e.g. OPEC) must be continually compared with genuinely re-volutionary alternatives, i.e. alternatives which begin with the basic need of the marginalised people of the world for material betterment and control over their own natural and social environment as the

objective of economic development and social change, rather than its derivative. [Girvan in Widstrand, 1975, p. 52].

The idealistic notion that economic control should be appropriated by the representatives of the 'people' and then redistributed in the best interests of the people by a socialist or communist government rests on assumptions about the omniscience and goodwill of those who have to make the crucial decisions about production and distribution which experience in the twentieth century should have dispelled.

Although the competition between economic and political systems might affect the multinationals in the future, it is possible that large global corporations will be extant when the distinctions between communism and capitalism as differing social orders have become blurred. This blurring of economic, financial and technological lines is already evident. A United Nations report (1973, p.21) noted that 'the centrally planned economies are more involved in the activities of the multinational corporations than a cursory examination of the standard data might indicate' and the involvement has deepened significantly in the last decade, in Eastern Europe, the Soviet Union, and China.

In the foreseeable future, therefore,

the need to identify its common interests and potential areas of conflict with many different nation–states is a continuing and never-ending operating requirement for international enterprises. The diversity and dynamic nature of these relations do not permit easy generalizations; nor is a general background adequate for an international manager. He must deal with specific business situations in relation to specific national environments. . . . The only certainties are that the situation will constantly be changing and that, in order to maintain its tenure, the international enterprise must be ever ready to justify to a nation–state not only its entry but its continued presence. [Robock et al, 1977, pp. 197 – 8.]

In considering the role of the multinationals in developing countries, Vaitsos (1977, London School of Economics conference paper), shows how the presence of multinationals makes contemporary integration processes different from earlier attempts at regional economic co–operation. In earlier times, tariff barriers often resulted in the physical exclusion of foreign economic actors; now the multinationals can reinforce their positions precisely because they can locate their activities behind regional protective walls in markets foreign to their home country. Moreover, in developing countries it is not often possible for local firms to combine effectively, if they exist in the first place, in the way for example that European companies did in order to meet adequately *le defi americain*. The aim of multinationals, it is argued, is to maximize the benefits that regional economic co–operation can generate and to reduce the risks that intergration can cause to their interests, so they are never passive about integration policies, but try to influence them.

Extrapolating to South Africa, it will not be easy for the Republic to supplant the multinationals in key sectors of the economy for some time to come. Furthermore, the process of economic integration in southern and sub–Saharan Africa, because of the conflict between White–ruled South Africa and the rest, is even more complex than the usual process which anyway implies benefit or damage to specific economic and political interests. Given this situation, it is arguable that, if anything, the role of the multinationals in the southern Africa region will be strengthened in future. This tendency towards increased participation by the multinationals will be reinforced by:

(a) the seeming ideological neutrality of large multinationals, as witness Gulf Oil in Angola, which enables them more easily to do business with everyone;
(b) the multinational's rational desire for business co–operation in the region;
(c) the South African government's support for regional economic co-operation, both for its own sake and in an attempt to bypass what appear to be intractable political problems preventing closer links with surrounding states; and
(d) by the economic needs of Black southern African states — even Zimbabwe will be dependent economically on South Africa for the foreseeable future — which can be served to a considerable extent by multinational corporations.

Although Vaitsos, for example, argues that multinationals tend to block effective regional co–operation which threatens their economic interests (he cites the case of the Andean pact countries), it may be that in southern Africa the multinationals are amongst the few actors who can surmount otherwise impenetrable barriers between countries and increase the economic prosperity of the region (at the same time as the political struggle continues to determine who will rule South Africa).

Indeed, Vaitsos shows clearly how the policy options open to developing countries when they attempt to integrate economic activity — such as market integration, common treatment of foreign investments and technology, and common industrial programming — often lead to a situation in which the multinationals are the true integrating force. Consequently, they can and do reorient the process of integration to meet their own corporate objectives rather than the development goals of the member countries.

Given that the international technology market is imperfect — since firms practise exclusion to maintain the value of their technology — there is no possibility of Paretian optimality in the production and use of technology in the world economy. The point has been summarized as follows 'The real problem of productive knowledge . . . is that the world has not found a better way to reward the private acquisition of knowledge, than by the granting of a monopoly of limited and uncertain duration' (Johnson, 1975, pp. 41 – 2).

Therefore the transfer of technology to South Africa and other developing countries in the region will pose problems for which there can only be second-best solutions (and it is pointless to berate the multinationals for providing a second-best solution when the alternative is no solution at all rather than a best one).

Also, given that there is 'no better way to reward the private acquisition of knowledge' than to consider it a private saleable commodity, it does not seem reasonable to argue (Cooper and Hoffman, 1977) that technology is in fact a public good, or that government intervention in the transfer of technology will promote greater welfare than a free market.

However, the argument for limited government intervention may be stronger in developing countries, at least as a temporary expedient; and the implications of the transfer process for the international distribution of welfare need careful attention. A 1975 UNCTAD report, for instance, show how firms place limitations on the access to technology:

(a) total prohibition of exports or requirement of previous approval;

(b) exports permitted to certain countries and prohibited to others;

(c) the specification of particular products which may be exported or of prices and quantities allowed, the designation of firms which are allowed to handle the export trade, and the prohibition of exports of substitute products;

(d) clauses which provide for guarantees concerning profits and royalties and concerning tax rates and tariffs and rates of exchange;

(e) provisions which result in restricting competition — and hence preventing a more rational utilization of resources — by imposing limitations of competitive imports, by preventing other enterprises from competing for local resources, or by obtaining local patents (thus eliminating possible competitors);

(f) provisions resulting in excessive reliance on expatriate skilled personnel, which hampers the formation of local skills and discourages the development of local technical and research and development capabilities.

The task of developing countries is to overcome these limitations without going so far as to make the transfer, or indeed the creation, of technology unattractive to business. There is a point at which both parties benefit without either exploiting the other, and the art of development management is to find that point in each case.

As an interim measure, developing countries like South Africa ought to develop even more than they have done, coherent policies towards foreign investment and perhaps institutions to deal with the transfer of technology in conjunction with domestic research and development. In the longer run, once local industry is sufficiently developed, these matters can be dealt with by private enterprise; otherwise there is the danger that institutions which are initially useful will become stultifying bureaucracies, analogously to the way in which 'infant industries' are still treated like infants and protected after twenty–five or fifty years.

Whereas it may be necessary at some stage of development to have a government body which will try to ensure that, for example, domestic interests hold a majority of the equity; and that the facilities for foreign investment in fields like taxation, tariffs and exchange control are such that there is a balance of benefits between foreign suppliers and the economy of the developing country, these bodies should play a temporary and advisory role.

As Roumeliotis points out (UNCTAD Seminar, November 1977), a number of writers on multinationals have argued that the activities of these firms in host countries and the policies of governments of these countries should be regarded as taking place in a bargaining framework. This view helps analysis of, for example, transfer pricing, which is probably the most controversial multinational activity after political interference and Lockheed-style bribery. The assumption is that the multinational has a set of preferences with a number of negotiable items, and so has the host government, but they are in inverse order to that of the multi-national; the final contract which the two parties consider as mutually acceptable will depend on their relative bargaining power. The practice of transfer pricing is one of the items around which bargaining takes place. This relative power approach takes both will and ability into account, in looking not only at the incentives but also at the possibilities open to both corporations and countries.

At some stages of development, countries may need a central-ized body to deal with the bargaining which must be conducted with foreign corporations.

> The big TNE's, for reasons associated with their size, technological know-how, links to the powerful states of the home countries etc., have a stronger bargaining position than a single host-country. Consequently, if transfer pricing is ranked high in their preferences, and here the policies of the nation-states are important, companies succeed in avoiding controls, or, in case they are pressured by governments to abstain from transfer pricing activities, they gain such concessions in their place that for the country concerned it is like sacrificing your right leg to save your left. [Roumeliotis, 1977, p. 3.]

Part of the problem with the multinationals is that intra-firm trade is beyond the market, and therefore not subject to market restraints. In order to present some countervailing power, govern-ments find it necessary to intervene in the intra-firm economics of multinationals, so that two major economic actors in a country are removed from Adam Smith's 'invisible hand'. Murray puts the argument in context: the neo-classical tradition sees international economic relations in terms of the market transactions of national firms and consumers. Trade takes place between independent national units so that both may increase their utilities. Governments have the power to regulate these international exchanges so that, taken together, they maximize a particular nation's social welfare, and they will do so not by attempting to block (for example, through quotas) or replace (through state trading) the private international market, but by altering the relative prices at which the exchanges take place.

Conventional trade theory has been challenged on value and institutional grounds. The latter suggests that neo–classical theory is based on assumptions which are inconsistent with the evident structures of contemporary international trade. Firstly, with the post–war expansion of foreign direct investment (which rose from $25 billion in 1951 to $287 billion in 1976), trade is increasingly dominated not by competitive national firms but by oligopolistic multinationals. For example, 69 per cent of United States exports are now associated with multinationals, as are 41 per cent of United States imports. Secondly, an increasing proportion of multi-national–related trade is intra–firm trade. A growing proportion of international trade, therefore, is not classical trade at all but transfers within single multinational corporations. Consequently, the prices on these intra–firm transfers are administered, and not market prices, so play a different role in economic activity to traditional market price. International transfer prices are primarily concerned with the accounting allocation of value between different branches of the same firm. They do not represent new values appropriated by one firm from another, as was the case with international market exchange.

South African economists and policymakers need to be aware that action which seeks to influence a firm's activity by changing relative prices may have unintended consequences. Devaluation, for example, may have the expected consequences of increasing exports and decreasing imports for national firms, but the mechanics are not the same with multinationals which have established an international division of labour, in which the foreign buyer and the foreign supplier are one and the same firm. The task of South African economic management includes ensuring that monetary policy and exchange controls are not bypassed by firms with the capacity to move company funds internationally by adjusting transfer prices; and that taxation is not affected by multinationals using transfer pricing to adjust what profit is declared where, according to comparative international tax rates and other fiscal incentives. In a nutshell the governments of developing countries, may have to play a role in safeguarding their power of internal economic management in the face of the substitution of transfer prices for market–prices.

> 'I hope it is now clear why transfer pricing ... assumes an importance which belies its unassuming technical appearance. It is one of the main points of contact between multinationals and nation–states, and highlights the crisis for national economic regulation which arises when the system of national economic prices (on which much state regulation is based) is rendered ambiguous by the growth of international transfer prices. Traditional theory (and much national economic practice) has not been able to address the problem adequately since transfer pricing strikes at the basis of its main assumptions: the prevalence of arm's length market relations, and the power of the state to regulate these relations by adjusting relative prices. The new theory — by starting from firms rather than states, and from intra–firm economics rather than the market — has raised these questions in a way which alternative theories and practices can no longer ignore. [Murray, 1981, p. 4.]

Assuming both the capacity and incentive for multinationals to undertake transfer pricing, there is then the question of a strategy of control. South Africa has to decide between two major approaches. The first is the restoration of the market system by:

(a) anti–trust action to reduce excessive profits and the monopoly abuse of transfer pricing, thus restoring the competitive if not the national private firm;
(b) a standardization of different national taxes and controls, thereby reducing the incentive to avoid one channel by using another, and an internationalization of income tax which would reduce the incentive to transfer price for tax reasons;
(c) an accounting comparison with arm's length prices.

This last approach is the most commonly used in both developed and underdeveloped countries. However, for some products there may be no comparable market price; the price may be a mono-polistic one; and even when it is competitive, neo–Ricardian trade theory suggests that they are not necessarily just prices, but may indeed, in Emmanuel's argument, be the means by which profit is transferred from low wage to high wage countries.

The approach of the transnational economists, as already

mentioned, is one which emphasizes bargaining. Cases should be dealt with individually. There is no objective 'just' price. World market prices could be used to strengthen a government's bargaining position and indicate the extent of surplus profit (or rent) hidden in a price. Governments in developing countries such as South Africa, according to this argument, ought not to be trying to restore a traditional version of market relations, but strengthening themselves *vis-à-vis* the multinational corporations which are tending to dominate the world economy.

South Africa, in common with all countries which host multinational corporations, has to address the question of mechanisms of control. One position which is adopted by the developed countries views the government's relationship with multinationals as equivalent to its relationship with individuals. Multinationals, like individuals, must be protected against the arbitrary use of state power. The burden of proof in transfer pricing, as in matters of crime, should be on the state and not on the accused. In this view, for example, information given in confidence to one government department should not be circulated to others; in many countries such confidentially is protected by law. A counter–argument is that multinationals cannot be equated to individuals, and that governments should develop a form of law which allows them scope and discretion in dealings with economic units which, in developing countries at least, are larger than themselves. Followers of this line of thought, for example, would suggest that governments should have the legal powers to acquire any corporate information which they might need.

Whichever of these approaches is adopted, in some cases there might be a need for strengthening the countervailing power of the state opposite the multinationals, so that there is a balance of benefits between them. This has implications in the fields of law, government organization and confidentiality, on the way in which data is collected and classified and so forth, so that countries are left 'not with a price system, let alone general government policies aimed at the macro–economy, but a multitude of serial relations with specific firms, whose unity is established not in the sphere of the private economy, but through some form of co–ordinating mechanism of the state' (Murray, 1981, p. 11).

Regrettably, through using transfer pricing, multinationals put themselves beyond the constraints of the open market, thereby opening the way — and giving the justification — for states and governments to do the same: the bilateral bargaining between governments and multinationals might well include non-economic issues and pressures, and allows for venal collusion between them to the detriment of the country's population in any given case.

The underlying assumption in all arguments for state involvement is that states, unlike the multinationals, act in the interests of the country's consumers — and this assumption may not always hold. As a tentative hypothesis, then, one could say that the more democratic a country, i.e. the more easily the government can be removed from power by the populace, the more it can be trusted to counter the power of the multinationals to the nation's benefit; an autocratic government may or may not act for the benefit of the nation. The multinationals, naturally, seek to achieve their own business aims, and equally naturally, take advantage of the opportunities and try to minimize the obstacles in their way. The essential part of the problem is to work out practical ways, in each specific situation, of ensuring that the consumers, the business corporation and the government achieve a new benefit from their interaction.

It is not easy to monitor transfer pricing and all the other activities of the multinationals, and even when effective monitoring is established, political considerations may prevail over economic ones. In Greece, for example, the transfer pricing commando unit which was established discovered instances of under–invoicing and over–invoicing which were never acted upon for political reasons (and indeed the operations of the unit were curtailed).

Some eonomists argue that the power of those in control of production (the multinationals in this case) will always tend to dominate those whose power is limited to the spheres of circulation (host country governments). To overcome the conflict between nation–states and multinationals it would be necessary to restore effective state control over the national economy by replacing private multinational production with public national production.

This argument has two weaknesses. Firstly, private production is likely to be more efficient and innovative over the long run. Secondly, placing all power of production into the hands of the state in South Africa (or most states for that matter) would result in a monopoly of power so total as to eclipse individual freedom. Indeed, the South African government itself is taking steps towards private enterprise (because the Whites no longer need so much protection). It is not necessary for the state to take over multinational production — it is enough for the state — representing the interests of all the country's consumers — to bargain over the terms of the multinationals' operations.

The socio–political arguments for not concentrating all power into the hands of the state are cogent, but so too is the purely economic argument for allowing private production by multinationals — and this holds for developing countries like South Africa.

> While the MNE cannot be expected to serve as a development agency (for this is the job of the government), it has been shown that the MNE is an efficient institution which responds to exogenous market imperfections. The MNE can be adapted to serve as an intermediary in the transfer of technology and can help to equalize the economic opportunities between poor and rich nations. In this way the MNE serves to promote the growth and development of all nations. [Rugman, 1981, pp. 154 – 5.]

Proponents of this type of argument suggest that the rationale for multinationals is that they reduce transaction costs (which are involved in mutually beneficial trading opportunities) by buying up complementary assets located in different nations and integrating their operations within a single unit of control. In so doing they create an 'internal market' for intermediate products. Transaction costs flow mainly from a change of ownership because change of ownership creates an incentive for both parties to haggle over price, and also an incentive to default. Neither of these incentives occur in an internal market so, it is suggested, in many instances an internal market is a more efficient institution for allocating resources than an external one. The theory of internalization predicts that the propensity to internalize is greater the greater is the volume of trade, and the frequency of transactions, between two units in the external market; if the frequency of transactions could be reduced, either by long–term contracts, or by purchasing more occasionally in greater bulk, then the incentive to internalize would diminish. In terms of this theory, one would expect firms with large–scale R&D producing a stream of innovations to internalize them, rather than one with a small R&D effort. Similarly, firms selling high–quality branded products are more likely to want to secure quality supplies through backward integration than firms selling unbranded goods, who would be more likely to shop around the world market for the cheapest supplies.

For sound economic reasons, businesses trying to produce goods and services on a worldwide basis tend to rely on internal markets. Rugman argues that internalization is the process of making a firm within a firm. The internal market of the firm substitutes for the regular or external market and solves the problems of allocation and distribution by administrative fiat. The internal prices, or transfer prices, of the firm lubricate the organization and permit the internal market to function as efficiently as a potential, but unrealized, regular market. Whenever there is a missing market (as in the pricing of intermediate products such as knowledge), or when the transaction costs of the regular market are excessive, then there will be a reason for internalization. Since the economy is characterized by many such market imperfections, there is always a strong motivation for firms to create internal markets. On a worldwide basis there are countless barriers to trade and other market imperfections so there are even stronger reasons for the emergence of multinational enterprises. Such firms internalize international market imperfections as well as domestic ones, and thereby increase global social welfare. 'We can say that internalisation is always a response to market imperfections and that both natural market failure and unnatural government regulations are everywhere . . . we now know that multinational enterprises exist due to worldwide market imperfections to which internal markets are the only viable economic response' (Rugman, 1981, p. 156). As long as governments persists in intervention in the market–place, they will create market imperfections and hence an incentive for internalization.

It is probably the case that South Africa is sufficiently developed, and has enough countervailing power, not to have to place barriers in the way of foreign direct investment by American and other multinational corporations. However, it is clear that if multinational corporations abuse any host country through unfair transfer pricing, (or in any other way, as witness recent allegations that collusion between cartel members pushed the price of electrical equipment bought by ESCOM in South African by 16 – 40 per cent) they are inviting government regulation, and, as discussed above, government participation in a bargaining process which ends in a deal. However, it should be borne in mind that a contractual agreement is unlikely to be as efficent as either an internal market used by multinationals in foreign direct investment, or as the regular market used in free trade. It is in both South Africa's (and this holds true whoever is in power) and the multinationals' long-term interests that they both adhere as closely as possible to good economics and the maximization of social welfare. The alternative is increased government intervention and a consequent multitude of market imperfections to which the multinationals will no longer be able to respond: social welfare is reduced and everyone is worse off. In addition, because South Africa is a developing country and has greater imperfections in the goods and factor markets that the developed countries of Europe and North America, it probably has even more to gain from the presence of the multinationals than would Germany or France.

Economic growth and political change

Both in the past and currently South Africa has shown awareness of these economic arguments, and has encouraged foreign investment. For example, in 1984 there was a prodigious effort by government to stimulate European investment in the country. South Africa, under whatever political dispensation, needs foreign capital and foreign direct investment and technology transfer to develop. Nevertheless, there probably needs to be further analysis and empirical verification where possible, of the theoretical arguments about economic development, about the relative efficacy of different economic systems in aiding development, and about the role of multinational corporations in aiding or hindering development. Already there has been long debate on the effects of economic growth on political change: will economic growth create exigencies which will destroy the apartheid system, or can economic growth adapt itself to the apartheid structure for the indefinite future? Whether some future version of a free enterprise system, and the multinationals which form an important part of international capitalism, are judged to be beneficial for South Africa (or indeed any developing country) will in turn depend on underlying assumptions about what constitutes that best kind of political economy and the most efficient way to develop the country towards that goal.

The conclusions reached could, of course, be applicable to all capitalist corporations and developing countries, with adjustments for particular circumstances: the adjustment that has to be made for South Africa is not only how these factors affect economic development, but also how they affect the racial structure of the country. Development economics perforce cross disciplinary boundaries into politics.

In this section it is suggested that the United States multinationals are useful to South Africa through capital formation, as well as through other economic and non–economic inputs.

> Few countries are blessed . . . by the augmentation of their supply of 'land' through the discovery and exploitation of rich deposits of natural resources that were previously unknown or unvalued. For all other countries, increase in productivity and income per worker must depend on the formation of physical capital, increase in the capability of labour, and innovation. Capital formation is a necessary member of the trio. Increase in output per unit of labour input is possible without capital formation — by managerial improvement, by improvement in labour skills, by technical inventions that require no added capital, in the production of many products by increase of scale, and in other ways — but there is no recorded case in which these have been sufficient to obviate the need for physical capital formation if there is to be sustained economic growth in the economy as a whole. [Hagan, 1980, p. 179.]

In South Africa, as with most developing countries, capital is scarce and labour plentiful relative to the high-income countries, but it is capital formation which is needed to increase the income per capita. Capital formation replaces capital that wears out, provides capital equipment for an increasing labour force, and increases the amount of capital per worker (i.e. per unit of labour input). These three effects, capital replacement, capital widening and capital deepening, are usually lumped together in considering the amount of capital needed. Lumping them together, it may require gross capital formation equal to, for example, only 2 per cent of GDP in one country, but in another country, 6 or 7 per cent of GDP to increase by 1 per cent the volume of goods that the country can produce. The ratio between the value of the added capital and that of the resulting increase in output per year — ranging from 2 to 7 in the figures just given — is the incremental capital – output ratio, or ICOR. The ICOR is a rough measurement because it includes not only capital formation, but also technical progress, changes in the scale of production, improvements in management and all other factors which affect the increase in productivity in the country.

To a significant extent, the task facing developing countries such as South Africa is to have a better, i.e. lower ICOR. The ICOR depends on a number of factors, including climate, natural resources, geographic size and population density, government policy as regards the capital – labour ratio, shifts from agricultural to industrial production, new mineral deposits, and so forth. If South Africa can achieve an ICOR of 3 through higher rates of capital formation (and this is where foreign direct investment is important), then one can work out how much capital formation is needed for an increase in output and income per capita: if South Africa's GNP is to grow at 5 per cent per year, ensuring rising income since this is faster than even the rapid 2 – 3 per cent per annum increase in the African population, then with an ICOR of 3 capital formation would have to equal 15 per cent of GDP. In sum, South Africa needs considerable annual investment even to keep abreast of, let alone make clear gains over, the increase in population, hence the importance of increased investment. The multinational corporations can aid development in a number of ways — but the onus is on the host country to develop a sound economic environment for both domestic and foreign investment.

Development issues in South Africa, however, are further complicated by the country's race policies. There are conflicting views on the effects of economic growth: some argue that growth is incompatible with apartheid, whereas others argue that growth will not alter the racial structure. A close examination of this issue is important to the topic under consideration, because nearly all South African businessmen — including the executives of foreign corporations — speak as though economic growth will, via certain mechanisms like the greater need for skilled Black labour, bring about the peaceful change towards an integrated South African society. The best-known variation of this approach is termed the Oppenheimer thesis, after the ex-Chairman of the Anglo – American Corporation. As stated succinctly by Oppenheimer himself in an address to the Foreign Policy Association in New York in October 1984, this thesis holds that:

It is just because the South African economy has moved forward rapidly that the original apartheid policy has had to be scrapped and that some changes for the better have come about.
    The fact is that continued domination of the blacks by the whites

could only continue if the economy were kept small enough for all, or anyhow most, skilled jobs to be reserved for the whites as they used to be in the past.

Other well–known writing on this subject by a South African businessman is that by Michael O'Dowd, also of the Anglo – American Corporation.

Like Oppenheimer and O'Dowd, most businessmen in South Africa tend to believe — or hope — that the government will opt for a 'rich and mixed' as opposed to a 'poor and White' South Africa. However, it remains to be seen whether this assumption is correct and whether economic richness and political whiteness are incompatible in the longer term.

> On the one hand, therefore, one cannot rule out O'Dowd's general modernisation and ensuing political liberalisation approach as a theoretical possibility (with perhaps a longer time–scale than that suggested by O'Dowd), although there are serious flaws in his view of change and the future of South Africa. On the other hand, it can be cogently argued that the political, social and economic forces at play are too complex and conflicting to permit a straightforward O'Dowdian four–phrase movement (confusion, repressive minority rule, old–fashioned liberalism, welfare state) towards a contented welfare state in South Africa early next century. [Razis, 1980, p. 90.]

While accepting the argument that simple economic growth by itself will not necessarily lead to the end of apartheid and the full incorporation of Blacks into the body politic of South Africa, the argument in this book is that growth actually does ease the political, social and economic constraints preventing the full inclusion of all South Africans into the political economy of the country. Full and final incorporation might well depend on political will and political action, but economic development can strengthen the will and pay for the action. Reforms need funding; and a state of poverty and backwardness is not a sound basis for self or group advancement.

In the massive academic literature on the subject, this liberalizing view is not being rejected as readily as it recently was:

> The implicit counter–factual for Houghton and Horwitz, or Hutt (1964), as for all the neo–classical economists or political scientists of the day, was what they took to be the mutually reinforcing indus-

trial and politically liberalising histories of England and America.
This led them to emphasise three things in particular: the importance of worker commitment and domestic consumers as conditions
for the realisation of capitalist profits; the efficiency of free markets
in assembling factors of production; and the manifest inefficiency of
the apartheid state on both counts. Until the mid–1970s Marxists
could safely scoff at this argument. Now I am not so sure. South
Africa's capitalists have been clamouring for larger domestic markets; the ethnic network of power looks vulnerable to black unemployment; many industrialists feel ready to risk trying out the power
of 'the essential civilising moment' as an alternative to the violence
of repression.
[Lonsdale, 1983, p.p.79–80.]

The well–known radical arguments, that economic growth in
South Africa will not by itself alter the racial structure (many of the
arguments go further to say that growth generates poverty for the
Blacks, while strengthening White privilege and White supremacy)
received support from an important 1980 publication by Stanley
Greenberg on *Race and State in Capitalist Development.* This
study looks at the persistence of racial conflict and domination in
four societies, mainly Alabama and South Africa, with Northern
Ireland and Israel included 'to help establish the generality of the
problem and process'.

And yet the events of Birmingham, Soweto, Derry and Nazareth are
hardly trivial or isolated. They highlight the bitter racial and ethnic
divisions in society that have managed high levels of urbanisation,
mass communication, economic growth, wage labour, trade union
organisation, bureaucratisation, political mobilisation, indeed, all
the essentials of developing capitalist societies. They leave us, therefore, with a difficult and unanswered question: What is the impact of
capitalist development on patterns of racial and ethnic domination?
The answer requires an appreciation of the dynamics of growth and
the tenacity of ethnic and racial differentiation.
[Greenberg, 1980. p.p. 6–7].

Greenberg says that in South Africa, White businessmen who
live with bitter divisions and violence maintain that racial barriers
are incompatible with rapid economic growth; given free rein,
businessmen would generate wealth and a new relationship
between Black and White. During a full century of industrial
development and increasing racial antagonisms in South Africa,

successive leaders like J.T. Jabavu, John Dube and Gatsha Buthelezi have allied themselves with liberal capitalists and have urged programmes of self–help and economic expansion. The study tentatively concludes that capitalist development in the research settings both preserves and remakes the racial order, extending and reinforcing racial barriers, but also creating new contradictions that paradoxically threaten to dismantle them. The state intervenes following demands by dominant class actors like commercial farmers, businessmen and (white) trade unions, creating a racial state apparatus which favours these groups and exploits subordinate groups.

Whether the racial order persists and in what form depends on the strength of the business challenge to the traditional racial hegemony (which with growth actually damages the interests of commerce and industry), but also on the resources and coherence of the racial state, and increasingly on the strength of the subordinate challenge.

The notion that economic growth alone is not enough to change the apartheid state, in other words, that overtly political action is also required, is one which is echoed by many thinkers on the subject. Cape Town University historian Giliomee, for example, says that growth and a free market is not a sufficient condition for political liberty: 'if businesses are interested in . . . worthwhile survival they must realise that the market cannot do it alone and that it is their task to help bring along the political decisions which are needed to lessen inequality and bring about a wider community' (F.M., 30 January, 1981, p. 334).

Elsewhere Giliomee has argued that if Greenberg is to be proved wrong (in postulating that the political and business elite in deeply divided societies usually fail to grasp the nettle of political reform unless driven to it by extreme pressures and only turn to rationality after all the alternatives have been exhausted) then the elite has to embark on a peaceful revolution of modernization. The revolution will have to transform all the systems by which South African society is organized — the political, social, economic, intellectual and psychological systems. These systems must be able to generate and absorb the vast changes which South African society will undergo in the next three decades as a result of the population and education explosion of Black South Africa. Business, which after Carltons I and II has become recognized by government as a bargaining partner, granted permanent rights of access, and accorded devolved powers such as under the new labour dispensation, will have to be a crucial actor in this transformation.

Now there is an apparent paradox in this urging of business to grasp the nettle of political reform in South Africa, namely that business is being asked to step out of the economic and firmly into the political arena, in order to bring about the sort of long–term stable South Africa in which they will be allowed to continue their business activities. However, the paradox is only apparent because, despite its protestations, business in South Africa historically has used the political level — the state — to act on its behalf. For example, a recent study by Yudelman argues that the years 1902–39 are historically noteworthy for the 'growing symbiotic relationship between the mining houses and the state, directed at the subjugation and control of organised labour, so that the mines could continue to make profits, and the state acquire the legitimacy and the solvency which it so desperately needed during the early turbulent years of Union' (Davenport, 1983, p.95). At this historical juncture, business could try to push the South African state towards allowing the economy to become a free–play area where accommodations are reached under free–market conditions.

Current business thinking seems to be in favour of freer relations of production: government intervention in the economy no longer appears to be in the best interests of the business community. This being the case, business is now happy to argue in favour of greatly decreased government intervention and unfettered markets. Although business might at last be doing the right thing for the wrong reasons, in terms of the ideal–type political economy used as a model in this work, the shift towards a diminished state and freer economic relations is nevertheless intrinsically good. On the way to freer economic relations it might be prudent for the state to spread wealth more evenly by social investment (for example, in education) in human capital, so that all South Africans have a greater chance to realize their economic potential.

The least attractive alternative would be a doctrinaire socialist state which could damage economic growth, and then spread the reduced benefits more evenly and thinly over the population, destroying economic incentive and finally running the real risk of turning South Africa into just one more poor, stagnating African state. Such a centralized state would, moreover, be ripe for commandeering by any group which could then rule with clear sectional interests in view, just as the Whites have done in the past.

Indeed, it sometimes sounds as though those who argue passionately for a powerful socialist state under Black rule simply and naturally wish to have their own hand in the honey jar for a change: but because the Whites used a strong repressive pro–capitalist state in their exclusive interests would not make it right as an ideal for which to strive for the Blacks to use a strong, repressive collectivist state in their exclusive interests — or that of a small elite among them. The aim should be to create a stable, just and prosperous South Africa, not to replace one flawed society by another flawed society for the satisfaction of seeing one's oppressors finally themselves oppressed.

In conclusion, in this book it is accepted that economic growth is unlikely, by itself, without further action on other fronts, to lead peacefully to an integrated, stable and equitable South Africa. However, it is suggested that genuine free enterprise economic growth is a necessary, but not sufficient, condition for any country which wishes to evolve towards political and social liberty. It would be damaging to the cause of individual freedom and material well-being, to better health, education and career opportunities, to either destroy the economy in the name of achieving some sort of political solution or to transform it into a socialist or communist economy, unresponsive to anything but the dictates of a new elite.

The next chapter examines the actual and potential impact of a limited section of the business community — the United States multinationals — but conclusions drawn about them could apply to the possible effects of all business in South Africa.

4 American business in South Africa: harnessing the workhorse

Why multinationals come to South Africa

South Africa was founded by a multinational corporation, the Dutch East India Company, which was also the world's first joint stock company. Jan van Riebeeck was a company executive, answerable to the Lords XVII, the businessmen who controlled the company from Amsterdam. The Dutch were among the first modern capitalists, and the settlement at the Cape was a purely commercial decision. The business of White South Africa, it seems, has always been business.

Investment is usually a function of risk and return, though other factors, such as strategic ones, might be added to the equation in certain circumstances. The American return on investment in South Africa was high (estimated by the United States Department of Commerce to be about 18 per cent) but fell in the autumn of 1985 to around 5 per cent because of political upheaval and South Africa's poor economic situation.

In 1981–2, for example, South Africa was the thirteenth most popular country for investors, ahead of such countries as Denmark, the United Kingdom, Ireland, and Greece, but behind Taiwan. The Swiss Beri–Institute in that year rated countries as follows:

(1) Switzerland	(11) Belgium
(2) Japan	(12) Australia
(3) Singapore	(13) South Africa
(4) United States	(14) Malaysia
(5) West Germany	(15) Sweden
(6) Netherlands	(16) United Kingdom
(7) Canada	(17) Denmark
(8) Saudi Arabia	(18) Ireland
(9) Taiwan	(19) France and
(10) Norway	(20) Greece

From a strictly business point of view, therefore, there was good and sufficient reason for American multinationals to do business in South Africa. Since September 1985 South Africa's international credit and investment rating have suffered badly and need to be rebuilt as an urgent necessity for the country's growth.

South Africa encourages business enterprise, both local and foreign, and welcomes foreign investment; and these were major reasons for its reasonable growth rate. The prevailing conditions concerning incentives, forms of investment, repatriation, taxation, the legal requirements of the Companies Act and related issues in which businessmen and particularly prospective investors are interested are available from a number of sources, such as commercial banks and government departments.

This book is concerned principally with American foreign direct investment, which is the investment of American non-residents in a South African organization in which they have a controlling interest; and the profile of American business in South Africa is described in more detail later in this chapter. Generally though, the relative importance of direct foreign liabilities, compared with non-direct liabilities, declined from 50 per cent at the end of 1956 to nearly 46 per cent of the total at the end of 1981.

With regard to foreign capital, the 1983 Nedbank appraisal of South Africa states that:

> The EEC was the most important source of foreign capital for the South African economy between 1956 and 1973, but its share of total foreign liabilities declined from 71 per cent at the end of 1956 to 66 per cent at the end of 1973. This occurred owing to a corresponding increase in the share of other West European countries and countries in North and South America. The contribution from countries in Asia, although still relatively small, also rose during the same period, while that of Africa first rose and then declined.
>
> The trends since 1973 reinforce the longer-term perspective, suggesting that North America has come to play an increasing role in satisfying South Africa's capital requirements, as shown in [Table 4.1]. From providing nearly 18 per cent of South Africa's net capital needs in 1973 the share of North and South America rose to nearly 24 per cent by 1981, while the share attributable to the EEC declined from nearly 66 per cent to just over 56 per cent. The sharpest rise in the American share took place between 1973 and 1976, suggesting that during the 1973 to 1975 economic downturn not only Britain, traditionally the chief supplier of South Africa's capital, but also the

European nations together drew in their horns. [Nedbank, 1983, pp. 143 − 4.]

Table 4.1. Origins of capital:* share of total

	EEC	Rest of Europe	N and S America	Africa	Asia	Oceania
	%	%	%	%	%	%
1973	65.9	9.6	17.8	3.8	2.1	0.8
1974	63.9	9.3	20.0	3.9	2.3	0.7
1975	62.2	10.1	21.8	3.1	2.2	0.5
1976	59.6	10.1	25.1	2.7	2.1	0.5
1977	59.5	9.8	24.9	3.0	2.3	0.4
1978	58.2	10.4	25.1	3.4	2.5	0.4
1979	59.0	12.2	22.9	3.1	2.4	0.5
1980	59.2	12.4	21.6	3.4	2.9	0.7
1981	56.3	13.2	23.7	2.4	3.6	0.8

* Excluding international organizations and unallocated items.
Source: S.A. Reserve Bank.

The Nedbank survey also includes Tables (4.2 and 4.3) which show the return on foreign investment in South Africa.

A classification of the earnings yield on direct investment of the United States according to type of economic activity [Table 4.2] indicates that the average yield in South Africa was higher for manufacturing and mining and smelting than the average for all countries during the period 1977 to 1981. However, rates of return on investment in trade and financing and insurance in South Africa were significantly lower than the average for all countries. Additionally, with the exception of mining and smelting and manufacturing, the earnings yield on US direct investment in South Africa was lower than that in other African countries. In particular, high earnings were received on investments in the petroleum industries of African countries.

The average rate of return on foreign investment in South Africa is shown for different periods in Table 4.3. This rate refers to the dividend and interest income of non-residents as well as their share in branch and partnership profits expressed as a ratio of total foreign investment in South Africa, before provision for non-resident tax. It shows that the average yield on foreign investments in South Africa remained relatively stable at 6 to 7 per cent between 1957 and 1981. [Nedbank, 1983, pp. 278 − 80.]

Table 4.2. Average earnings yield on American foreign direct investment according to main economic activity, 1977–81*

	Mining and smelting	Petroleum	Manufacturing	Trade	Insurance	Total
Australia	23.2	21.5	8.6	10.4	16.0	14.6
Canada	11.2	14.1	9.2	9.5	8.6	10.6
New Zealand	na†	na†	9.7	10.1	16.9	8.1
Norway	6.7	28.6	12.6	12.9	2.9	7.5
Spain	5.8	2.9	4.9	12.3	11.2	17.4
South Africa	25.0	na†	18.4	13.9	13.0	27.7
Other African countries	na†	38.9	14.7	13.9	13.0	27.7
All countries	3.7	23.9	12.6	14.6	14.6	15.8

* The earnings used in this comparison consist of the US parent companies' shares in the earnings (net of foreign income taxes) of their foreign affiliates, plus net interest of inter-company current accounts, less foreign withholding taxes. This information is, therefore, not comparable with the rates of return presented in Table 3.
† Figures not made available—to prevent disclosure of information on individual companies.
Source: United States Department of Commerce.

Table 4.3. Average rate of return on foreign investment
in South Africa, 1957–81

Period	Direct investment	Non-direct investment	Total investment
1957–61	6.5	6.5	6.5
1962–66	6.3	6.6	6.4
1967–71	7.1	6.7	6.9
1972–76	5.5	7.4	6.5
1977–81	5.6	8.2	7.0
1957–81	6.2	7.1	6.7

Source: S.A. Reserve Bank.

South Africa was generally viewed by foreign business executives as having a sound investment climate. This perception was reinforced by the fact of South Africa's historical record of financial responsibility, (but this was badly tarnished by the South African moratorium on the capital repayments in 1985).

On 30 April 1982 there were 146 members of the International Monetary Fund. Of these 54 members had accepted the obligations of currency convertability required by Article VIII. South Africa joined the group in September 1973 and, along with twelve industrial country IMF members, does not impose restrictions on the making of payments and transfers for current international transactions (except by permissible exchange control regulations imposed on residents). Exchange controls over non–residents, in force from 1961, were abolished in February 1983. The country does not engage in discriminating currency arrangements. It stands ready to convert foreign held balances that have recently been acquired as a result of current transactions or are being converted to make payments for current transactions.

The Republic of South Africa is the only state on the continent of Africa to have acceped IMF Article VIII obligations and, in doing so, the associated commitments in terms of the General Agreement of Tariffs and Trade (GATT).

In 1979 a cut–off point of $380 of per capita income per annum was used by the World Bank to determine whether a developing country was placed in the 'middle–income' category or not. South Africa's gnp per capita at the time was $1720 — or more than four times the minimum level. But it was less than the gdp per capita of thirteen of the countries that were current borrowers from the World

Bank in 1979. South Africa's economic dualism, however, dictated that, together with Austrialia, Belgium, Finland, Iceland, Ireland and New Zealand, it joined the 'industrialised countries' in making up the Part I (major contributor) list to the IDA's resources. Its contribution of $7 million to the Fourth Replenishment is the fourth smallest and is only 0.2 per cent of the total of Part I. But the fact that it was made demonstrates again that South Africa perceived itself (and was thought of by others to be) a wealthy industrialised donor nation. But because of its backward sectors, it could, as validly, be regarded as a potential recipient of soft loans or other development aid. [Nedbank, 1983, p.p. 20 — 2].

The complete rebuilding of a sound investment climate is imperative for the future growth of the South African economy.

A striking example of a developing country which has successfully used foreign direct investment for economic growth is Singapore. It is understandable that Singapore should rate so highly as a country in which to invest (third in the Beri listing cited earlier), and that its current per capita income is around $5000, higher than most of Latin America, Asia, Africa and Eastern Europe, and that its average real growth rate is 9.5 per cent per annum. A doctrinaire socialist in his youth, Prime Minister Lee Kuan Yew progressively adopted free enterprise principles; placed multinational corporations at the centre of Singapore's social structure (so that there is mutual commitment between employers and employees along Japanese lines); reduced corporate tax for firms which invested in new plants and machinery; encouraged capital intensive and high technology industry (which in turn increased productivity per employee and justified higher salaries and wages); and allowed all banks (which included the spectrum from Chase Manhattan to Moscow Narodny) in Singapore to accept deposits in foreign currency, which, together with tax exemption for depositors and strict secrecy, have made Singapore the financial capital of South–East Asia. The Prime Minister of Singapore acknowledges that it is the corporations which produce the golden eggs; his actions are consonant with this belief, and his nation has prospered accordingly.

South Africa until the autumn of 1985 offered attractive conditions for foreign investment. These conditions can — and it is argued here — should, be improved all the time. While there are strict political controls on such vital factors of production as land

and labour, the economy cannot be characterized as genuine free enterprise. It should be opened up further, and artificial barriers — paticularly on labour—removed, taxes reduced, exchange control regulations made even more flexible or done away with, free ports created, so that South Africa grows faster to join the developing countries like Singapore, which are elevating their people beyond the problems of food, shelter, literacy and basic security in which most of the Third World is mired.

In 1981–2, for example, although recession affected much of the world, the non–communist Asian nations achieved growth rates of between 3 – 7 per cent for the year. In Hong Kong and Singapore, output grew by 10 per cent. These nations contributed more to the increase in world production than the United States, Canada, and Europe combined. Taiwan, South Korea, and Singapore are following Japan's export-led growth. Their economies are moving into heavy industry and consumer electronics; Singapore is second to the United States in building oil–drilling rigs; South Korea has become a major force in world steel production and shipbuilding and is exporting television sets to America and cars to Britain; Taiwan is the fourth largest supplier of machine tools to the United States and has moved into microcomputers.

This development is taking place at the same time as the world's command economies, from the largest (the Soviet Union, Poland) to the smallest (Cambodia), are chronically unable to feed their peoples, let along provide them with rising standards of living. These comparisons are often ignored by the critics of business, whose activities make the growth of the free enterprise economies possible.

The importance of American multinationals to the South African economy

The American business direct investment in South Africa arouses so much fierce feeling that it is all the more important, as it is always correct, to retain a sense of proportion and responsibility in examining the importance of the American connection. The facts and figures in this section help to place American business involvement into perspective — and show that the passions generated perhaps owe more to symbolic than to concrete reasons of America importance.

Before assessing the significance of direct American investment, it is essential to note that trade with the United States is
indeed of considerable value to South Africa. The United States has
taken over from the former colonial power, Britain, as South
Africa's major trading partner in the world. Table 4.4 shows South
African exports to the United States; however, the figures do not
include the $9 billion or so of gold which is annually sold to Zurich,
but most of which finds it way to the United States. Table 4.5 shows
South African imports from the United States, but these United
States Department of Commerce figures exclude oil shipments.
Table 4.6 shows American trade with Africa. What is interesting
here is that of the total $27 billion American imports from Africa,
some $20 billion are oil imports from Algeria, Libya and Nigeria;
whereas only $2.4 billion of goods are imported from South Africa,
some of them admittedly strategic minerals.

From the State Department's and oil companies' point of view,
the trade–off, if one were forced, would be between oil supplies
from countries which have the advantage of being relatively close
to the American east coast harbours and not embroiled in the
Middle East maelstrom, though not necessarily reliable friends of
the United States, and the much smaller quantity of nevertheless
important imports from South Africa, which is possibly a more
dependable friend to the United States. However, while everyone
wants to sell, a forced trade–off is not likely. From the point of view
of American business, exports are important, and here South
Africa is the biggest market in Africa, followed by Egypt and
Nigeria. The only African nation to have measurable countervailing economic power to that of South Africa on the African
continent vis–à–vis the United States is Nigeria.

American exporters to South Africa need to comply with the
trade restraints of Export Regulation 175 which prohibits the sale of
goods and technical data to the South African military or police.
The American Chamber of Commerce in South Africa says that 'the
end result of the effects of Export Regulation 175 is that United
Kingdom, European and Japanese companies gained where the
United States lost out' (Amcham report, 1984, p.19). Over 6000
American companies trade with South Africa, and have
contributed directly to making the United States South Africa's
major trading partner.

However, as far as direct foreign investment is concerned, the
United Kingdom is still considerably more important to South

Table 4.4. South African trade exports to the United States, 1980–2 ($000 customs value)

Description	1980	1981	1982
Metal coins	941,004	381,774	363,564
Platinum metals, unwrought	616,653	484,593	340,044
Natural precious and semiprecious	665,267	284,101	200,739
Uranium oxide	29,811	45,881	139,557
Ferromanganese > 4% carbon	68,011	85,169	67,057
Uranium compounds	1,252	38,981	60,659
Diamonds, >0.5 carat	43,100	48,266	51,744
Iron/steel plates, not alloy	24,105	25,467	42,015
Angles, not alloy	29,634	40,820	38,141
Gold or silver bullion/ore	33,377	188,292	38,135
Industrial diamonds	52,182	43,322	28,234
US goods returned	12,497	17,242	27,106
Diamonds, ≤0.5 carat	25,627	27,857	24,211
Iron or steel ingots, blooms	0	0	23,745
Wood pulp; rag pulp; and other	26,983	33,762	21,739
Ferrochromium, ≤3% carbon	90,895	101,996	19,343
Shellfish other than clams	23,592	24,955	19,165
Unwrought nickel	21,725	24,168	18,950
Fluorspar	21,177	28,526	18,123
Welded pipes, >0.375 inch	18,175	21,347	16,838
Plates and sheets of iron	18,873	15,709	16,374
Coal	16,948	19,877	15,568
Chrome ore	19,005	23,775	14,666
Sheets of iron and steel	25,961	13,781	13,870
Total, all items imported from Republic of South Africa	$3,309,700	$2,435,797	$1,958,778

Note: Most South African gold is sold to Switzerland, from where it finds its way to other parts of the world, including the United States.

Source: Compiled from official statistics of the US Department of Commerce.

Table 4.5. South African trade imports from the United States, 1980–2 ($000 f.o.b. value)

Description	1980	1981	1982
Aircraft	179,274	116,484	126,506
Mech shovels	156,943	158,501	143,893
Digital cups	64,279	82,347	104,687
Aircraft, parts	61,160	81,240	66,141
Chassis, parts	59,658	81,842	50,362
Rice, not parboiled	43,965	54,394	47,292
Parts of office mach, other	26,471	41,430	43,466
Chem mixtures and preps	41,035	62,138	42,346
Rail locomotives	0	0	35,187
Paper impregnated	13,904	26,642	34,800
Chem wood pulp	42,751	42,324	30,529
Electrical switches	22,152	29,895	28,873
Pressure gauges	32,636	42,610	23,958
Mach for soil prep	13,155	35,171	23,827
Generators	13,951	31,010	23,611
Parts for tool holders	7,306	10,110	23,213
Tractors, wheel type, parts	27,544	38,636	22,005
Digital machines	20,659	22,361	21,840
Printing machines	8,416	7,583	20,708
Film, not motion picture	22,419	32,082	20,632
Tractors wheel type, agr use	14,058	30,589	20,085
Non-piston-type engines	3,513	10,657	19,515
Mixtures of petro hydrocarbons	14,580	23,228	19,468
Parts, for locomotives	25,750	22,980	19,123
General merchandise < $500	29,567	36,005	18,806
Total all items exported to Republic of South Africa	$2,452,543	$2,900,600	$2,359,891

Source: Compiled from official statistics of the US Department of Commerce.

Table 4.6. American trade with Africa

Country	US imports from Africa ($ millions FAS*) 1981	US exports to Africa ($ millions FAS) 1981
Algeria	5,038.1	717.3
Angola	904.1	268.3
Benin	0.5	18.7
Botswana	131.6	6.4
Burundi	28.0	3.8
Cameroon	625.4	152.1
Central African Republic	6.4	0.8
Chad	(Z)	0.8
Congo	287.6	25.0
Djibouti	—	7.2
Egypt	397.3	2,159.4
Equatorial Guinea	0.2	0.7
Ethiopia	83.0	62.2
Gabon	431.9	128.0
Gambia	0.4	3.5
Ghana	245.5	153.6
Guinea	95.8	53.0
Ivory Coast	344.4	129.7
Kenya	51.8	150.3
Lesotho	0.1	8.7
Liberia	113.1	128.4
Libya	5,300.9	813.4
Madagascar	69.3	16.2
Malawi	61.6	5.0
Mali	0.9	5.0
Mauritania	0.2	26.9
Mauritius	19.7	18.2
Morocco	36.2	429.0
Mozambique	83.1	35.0
Namibia	7.6	12.9
Niger	(Z)	12.3
Nigeria	9,249.0	1,522.7
Rwanda	40.5	6.2
Senegal	1.4	42.3

Table 4.6 (*cont.*)

Country	US imports from Africa ($ millions FAS*) 1981	US exports to Africa ($ millions FAS) 1981
Seychelles	0.4	3.9
Sierra Leone	45.0	26.3
Somalia	0.2	58.8
South Africa	2,445.3	2,911.7
Sudan	58.0	208.4
Swaziland	65.6	7.2
Tanzania	18.8	47.7
Togo	9.2	24.2
Tunisia	10.4	222.2
Uganda	101.0	6.8
Upper Volta	0.1	22.2
Zaïre	423.4	141.3
Zambia	113.6	68.3
Zimbabwe	109.0	32.4
	$27,055.6	$10,904.4

* = free alongside ship. (Z) = less than $500,000.
Source: US Department of Commerce.

Africa than is the United States. The United Kingdom stake, including invisible investments such as financial services, may be as high as nearly 50 per cent of total foreign investment. By contrast, the direct American investment of ± $3 bn is about 17 per cent of total foreign investment and 2 per cent of total investment in South Africa. About 350 United States companies (the list is obtainable from a variety of sources), employing less than 120,000 people (Barlow Rand alone has over 200,000 employees in South Africa) have subsidiaries in the Republic. About 1.7 per cent of the South African workforce is employed by American companies. The flagships of American direct investment are Ford, General Motors, Mobil and Caltex but most of the famous names are in South Africa. American subsidiaries (together with those of South Africa's other major trading partners like the United Kingdom, Japan, Germany and France), have come to dominate the car industry, oil–refining and petrochemicals, the telecommunications and computer industries, and the ethical medicines industry; American business is also involved in agricultural heavy equipment and mining equipment. American firms have brought valuable computer hardware and software technology into South Africa, as well as other varied technologies ranging from bio-genetics to solar energy. The role of American companies in export promotion is small to date, though there are plans to intensify that role. American companies are recognized as progressive in terms of wage rates, fringe benefits and training. Nevertheless, the actual economic importance of American business in South Africa should not be exaggerated. Table 4.7, drawn from figures supplied by the United States Department of Commerce, shows the sectoral breakdown of cumulative American direct investment in South Africa up to 1982. Table 4.7 also shows equity and intercompany outflows, the reinvested earnings of corporate affiliates, income, and capital expenditures by majority–owed foreign affiliates of United States companies in 1982. What is striking about all these figures is that they are relatively small, that is, insignificant in terms of the South African economy. This may be due, at least partly, to strict control of subsidiaries by American multinationals.

In a 1979 Stellenbosch University doctoral thesis on capital budgeting of foreign multinationals in South Africa, Dr R. Bishton said there was some indication that 'USA subsidiaries are more rigidly controlled than those of their counterparts (United Kingdom and European multinationals) participating in the study' (Bishton, 1979, p. 13). This researcher affirmed (pp.14, 151–2, 380–1) that political sensitivity, particularly of American firms, was an inhibiting factor in trying to determine multinational corporate strategy with regard to investment. Surprisingly, for it is American academics and business who have made the advances, Bishton's findings indicate that American subsidiaries in South Africa tend to use the traditional payback and return on investment methods of capital budgeting, rather than discounted cash flow (net present value and internal rate of return) methods, which take cognizance of the time value of the money. Whatever capital budgeting model is used, though, Bishton's research points to the smallness of the actual amounts as far as American subsidiaries are concerned:

> it is apparent that more European subsidiaries have annual capital budgets in the categories exceeding R2 million per annum than do the local companies of either USA or UK multinational corporations. In fact it is surprising to find that both UK and USA—based

Table 4.7. Survey of current business

| | All industries | Mining | Petroleum | Manufacturing | | | | | | | | Trade | Banking | Finance (except banking), insurance and real estate | Other industries |
				Total	Food and kindred products	Chemicals and allied products	Primary and fabricated metals	Machinery except electrical	Electric and electronic equipment	Transportation equipment	Other manufacturing				
US direct investment position abroad, year end 1982 (Millions of dollars)															
South Africa	2,513	177	*	1,128	167	256	114	236	69	*	*	401	*	31	65
Equity and intercompany account outflows, 1982 (Millions of dollars, inflows (−))															
South Africa	−14	1	*	−13	−8	2	*	−2	−2	*	*	−16	0	−11	*
Reinvested earnings of incorporated affiliates, 1982 (Millions of dollars)															
South Africa	−36	−16	*	−33	9	8	*	7	*	*	*	16	2	−3	*
Income, 1982 ($m)															
South Africa (August 1983)	194	−9	*	78	50	27	13	14	5	−27	−5	47	2	−2	*
Capital expenditures by majority-owned foreign affiliates of US companies in 1982 ($m)															
South Africa (September 1983)	391	24	*	211	52	24	33	18	3	48	34	111		†	*

* Suppressed to avoid disclosure of data of individual companies.
† Less than $500,000 (±).
Source: US Department of Commerce.

subsidiaries are more heavily represented in the under R2 million group than European companies. This variation is quite significant if cognisance is taken that only 45.4% European respondents are categorised below the R2 million value grouping as compared with the 66.7% and 62.9% of the USA and UK companies respectively. In taking a brief look at the sectoral components of the respondents, it is noted for example that only one of the five local petroleum companies participating has its origins in Europe. Apart from the powerful Petroleum sector, it will be seen that the Motor Assembly and Tyre Manufacturing sector, which is another financially powerful grouping, contains only four subsidiaries of European origin. The European companies are therefore not reinforced by the high level capital-intensive petroleum or motor industries as are USA and UK Company budget values, yet they are reflected in the upper-level of the budget value scale. [Bishton, 1979, pp. 226–7]

American companies were also found to be more sensitive to risk than subsidiaries of EEC companies in South Africa.

The value of American bank loans, too, are small relative to those of the British based banks, which, together with indigenous banks, dominate the banking sector in South Africa. The figures in Table 4.8 are drawn from the United States Federal Financial Institution Examination Council, and show a total of $4.6 billion in bank loans to South Africa.

In view of the foregoing analysis, what are the likely results of significant or complete American disinvestment? The real problem is that American disinvestment might have consequences which are unforeseeable and potentially far-reaching (e.g. acting as encouragement to violent uprising in South Africa or causing other foreign investors to withdraw), as well as more obvious and limited areas. The foreseeable ones are that South Africa would lose even more of the peak investment of $15 billion (in bank loans, American-owned shares on the Johannesburg Stock Exchange and direct investment), which would undoubtedly affect economic growth and employment, and damage business confidence in the country. Indeed, the capital boycott by major American banks has already implemented sanctions more effectively than the 'political' ones imposed by the Reagan Administration and the EEC governments. The banks' move was probably unnecessary and profoundly damaged business confidence, as well as imposing continuing downward pressure on the rand and injecting new uncertainty into a climate of unrest. As far as direct investment is

Table 4.8. Lending by major American banks to South African public and private sector borrowers ($m)

	June 1978	June 1979	June 1980	June 1981	June 1982	June 1983	Dec 1983
Value of loans by all US banks to all South African borrowers	2,248.1	1,661.2	1,368.0	1,848.8	3,655.2	3,883.0	4,637.1
Loans by top 9 US banks*	1,521.2	1,143.8	1,015.0	1,348.6	2,361.9	2,540.7	3,158.5
Loans by 15 next largest US banks†	309.9	206.1	170.1	304.4	669.3	750.3	837.9
Value of loans by all US banks to public sector borrowers	794.0	519.7	350.3	278.1	623.4	326.7	487.9
Loans by top 9 US banks*	398.5	271.9	188.9	216.9	346.8	157.0	221.5
Loans by the top 9 US banks*	748.8	545.9	373.1	320.2	587.5	858.9	946.4
Loans by 15 next largest US banks†	184.2	83.1	54.5	39.0	212.8	123.9	172.9
Value of loans by all US banks to private sector borrowers (excluding banks)	914.9	685.1	442.7	495.2	868.6	1,179.0	1,212.8
Loans by 15 next largest US banks†	58.9	42.8	26.0	100.1	32.9	68.9	103.5
Value of loans by all US banks to South African banks	539.1	456.3	574.9	1,075.5	2,163.2	2,337.2	2,936.3
Loans by top 9 US Banks*	373.9	326.0	453.0	811.5	1,427.6	2,524.8	1,990.6
Loans by 15 next largest US banks†	66.7	80.1	89.5	165.1	424.4	557.4	561.4

* 'Top 9 US banks' refers to the nine largest US banks in terms of total capital. For the years shown, the nine largest banks were: Bank America, Bankers Trust, Chase Manhattan, Chemical, Citibank, Continental Illinois, First Chicago, Manufacturers Hanover and J. P. Morgan.
† '15 next largest US banks' refers to the tenth through twenty-fourth largest US banks in terms of total capital. For June 1982, the 15 next largest banks were: Bank of New York, Crocker National, First Boston, First City National Bank of Houston, First Interstate Bank of California, InterFirst Bank of Dallas, Irving Trust, Marine Midland, Mellon Bank, National Bank of Detroit, Republic Bank (Dallas), Seattle First National, Security Pacific, Texas Commerce Bank and Wells Fargo.

concerned, in the short run South Africa would lose the finance, managerial skills, technology and expertise of the American companies, as well.as their social responsibility approach and the worthwhile projects which they are undertaking.

As mentioned in the introduction, these are all serious effects, but it is doubtful whether they could, by themselves, cause the overthrow of apartheid. Since the numbers of people employed and the proportion of GNP generated by American firms is relatively small, the loss could probably be absorbed. South African capital could take over American subsidiaries: the process of local buying of shares in American companies has been going on for a while. Most of the management is South African. In addition, the Euopeans, Japanese, Koreans, Taiwanese and others might be willing to take over former American investments which might once again yield high returns by world standards.

The implication is that, unless the other major foreign investors also disinvest (the EEC has already shown a willingness to follow the American example in matters of selective sanctions), the impact of American withdrawal ultimately could be contained — at some considerable cost — without achieving its primary objective: the demise of apartheid. American disinvestment would cause economic disruption and increase unemployment in the region, therefore, without necessarily achieving corresponding gains in political terms. Nevertheless, American disinvestment should be opposed, not to support apartheid, but because it is a high–cost, high–risk strategy with no determinate outcome of political benefits such as genuine democratization. Moreover, the loss of the main (business) connection with the United States, or 'any steps taken at home which would remove or limit our presence here can only reduce our capacity to project these [American] values, to contribute to understanding, and to the institutional structures which are necessary to peaceful change, equality and business progress' (Amcham report, 1984, p.4). An early statement of this view can be seen in the report of an interview with Ronald Reagan in 1978.

> Reagan: And this is what I mean by an America that can disagree with apartheid, but can still feel a friendly allied feeling and say, we understand, we have had the problem — not exactly the same problem — but had such a problem that wherever we can be of help we want to be of help. You don't

help by suddenly throwing economic roadblocks at your allies and turning your back, but by being there. For example, American firms by the way they treat Black employees, can be setting a standard for industry and business in South Africa. They could be showing, just by example, that the mix is possible, because I am sure that they are acting very much like they would in America with regard to labour.

Feldberg: So you would see United States companies as a force for positive change in South Africa?

Reagan: Yes, and be there with an idea of lending a hand where possible to bring about the very thing that they say many South Africans are trying to bring about.

[Quoted from Meyer Feldberg, 'Interviews with five prominent Americans on U.S. Investment in South Africa', 1978, p.6]

This interview shows clear indications of the attitude which led to the policy of constructive engagement in the 1980s.

Increased American investment might form a better lever for producing changes in the South African economy and political power structure than the withdrawal of the American presence (which might lead through a snowball effect to the total political isolation of South Africa). Special projects undertaken by American companies range from intensive technical training and educational programmes, through a Black Youth Leadership Programme to the provision of quality housing. Nearly all American companies now pay equal wages for equal work, and Black wages have increased by an average of more than 20 per cent per year over the past four years. American companies stress training and education to accelerate the upward mobility of Blacks. Examples include the 'Adopt-a-School' programme, through which seventy-six American corporations have adopted 150 schools — providing facilities, support for teachers, materials, audio-visual aids and computer assisted education. This programme is now being extended to the entire business community of South Africa. Adult education, in-service teacher training, and Pace Commercial College for Blacks in Soweto are all fruits of efforts by United States corporations and Amcham. Collectively, American companies are spending millions to develop a skilled workforce covering toolmakers, machinists, electricians, boiler–makers, skilled clerical, administrative, sales, and service personnel.

The influence of American companies and the Sullivan Code is analysed in the next two chapters. As far as Black business development is concerned, American companies in South Africa have played a significant rôle through in–house business training, as well as sponsored academic training locally and abroad. There are currently several hundred Blacks following management–related courses in the United States, sponsored by American corporations. Several American companies have assisted Blacks to set up franchise operations of their own. Many American corporations are associate members of the National African Federated Chamber of Commerce, and assist NAFCOC in its activities. Health care and the improvement of the quality of life in Black communities have received substantial support from the American business community. In the industrial relations field, many recognition agreements with both registered and un-registered unions are now in operation. Most American companies have set up grievance procedures to ensure shop–floor justice and many companies provide both management and workers with training in industrial relations and negotiating skills.

All of these special projects, plus the contribution of American corporations to employment and GDP are positive, measurable, concrete gains for a developing country like South Africa, and may have wider effects in the political economy through example. American companies are helping to establish models of corporate social responsibility in South Africa. It would be a peculiarly hollow political point that would be made by forcing American disinvestment in South Africa.

Why do American multinationals remain in South Africa? If South Africa slid quietly under the cold waves of the South Atlantic and Indian oceans overnight, the United States would still have 99 per cent of its total foreign investment left the following morning. Is 1 per cent worth the trouble? After all, whatever American corporations achieve, there are critics in both America and South Africa to whom these achievements mean nothing: they will not be satisfied until there is a Black socialist Azania. This situation lends some strength to the Friedmanite argument that it is pointless for business to go beyond being efficient and making a profit. Ford's global headquarters has a department which deals with political

issues emanating from its world–wide investments: although only
1 per cent of Ford's foreign investment is in South Africa, that
department spends 85 per cent of its time on South African
problems — an absurd misallocation of resources.

Despite this skewed situation, it is argued here that American
companies should stay, for a number of reasons. Firstly, if the
business criteria for investment are satisfied, then corporations
must go ahead or they will cease to be in business after a while. It is
inherent in the nature of successful business enterprises that they
cannot afford to overlook any opportunity — however small — in a
competitive global business system. American companies must be
on the ground in South Africa to make the most of the opportunities
which exist. They might also one day be able to service a much
larger part of sub–Saharan Africa from the powerful industrial base
of South Africa. It has been suggested that American companies
are helping to ease the constraints in the way of rational business
and economic pursuits in South Africa. It has also been argued in
this work that American companies are the strongest representatives of the United States in South Africa. American business and
the American government have co–operated in recent years
because they have realized they have common goals in pursuing a
policy of constructive engagement and in promoting change in
South Africa. This closer working relationship is manifested in
many ways, according to Amcham:

(a)   quarterly briefings on political and economic developments by
      United States mission officers;
(b)   the United States Ambassador's major policy address at its
      annual business meeting in February 1983;
(c)   United States mission officers serving as members of Amcham
      committees;
(d)   soliciting by the Embassy of Amcham views prior to the annual
      review of export administration regulations;
(e)   focusing of United States Government programs on black
      businessmen (exchange programs, visiting experts, a United
      States AID–financed training project for the National African
      Federated Chamber of Commerce) and a continuing, close
      consultation on a number of current issues between senior
      Amcham officials and the Ambassador and his staff.

This sound relationship is mutually beneficial and both the

Embassy and Amcham are committed to maintaining and strengthening it.

Every Boeing operated by the South African commercial fleet is another connection with the United States. The satellite–tracking station in the Transvaal is important to the American use of space. South Africa is the only country in the southern hemisphere which has the technical knowledge to assist in the United States–led international effort to establish global tracking stations, especially in the ocean, to obtain metereological data (which in turn can help plan against disasters like storms and drought). Nor is the flow of technology one–way: SASOL oil–from–coal technology has been imported into the United States from South Africa. There is co-operation in research. Some of these American connections straddle the concerns of the private sector and the government in both countries, and go beyond narrower business and state concerns to, for example, the advancement of science which can help to develop South Africa.

Perhaps the most important point raised in this book is that through the presence of American business, there is a working relationship between South Africa and the United States. This working relationship is beneficial to all South Africans, for reasons varying from the transmission of worthwhile values (defined in terms of the ideal–type political economy adhered to in this book), through increased employment to scientific co–operation. It is a relationship worth preserving.

Unconvinced critics might say, 'fine, so the United States corporations do make a contribution, but at what cost?', implying that they strengthen the White establishment. Reality is more complex and more subtle, and the contributions of American multinationals might be characterized as a double–edged sword which does strengthen the Whites mainly in indirect economic ways, but simultaneously strengthens the Blacks even more in a number of direct ways as well as indirect ways. And all South Africans gain from the presence of foreign multinationals:

> The multinational corporations (MNCs) have a special role to play. Experience teaches that mere infusions of money, even given productive potential in particular spheres, are not sufficient to spark off sustainable expansion. To absorb capital productively requires something else — the technology and managerial skills necessary to

complement the investment. It is no wonder that those countries which have been prepared to accept MNCs as a source of technology, product innovation and economic dynamism have developed much faster than those which have rejected them as offensive to national sovereignty.

As I see it, therefore, the challenge for the next five years — and well beyond — is to accept that solutions to our manifold problems must be sought not in institutions and government regulation but in the market place. Keynes reminded us nearly fifty years ago of the dangers of dimming the 'animal spirits' and spontaneous optimism of businessmen and emphasised how essential it was to generate a political and social atmosphere congenial to investment. To my mind this is fundamental, if we are really committed to our desire to harness the forces of enterprise, both domestic and foreign, which have faith in Africa as a continent whose time has yet to come.' [GWH Relly, Chairman of the Anglo–American Corporation, *Optima*, vol. 32, No. 2, p. 63.]

It is clear that American investment has helped shape the South African economy, particularly in areas such as automobiles, petrochemicals, telecommunications, and computers.

In addition, as the Amcham report concludes:

The influence of United States companies in changing the character of South African society has been significant. It is continuing to achieve equality of opportunity and social justice in the work place. Its success in the promotion and monitoring of the quality of education, health and housing is exerting an influence out of proportion to the size of United States investment in the country. American business is evolving strategies that can make even greater progress and have an even stronger impact if its efforts are encouraged and supported in the United States. If moves to bring about disinvestment (or divestment) are successful, then this progress will die away and the black people in the country will be the ones that will most severely suffer from such a retrogressive step. [Amcham, 1984, p. 20.]

*Historical background figures**

*Most of the historical background figures in the following pages are obtained from the Study Commission on U.S. Policy toward Southern Africa (1981) called *Time Running Out*.

The Study Commission (pp. 133–43) describes the historical importance of foreign economic relations for South Africa, and provides considerable useful detail. Total foreign investment in South Africa at the beginning of 1979 was $26.3 bn, an amount equivalent to 20 per cent of the value of South Africa's industrial plant. Of this, approximately 40 per cent was direct investment (primarily foreign company ownership in South African subsidiaries or affiliates), and 60 per cent was indirect investment (international bank loans and foreign ownership of stock in South African firms).

Five countries — Britain, the United States, West Germany, Switzerland and France — held 80 per cent of the foreign investment in South Africa. Britain had an estimated 40 per cent, or more than $10 billion, the United States 20 per cent, West Germany 10 per cent, and Switzerland and France approximately 5 per cent each. In all, two-thirds of foreign investment in South Africa was held by European countries, 20 per cent by the United States, and 15 per cent by the rest of the world. A decade earlier Britain had held 60 per cent of total foreign investment, the rest of Europe 20 per cent, and the United States 15 per cent. In dollar amounts British investment had declined slightly over the previous ten years, while that of the United States and West Germany had increased.

Foreign trade and investment have been of fundamental importance to the South African economy, helping to offset the balance of payments deficits which have tended to accompany periods of rapid economic growth (though the gold boom helped during the 8 per cent growth which South Africa achieved in 1980), and providing the foreign exchange required for industrialization and for the expansion of an increasingly capital–intensive economy.

It is estimated that foreign capital is responsible for about one–third of the growth in the country's gross domestic product. It has provided funds to key growth sectors of the South African economy, such as computers, electronics, telecommunications, petroleum processing, motor vehicle production, and, to a lesser, though still important degree, to mining. If the gross domestic product grows at about 6 per cent, then 2 per cent of that growth is generated by foreign capital.

Foreign investment has been important (Myers, 1980, p.39) not just for the capital provided but also for the technology that has accompanied it. A former Director of Barclays National Bank of South Africa has said that figures on foreign investment 'can be misleading in that they do not reflect the true extent to which we have had to rely on foreign investment (and in particular the know-how skills normally accompanying foreign investment) in respect of specific projects or key economic sectors'. One British econo-mist, John Suckling of York University, suggests that foreign tech-nology accounted for 40 per cent of the growth in South Africa's gross domestic product during the period between 1957 and 1972.

Foreign companies dominate several of the most important sectors of the South African economy. Five multinationals, Shell, British Petroleum, Mobil, Caltex and Total, collectively control close to 83 per cent of the petroleum market in South Africa and generate 91 per cent of the service stations. Volkswagen, Ford, GM, Datsun, and Toyota hold the major share of the automobile market; the sole South African company, Sigma Motors, has acquired 14 per cent of the market by manufacturing Chrysler, Peugeot, Citroën, Mazda, and Leyland cars. Mainframe computer sales are split between IBM and British-owned ICL, each with one-third of the market, and Burroughs, Control Data, Sperry Univac, and Siemens play lesser roles. Only in mining and agriculture are the companies and operations primarily South African, and even in those sectors some major international corporations like Exxon, Union Carbide, US Steel, Phelps Dodge, Del Monte, Tate and Lyle, Rio Tinto Zinc, and Newmont Mining play an important role.

The Study Commission says that at the beginning of 1979 direct foreign investment was $11 billion, with $8 billion held by Europe and $2 billion by the United States. Britain, which for historic reasons had the closest economic ties with South Africa, may have had as much as $6 bn directly invested in the country. The British figure was equivalent to 10 per cent of its worldwide foreign investment, while the United States total represented approximately 1 per cent of its worldwide investment. Although the Commission does not say so, this suggests that American moves towards South Africa will be constrained to some extent by its concern for the investments of Britain and other European allies. The United States itself has a relatively freer hand in that only 1 per cent of its direct investment abroad is the maximum that can be lost in a worst-case scenario. In the past decade foreign direct investment in South Africa has increased only negligibly in real terms. Fifty per cent of this investment is in manufacturing, 25 per cent in finance, 15 per cent in trade, and less than 10 per cent in mining. Many of the world's major automobile and oil companies are represented in the manufacturing sector (in October 1981 Mercedes Benz announced plans to invest a further R200 million in South Africa). The bulk of the investment in finance is held by subsidiaries of British banks, notably Standard Bank and Barclays Bank International.

American direct investment in South Africa had increased an average of $100 million a year since the mid–1960s when it stood at $500 million, a very rapid increase. In the 1970s most American investment came from the reinvested earnings of South African subsidiaries. Return on all American investment averaged over 15 per cent for 1970 – 4, declined to 9 per cent in 1975, and then rose to 14 per cent for the period 1976–8. Over 50 per cent of direct American investment is held by four companies: Ford, General Motors, Mobil, and Caltex Oil. Altogether, some 350 American companies have subsidiaries in South Africa and over 6000 do business in the country.

At the beginning of 1979 indirect foreign investment in South Africa was between $13 billion and $15 billion, 80 per cent of which consisted of United States and European bank loans. The American portions of international bank lending had declined over the past few years, from over $2 billion in 1976 to $1.3 billion in 1979. American banks had also become temporarily more reluctant to make long–term loans to South Africa — in 1976, 57 per cent of American loans had maturities of more than one year, but by 1980 only 41 per cent were long term.

> Although it is difficult to determine the precise reasons for this large drop in United States lending, the following factors appear to have played a part:
> (1) a post–Soweto reluctance to lend to an economically and politically unstable South Africa;
> (2) a general cutting back by United States banks on their loan exposure in less-developed countries;
> (3) increasing domestic pressure on banks not to lend to South Africa; and (4) the reduced need for South Africa to seek international credit because of large balance of payments surpluses generated by higher gold prices. [Study Commission, 1981, p. 135.]

Foreign government trade credit agencies and the International Monetary Fund also on occasion provide loans or loan guarantees

to South Africa. However, American government credit agencies —
the Export/Import Bank and the Department of Agriculture
Commodity Credit Corporation — have not done business with
South Africa since 1978.

Portfolio investment, especially the foreign ownership of South
African gold–mining stock, was also an important component of
indirect investment. Americans alone held 25 per cent, or $2
billion, of South Africa's total gold–mining stock, and foreign
ownership overall was approximately $3 billion.

As Myers *et al* point out, foreign capital has also served to spur
international trade. South Africa relies heavily on foreign trade; its
exports in 1978 amounted to $15.3 billion including gold and
services against $13.7 billion in imports. A study in 1978 by the
South African bank Nedbank shows that machinery and transport
equipment account for more than half of the imports from South
Africa's six major trading partners, and the study concludes that
'unless the South African manufacturing industry makes
fundamental adjustments to its production processes, or greatly
expands its domestic market, it will remain very dependent on
imported capital goods'. In addition to high technology goods in
data processing, electronics and telecommunications, South
Africa depends on imported heavy machinery such as earth movers
and long wall miners for its mining industry.

South Africa is a developing country in which there might be as
many as 1.5 to 2 million unemployed or underemployed Blacks, or
about 25 per cent of the potential workforce. Disguised unemployment makes the figures difficult to determine, but it is
probably of the right order of magnitude to suggest that an average
growth rate of about 5.5 per cent will be required in future years to
absorb the workers coming on the job market, and this in turn
depends on between $1 billion and $2 billion a year in new foreign
capital.

After the 1985 moratorium, South Africa might continue to
receive foreign capital; it has been an attractive investment prospect for a long time, and there are generous investment terms.
Normally, all current income may be repatriated, and the
government offers numerous concessions to companies interested
in establishing operations in government–designated growth
areas, including low–interest loans, preferential transportation
rates, cash rebates, and tax concessions. The rate of return on

investment in the Republic has until recently outpaced investment elsewhere in the world.

The American multinationals do have some effect on local employment in terms of direct hiring by American firms, but it is not significant. It is estimated that United States companies employ about 120,000 people in South Africa, around half to three-quarters of whom are Black. The South African employees of American firms account for less that 2 per cent of the labour force in South Africa (other foreign firms may employ an additional 5 — 6 per cent of the total work force). This is important in evaluating the direct impact of American firms' labour practices in South Africa: whether good, bad, or indifferent, United States firms can only have a negligible direct effect relative to the entire labour force.

The example set by these firms, however, can have far wider repercussions, so that the demonstration effect of practices adopted by American firms will eventually affect a much larger percentage of the work force. In actual numbers, based on the assumption that one Black worker supports a family of five, the American firms in South Africa may indirectly be supporting about 300,000 to 350,000 Blacks and around 165,000 Whites. Clearly, the labour practices of South African firms are the crucial ones for more than 90 per cent of the work force. As mentioned earlier, Barlow Rand alone employs far more Blacks (around 200,000) than all the Sullivan signatories put together.

The demonstration effect of American employment practices is discussed later in greater detail.

Criticism of American corporations in South Africa

On purely economic grounds, it appears that all the foreign involvement in the South African economy is not only essential but probably beneficial to all South Africans in varying degrees. However,

> as frustration mounts, there is growing evidence that urban Blacks — many of whom have extolled the benefits that foreign companies bring to Blacks — are increasingly questioning the role of foreign investment in South Africa, although accurate assessment of this change is extremely difficult. There are real limits on the extent to which Blacks can speak openly. Publicly calling for withdrawal of

foreign investment, for example, could be interpreted as a crime punishable under the Terrorism Act. And there are few organisations that provide political representation or participation for Blacks. In addition, a number of important Black leaders have been arrested, detained, banned or forced underground and several have died in demonstrations or in detention. [Myers, 1980, p.49.]

As the Investor Responsibility Research Center points out, Black attitudes towards foreign investment have been varied. Many have argued that foreign investment creates jobs, improves the economy, provides trickle–down benefits, and gives companies an opportunity to influence the situation in South Africa by following model employment practices and by improving working and living conditions for Black employees. Lucy Mvubelo, head of the 24,000 member Black clothing workers' union, stated that 'the multi-national companies have been an asset to us. . . . Why should the world be so cruel as to call for these companies to withdraw when we are only now getting some sunshine in that very dark country of ours?'

Chief Buthelezi argues that

It is morally imperative that American firms remain active here and support us in our struggle. . . . As industry expands, propelled by domestic and foreign investment, a severe shortage of skilled men is increasingly appearing, and Black people are of necessity being advanced to more responsible positions. . . . A call for a slow down on investment, or actual disinvestment, is a call for an aggravation of exactly the conditions we are struggling against. . . . What kind of a struggle for independence can you wage from a level of utter impoverishment?

Both Mvubelo and Buthelezi put caveats on the performance of companies operating in South Africa, stressing that they ought to be active in promoting the Black cause through peaceful change.

Inevitably, in the absence of government response to decades of protest and their own inability to effect change, there have been growing demands among Blacks for foreign countries to take action to affect the situation, and for an end to foreign trade and investment, whatever the cost to Blacks themselves. The United States Ambassador, William Bowdler, wrote in a diplomatic cable in March 1978 that:

among more politically oriented Blacks, the question is increasingly being weighed of whether foreign investment should be seen as an ally or obstacle in pursuing the goal of a more democratic and non-racial society . . . . with radicalization of Black attitudes, the tendency to call for disinvestment grows stronger . . . . the role of American firms here will become increasingly controversial and the rationale for continued presence may become less and less persuasive to increasing numbers of Blacks.

It seems that the use of economic means to achieve political ends will become a predominant feature of the South African landscape; foreign trade and investment provide a powerful potential lever for protest against apartheid. The South African Council of Churches, for example, has said that: 'foreign investments and loans have largely been used to support the prevailing patterns of powers and privileges' in South Africa, and asked foreign countries to revise their investment policies to benefit the total population. The Council's general secretary, Bishop Desmond Tutu, has called for selective boycotts, arguing that any suffering by Blacks resulting from such actions, would be 'suffering with a purpose'.

As always in South African affairs, whatever line of enquiry is pursued, there comes a point at which the entire existing political economy is called into question by those who advocate or work for a new dispensation. From this perspective, the multinationals are viewed as purely bad:

The ongoing struggle of the peoples of southern Africa to uproot, once and for all, the exploitative regional system had emerged, by the beginning of the 1980s, as a crucial phase of the worldwide process of social transformation.

In this historical context, the transnational corporations pressed their governments to co-operate with the South African regime in negotiating 'moderate' solutions: the installation in public office of a few wealthy blacks, creating a supportive black 'middle class', while leaving the exploitative status quo intact. The minority regime itself, preparing if necessary to block the wheels of history by sheer military might, continued to produce and buy the most sophisticated technologies of modern warfare: computerised systems of population control, guns, tanks, planes, missiles, even nuclear weapons. It jailed, tortured and murdered opponents at home. Its troops, armed with automatic weapons, repeatedly invaded

neighbouring countries. They bombed villages and industrial
installations. They aimed to cow the liberation movements into
submission. [Seidman and Makgetla, 1980, pp. viii — ix.]

Seidman and Makgetla attempt to show how technological
changes increased the size and productivity of corporations in the
core industrial capitalist economies, and how the collapse of
colonial empires forced the multinationals to discover new ways to
secure sources of raw materials and markets for their industrial
goods. This situation forced the multinationals to invest in and sell
technology to 'oppressive militaristic regional sub-centres' like
South Africa, Brazil, and Iran. Far from stimulating social advance,
they argue, multinationals provide South Africa with the industrial
infrastructure and military equipment to block the struggle for
change. They also examine the options available to neighbouring
countries seeking to break their dependence on 'the South
African–transnational corporate alliance that continues to distort
their national development'.

The solution, they would argue, is not change within the system,
but change of the system itself to a socialist one. Yet nowhere do the
authors examine their implicit assumptions that a socialist state
would be politically more democratic and economically more
efficient than a free enterprise alternative, and it is precisely these
assumptions which require thorough examination. It is not clear
why the multinationals should be cast in the role of (right-wing)
villains when, as the authors point out themselves, they do
business wherever they can:

> Gulf Oil, for instance, reports that the MPLA government in Angola,
> planning long term growth to meet its citizens' needs, provides an
> unusually stable, strong framework for a mutually beneficial
> relationship. Gulf has agreed to turn over a majority share of its local
> affiliate to the government, to train more Angolans, and to prepare
> for the eventual loss of managerial control. In return, it is able to
> pump increasing amounts of oil from Angolan wells for profitable
> world markets. A Gulf spokesman testified in Washington D.C. in
> early 1979 that Angola provided an outstanding investment
> environment. [Seidman and Makgetla, 1980, pp. 352 — 3.]

According to Seidman and Makgetla, the multinationals are good
when they form a 'mutually beneficial relationship' with a government of which the authors approve, and bad when they do the same
with a government of which they disapprove, and it does not matter

whether the latter also forms an 'outstanding investment environment' from a business point of view

Abstracting the multinationals from any particular political setting in the developing countries, there are legitimate economic concerns about their activities. For example, if exhaustible natural resources such as minerals or oil are involved, the primary wealth of the host nation may be drained off without regard for the local economy. The host country may lose tax revenues because the foreign corporation reports lower profits by manipulating transfer prices between subsidiaries. When parent companies use their financial network to pull funds out of a country with a balance of payments problem, or to move money into one struggling to reduce inflation, host governments lose some control over their domestic economy. Multinationals can simply pull out of a country, causing economic dislocation.

However, the criterion for judging multinationals ought to be whether they make a net contribution to the host country's economy. The acceptability of the host country itself is strictly not a business issue. Were multinationals to do business with only those countries in which there is a significant degree of individual, political, press, judicial, religious, racial, and other freedom, there would be very few countries with which they could do business. To the extent that multinationals do interfere with political processes, they open themselves to political judgement, but then approval or disapproval becomes a political issue, and not an economic one. Political interference is an aberration on the part of business corporations, whereas making a net economic contribution to host countries is a consequence of their normal business functioning.

The work of the multinationals in South Africa is rarely judged on economic grounds: generally those who prefer a free enterprise system and wish to see evolutionary change tend to argue in favour of the multinationals, whereas those who prefer socialism and wish for revolutionary change tend to argue against them. In, 'Decoding Corporate Camouflage', for example, Elizabeth Schmidt (1980, p.82) says that

'Reform is illusory in South Africa. Modifications in the work environment and superficial changes in trade union laws do not alter the basic structure of apartheid. The homelands policy remains intact. Migratory labour, influx control, and the pass laws continue unabated. South Africa's black millions remain disenfranchised and dispossessed, while American companies continue to reap the benefits of a 'good investment climate'. Workplace reforms do not alter the importance of American companies to the South African economy. They do not weaken the links of corporate collaboration or soften the blows of government repression . . .'

Schmidt considers a number of key industries and her conclusion, in common with those of many opponents of American business involvement in South Africa, is that the multinationals supply an infrastructure for the apartheid state. Superficially that might appear to be the case, until it is realized that the multinationals, and the entire business community, would continue providing an infrastructure for a different, democratic state — indeed, for any state which allowed business to function normally. (Multinationals which were once accused of supporting the 'Portuguese colonial oppressors' are now propping up the Marxist government in Angola.) The business community can continue to serve the nation as a whole under a wide variety of types of state.

Economic institutions which work should not be destroyed simply because they coexist, at a point in time, with an unacceptable state — this question of politics versus economics is considered further in the next section. What needs to be noted here is that the proper focus of criticism should be the ideologically-driven state: it is ironic that many of the critics of multinationals would be happy to replace the apartheid state with another form of social–engineering state along socialist/communist lines. The fundamental problem is the nature of the state itself in the twentieth century:

> Disillusionment with socialism and other forms of collectivism was only one aspect of a much wider loss of faith in the state as an agency of benevolence. The state was the great gainer of the twentieth century; and the central failure. Up to 1914, it was rare for the public sector to embrace more than 10 per cent of economy; by the 1970s, even in liberal countries, the state took up to 45 per cent of the GNP. But whereas, at the time of the Versailles Treaty, most intelligent people believed that an enlarged state could increase the sum total of human happiness, by the 1980s the view was held by no one outside a small diminishing and dispirited band of zealots. The experiment had been tried in innumerable ways; and it had failed in nearly all of them. The state had proved itself an insatiable spender, an unrivalled waster. Indeed, in the twentieth century it had also proved itself the

great killer of all time. By the 1980s, state action had been responsible for the violent or unnatural deaths of over 100 million people, more perhaps,than it had hitherto succeeded in destroying during the whole of human history up to 1900. Its inhuman malevolence had more then kept pace with its growing size and expanding means. [Johnson, 1983, p. 729.]

Although there is a socialist challenge to South Africa, represented by a considerable amount of Marxist as well as non-Marxist thought which advocates social engineering, it is beyond the scope of this book to discuss it.

Economics versus politics?

Overtly political analyses do not address important economic questions about the interaction of multinationals and developing countries — interactions that would probably be significant for South Africa even under a different, Black-ruled system. Indeed, it is likely that when some of the older-established American multinationals were first located in South Africa, there was every intention of using South Africa as a base for supplying the entire sub-Saharan African market, and achieving worthwhile economies of scale by supplying this much larger market. Representatives of American corporations used to travel regularly from South Africa to all other parts of the continent, supplying goods and services, until the collapse of the European colonial empires, African nationalism and the ostracism of South Africa made such contacts far more difficult.

The American penchant to view rational business considerations as able to overcome most barriers foundered on the rock of African politics. It is possible that in boardrooms in the United States there are directors who are awaiting a political solution in South Africa which would allow open access to business between southern Africa and the rest of Africa, thereby making their South African investments really worthwhile — and it is not inconceivable that they would view a basically free-enterprise Black government as a viable alternative to the current situation which renders them vulnerable to criticism and has inherent potential instability.

Given the likelihood that the multinationals will continue to have a businesslike approach to South Africa, largely irrespective of who is in power at any given time, then *economic* questions about the activities of multinationals become of paramount importance, because they will have to be faced by whatever government is in power.

In a developing country like South Africa, for example, high profitability registered by a foreign subsidiary might reflect either or both of the following. It might be the result of competent management, superior technology, and the availability of inputs (both local and foreign) at relatively low market prices. High profitability could also reflect the existence of monopoly rents which accrue from tariff and non-tariff protection against foreign competition; from practices which reduce domestic competition (such as domestic horizontal integration through acquisition of national firms or the use of scarce local factors such as bank loans creating availability problems to potential competitors; and from legal and other protection against both foreign and local competition such as that resulting from patent laws). High profitability which stems from increased efficiency will imply, from the international point of view, gains from the reduction of resource costs resulting from such efficiency. From the national point of view, though, gains will take place only if the fruits of efficiency are shared partly by the host government through higher tax revenues from profits, or if local factors of production obtain higher returns than otherwise from the operations of foreign subsidiaries, or if efficiency is passed on to the consumers from lower prices (Vaitsos, 1974, p.66). These are the sorts of issues with which national economic policy towards multinationals should be concerned in South Africa.

The value of foreign direct investment

An interim conclusion that can be reached here is that both in theory and in practice, as evidenced by the figures and economic arguments, the presence of the multinational corporations is vital to the continued growth of the South African economy. The economic usefulness of the multinationals can be castigated by those who wish for political reasons to see the economy falter and preferably fail in order to facilitate a Black uprising to overthrow White domination of the country — but they are in a sense proving the case for the multinationals by regarding them as being so important. In truth they are powerful, but primarily economically rather than politically; they would presumably continue to serve a Black-ruled South Africa, if allowed to do so, in the same way that they are serving the country's economy under a White-ruled South Africa. If some of the resources of the multinationals are being used by Whites to strengthen themselves, the multinationals are also helping to strengthen the Blacks — everyone gains through economic growth fuelled by foreign investment, though the Blacks would probably gain proportionately more if they were part of the power structure. It appears shortsighted to want to destroy productive capacity, particularly when it is economically efficient; it makes more sense for everyone to support economic develop-ment, while simultaneously struggling in another arena, the political one, to determine how the benefits accruing from this production are to be distributed equitably. One Black leader who has supported a realistic approach time and again is Chief Gatsha Buthelezi: he has reiterated that

> the view that Blacks must suffer even greater want than they already experience in order that we may be better prepared for revolution is outrageous. Those who advocate disinvestment hold this view. They propagate the notion that Black South Africans want foreign capital to be withdrawn so that the central economy could be weakened. They want Blacks to be jobless and starving so that they would more willingly be prepared to go on suicidal missions to boost the images of certain exiles abroad. . . . Poverty demoralises a people. Real poverty, the kind of poverty that gives rise to high infant mortality rates, high incidences of malnutrition and related diseases, and shortened life expectancies, poverty like this found in South Africa's depressed Black areas demoralises. Poverty is disruptive of social values and social norms, when it is accompanied by a sense of hopelessness.
>
> Social reconstruction which this country needs cannot be achieved on the smoke and ashes of economic ruin. President Machel is grateful that the Cabora Bassa power plant remains intact. President Nyerere is deeply aware of the fact that his Ujamaa programme faltered because there was insufficient industrial development in Tanzania before he took over. President Kaunda does not regret the mining industry he inherited when he took over. Other Presidents, such as Kenyatta, Sir Seretse Khama, Chief Jonathan or King Sobhuza II have battled against tremendous odds because they have taken over governments of countries which did not have a sufficiently strong industrial backbone.

Today even a great country like Russia is dependent on capitalist states like the United States for its grain requirement.

South Africa, more than any country in Africa, needs industrialisation. It needs industrialisation now. It will need industrialisation after liberation. The creation of jobs will continue to be a national priority deep into the future.

Whatever system of economic and political management we may have in South Africa in the years to come, jobs will remain important. . . . It is irresponsible to advocate any course of action which results in less jobs for the hungry. We already face a very difficult future because there seems little prospect of job creation running ahead of population increases. If we damaged the job-creating industries in the South African economy, we would do irreparable harm to future prospects of social, economic and political reorganisation.

Michael O'Dowd, himself an executive of a South African multinational, echoes Buthelezi's view in saying that

the hope is, that in the absence of capital inflow there would be so little economic development in South Africa that the conditions of life of the major section of the Black population would deteriorate until they were prepared to face the terrible consequences of revolt and in this way a revolution would be brought about. It is not that the advocates of 'disinvestment' do not know that if the 'disinvestment' was effective, it is the Blacks that it would injure; it is the Blacks it is intended to injure. The theory is that what the masses need is revolution but they first have to be starved by their friends abroad into recognising this fact. [O'Dowd, 1980, p.4]

These views are not confined to South Africans who might be said to have a stake in the system. Professor Ali Mazrui, Kenyan-born analyst of African affairs has said that Western investment will help create conditions for a revolutionary situation in South Africa before the end of the century, on the reasoning that revolutionary situations often occur when progress is being made, but not fast enough to overtake expectations. Indeed, a part of the case for the multinationals is that their business activities, and the economic growth to which they contribute, by themselves cannot be expected to change the political system in South Africa, so they should not be pilloried politically until and unless they go beyond doing business into using force of some sort for political ends. Most of the top executives interviewed affirmed that their corporations had long-term plans to be in South Africa, irrespective of who might be in power. The argument here is that South Africa gains considerably from the presence of the multinationals, again irrespective of who might be in power, provided the corporations are allowed to do business.

Despite the potential for political instability in South Africa, and harassment at home in the United States for operating in the Republic, many American multinationals show determination to continue to do business in South Africa. Their confidence is backed by other important American economic actors, like the 6,000 American companies that trade with South Africa, and to a lessening extent the banks that lend money, and the private investors who include South African shares in their portfolios.

The President of the South African Federated Chamber of Industries said in November 1984 that the United States consulate in Johannesburg found that, besides the ± $3 billion direct American investment, private American assets in South Africa amounted to ± $13 billion including more that $4 billion of bank loans and nearly $8 billion American-owned shares listed on the Johannesburg Stock Exchange. This latter figure represented about 60 per cent of all the foreign-owned holdings on the exchange. When an annual trade figure of around $5 billion is added (excluding items like gold bullion, uranium and oil), then the American economic stake in South Africa is a sizeable one, at least from South Africa's point of view. To the United States, with its $3.5 trillion economy, an economy which is so very much smaller has little economic leverage. In theory, therefore, the proponents of divestment and disinvestment might argue that it will hurt the United States little, and the White South African establishment much more, if their campaign is successful. In practice it seems less likely that American corporations will succumb to the pressure, because it would form a dangerous precedent of making investment decisions on criteria that have nothing to do with business pursuits. The disinvestment campaign, if successful, would challenge the very essence of the systems — democracy and free enterprise — by which power and resources are allocated in the United States. This would be much too high a price for the United States to pay to do what Congressman Solarz referred to as 'serving notice to the White establishment in South Africa that they cannot hope for any significant or sustained improvement in relations with the United States as long as apartheid continues'.

Nevertheless, the disinvestment campaign has gained momentum. Table 4.9 shows a recent situation with regard to legislation in the United States:

Table 4.9. Divestment Legislation

Cities and states that have passed divestment legislation	Cities and states that have passed non–binding legislation
States	
Nebraska	Kansas
Michigan	Atlanta
Massachusetts	Portland, Ore.
Connecticut	East Lansing, Mich.
Maryland	Grand Rapids, Mich.
	Multnomah County, Mich.
Cities	
	States where legislation is pending
Cotati, Calif.	
Newark, N.J.	
Cambridge, Mass.	New York
Cuyahoga County (Cleveland)	New Jersey
Philadelphia	Florida
New York	Georgia
Boston	Illinois
Wilmington, Del.	Ohio
Hartford, Conn.	Pennsylvania
Berkeley, Calif.	
Davis, Calif.	
Santa Cruz, Calif.	
Washington D.C.	

Source: Christian Science Monitor 20 September 1984.

Mr Dumisani Kumalo, a former South African journalist who is a key figure behind this campaign argues that disinvestment is the most direct, non-violent means to help weaken the South African government.

The campaign raises a number of disturbing questions. For example, what is the evidence that weakening the economy, even severely, will cause the Whites to abdicate control? To justify the human and economic cost involved in damaging the South African economy it would be necessary to show fairly conclusively, that sanctions would bring about a democratic dispensation in South Africa. Is not damaging the South African economy too destructive a way of 'sending a signal' to both White and Black South Africans? Are the costs to the American system itself of subverting rational economic decisions for doubtful political gains not too high?

The inner logic of the campaign suggests that some of the more militant proponents will not rest even if all American business withdrew from South Africa, until the country is entirely isolated in all spheres from the rest of the world. Is it likely that this total isolation and its attendant hardship will cause the races in South Africa to come to reasonable terms with each other?

These questions raise an even more fundamental question: millions of words (and millions of dollars) have been spent by all the various opponents of apartheid in analysing its obvious and generally accepted iniquities, but relatively few of the opponents have actually spelt out in precise detail what type of political economy should take its place. Rational discourse is difficult with those who wish to destroy apartheid — almost at any cost to the nation and its people — if they do not also propose workable alternatives that can be judged on their merits. Moral outrage and impetuous action are poor substitutes for a careful, practical assessment of the best alternatives for moving towards a better society.

One of the key Congressional proponents of American economic disengagement from South Africa is Stephen Solarz, who is articulate on the motives for economic sanctions. The following explanation is from an interview with him in *Leadership S.A.* (Third Quarter 1984, vol. 3, no. 3, p. 114-17):

Murray: There seems to be a feeling in Southern Africa that any form of economic sanction or anything that interferes with the process of free trade, particularly in the current climate of renewed links in the sub-region, would be counterproductive for black South Africans and, in fact, the people in the Frontline States.

Solarz: We, of course, reject that, otherwise we wouldn't be promoting this particular legislation. We reject it for a number of reasons. First of all, we have a very significant interest in fundamental change in South Africa — the kind of change that will result in the elimination of apartheid, and the establishment of a new dispensation that will be acceptable to all the different communities of the country. We believe that in the absence of such change a cataclysmic confrontation in South Africa is likely to take place which would have terribly adverse consequences, not only for South Africa and for the region but potentially for the United States as well. The question then becomes: How could the United States best go about bringing about the sort of change which is compatible with our interests as well as our principles? And here, I would say that those of us involved with this effort believe very strongly that first and foremost the future of South Africa will be determined as it should be, by the people of South Africa themselves.

The United States, to the extent that it can have an impact on the future of South African law, is likely to have that impact really only at the margin. Nevertheless, we believe that the prospects for meaningful change in South Africa require a combination of increasing internal as well as external pressure. If you look at history, it is very difficult to be optimistic about the willingness of white South Africans to voluntarily divest themselves of their power, their purpose and their privileges. Only in the context of increasing internal as well as external pressures will the Government of South Africa be willing to consider the kind of changes that are necessary.

We also fundamentally reject the view that America's investment can play a significant, let alone fundamental, role in serving as a catalyst for truly significant changes in South Africa. First of all, less than one per cent of the entire work force is engaged by American firms in South Africa. Individuals who work for those firms may personally benefit from their appointment, but it's hard to see how American investment is going to produce really significant change in South Africa. By the way, just as I reject the argument of those who believe that increasing American investment is likely to bring about fundamental change in South Africa, I also reject the argument of those who would say that by withdrawing all American investment, we can bring about fundamental change in South Africa. I think that the impact of American investment, whether it's expanded or contracted, on the future of South Africa is likely to be very limited insofar as the economy is concerned. I do think, however, that restricting additional investment can have a useful political impact in a number of ways.

Murray: In what ways?

Solarz: First it would serve notice on the white establishment in South Africa that they cannot hope for any significant or sustained improvement in relations with the United States so long as apartheid continues.

In that sense it will help to eliminate whatever illusions may have been created by the policy of constructive engagement. Obviously, this constitutes in essence a repudiation of the policy of constructive engagement as it's been described and developed by the Reagan Administration. Secondly, I think it sends a useful signal to the black majority in South Africa, that the United States is on the side of change rather than on the side of the status quo. If one assumes, as we do, that sooner or later the black majority will be in a position to determine the destiny of South Africa, our prospects for a constructive relationship with South Africa will be enhanced if the black majority feel that we have been working for change rather than supporting the status quo. And thirdly, I think it sends a useful signal to the rest of the countries in the continent and elsewhere throughout the Third World, that the United States is opposed to apartheid by deed as well as by word. This, I think, can redound to the political and diplomatic benefit of our country given the extent to which many people throughout the world believe that in spite of our rhetorical opposition to apartheid, we are not all that uncomfortable with it. So, for all these reasons, I think that the adoption of this legislation will be helpful to the United States and ultimately would be a cause in eliminating apartheid in South Africa.

Murray: What is your view on how blacks in SA would receive your proposals?

Solarz: Let me say that it is my impression that this legislation would, in fact, be welcomed by most of the black people in South Africa–just as I think most of the blacks in Rhodesia welcomed sanctions against their country. And the argument is often made here by the opponents of the legislation that we are hurting the people we want to help. To a certain extent and a limited sense that may be true, but in larger terms — in terms of facilitating achievement of the ultimate objective, namely the elimination of apartheid — I think we are actually helping them.

Murray: To what kind of sanctions are you referring?

Solarz: I think if sanctions are going to have an impact they've obviously got to be international. Unilateral sanctions by the United States will have a very limited impact.

The Director of the Institute of American Studies at RAU has collated a number of South African and United States views against American disengagement (Nöffke, 22/11/1984 speech to the Manpower Management Foundation).

*The views of some South Africans against disinvestment**

Professor Lawrence Schlemmer, head of the Centre for Applied Social Sciences at Natal University conducted a survey in 1984 which was commissioned by the United States State Department. The study found that three-quarters of South African Black production workers support foreign investment in South Africa and reject divestment and boycotts as a strategy for advancing Black liberation.

Chief Gatsha Butelezi, leader of the Zulu nation, calls divestment 'tactical madness'. He said divestment 'will destroy the economic basis that the new society we strive for will rest upon'.

Llewellyn Mehlomakulu, a Black banker in Soweto, told Allan Brownfeld, an American columnist, on 18 June 1984: 'The majority of Blacks in South Africa are for continuing United States business involvement, providing it contributes to evolutionary change.'

Mr Harry Oppenheimer, former Chairman of the Anglo American Corporation, addressed the Foreign Policy Association in New York on 11 October 1984 on the divestment issue. Stressing that external pressure, if it is to be of value, must attempt to bring about reform, not revolution, Mr Oppenheimer warned: 'The trouble with the policy of disinvestment and economic sanctions is that it works, if it works at all, for violent and not peaceful solutions.'

Mr Alan Paton, in congratulating Nobel Peace Prize winner Bishop Tutu, said: 'Bishop Tutu, I want to ask you a last question. I do not understand how your Christian conscience allows you to advocate disinvestment. I do not understand how you can put a man out of work for a high moral principle.'

* It is illegal in South Africa to advocate economic sanctions.

Views of some Americans who disapprove of disinvestment

This argument (divestment) reflects the hope that we can achieve moral purity by separating oneself entirely from evil practices. Aspirations of this kind can be criticized for counselling us to run from evil rather than work to overcome it.

[Dr Derek Bok, President of Harvard University]

If we cut off investments we would lose jobs in this country and we wouldn't necessarily help Blacks in that country.

[Former United States Ambassador to the United Nations,
Mr Andrew Young]

State disinvestment laws are counter-productive. They undermine international trade and the positive climate for investment. Further, from the standpoint of social change, the facts clearly show that American firms operating in South Africa can do a great deal of good by stimulating economic activity and initiating change toward equal opportunity.

[Mr William E. Brock, United States Trade Representative]

If the record of United States business in South Africa was understood, there would be little reason for the rash of disinvestment bills.

[Mr George Shultz, United States Secretary of State]

Constructive engagement does not mean waging economic warfare against the Republic, nor does it mean erecting foolish principles that only erode the American position in South African and world markets.

[Dr Chester Crocker, United States Deputy Secretary of State for African Affairs.]

Let us, for the sake of argument, suppose that we can agree on a code of morality, and that the practices of the South African regime clearly violate it. Suppose we agree to divest our shares of all companies that do any business in South Africa and that the total amount of disinvestment is large enough to cause many United States companies to completely pull out of South Africa. Now we have to ask ourselves, is our decision to disinvest likely to help or harm those whose oppressed condition was the cause of our decision. In other words, in our rush to attain moral purity by disinvesting, are we condemning millions of South African Blacks to an even darker, more hopeless, more desperate, more violent and more tragic future?

The argument over disinvestment, it seems to me, comes down to this proposition: Do you want to accelerate the South African economy, improve the lot of black workers, and use the pressure of a growing economy to break down the barriers of apartheid? Or do you want to destroy the South African economy, force a terrible bloodbath, and hope that something resembling justice and prosperity eventually returns to benefit the survivors? The choice, it seems to me, is clear.

[Mr William E. Simon, former United States Secretary
of the Treasury]

The effects of impetuous action would affect not only South Africans, but also Americans. For example, early in 1984, at the request of the Washington DC Retirement Board, Meidinger Asset Planning Services Inc. of Chicago conducted a survey of the divestment effect on United States pension funds.

Meidinger estimated that divestment would bar investments in between 40-50 per cent of the total United States stock market. Investments would be blocked in thirty-two of the top fifty American corporations. These companies alone represent over $300 bn in total market capitalization of the liquidity market. It would also exclude more than 30 per cent in value of total American equities, and would prevent investments in any of the giants in the electronic, pharmaceutical or chemical industries, such as General Electric, Westinghouse, RCA, Eli Lilly, Merck, Squibb, Bristol-Myers, Dow Chemical, Du Pont, and Monsanto.

The survey also disclosed that a team of investigators appointed by the Governor of Connecticut concluded that the following American investments would be precluded by divestment legislation:

(a) 82 per cent of the market value of shares in the aviation industry;
(b) 81 per cent of the market value of shares of companies manufacturing hospital equipment;
(c) 81 per cent of the market value of companies manufacturing office and business equipment;
(d) 100 per cent of the market value of shares in multinational oil companies.

It was also disclosed that three out of every four investment managers concluded that divestment would weaken the entire United States share portfolio.

Meidinger feels that a compulsory ban on investments in United States companies operating in South Africa would harm the ability of investment managers to meet their objectives, would cause the funds to be more volatile, would force managers to acquire securities of lower overall quality and could reduce future fund performances.

Meidinger also conducted a study of the consequences of divestiture on pension funds, and therefore the effect on the income of pensioners. He used the Ohio Pension Fund as a hypothetical case, the current net worth of the fund being approximately $20 bn. Prime industrial groups to be eliminated from potential investments include all the major electronic firms, all the major chemical corporations, all the major drug companies and most of the new computer and hi-tech companies.

The survey concluded:

> If one calculates that these restrictions will merely reduce the rate of earnings in that pension fund by 1 per cent per year — and that may be a very conservative estimate — and if one assumes that the rate of return for the next 30 years is thereby reduced from 11 per cent to 10 per cent a year, then at the end of 30 years the Ohio Pension Fund would have lost $100 billion in growth potential from its current holdings . . . One may be incredulous about that figure, but it is correct. It represents the dramatic effect of compound interest.

The disinvestment campaign has a number of major weaknesses. In the first instance, it cuts right across the grain of American democratic free enterprise, and therefore challenges the United States as much as South Africa. It also exhibits the moral weakness of emphasizing that the ends justify the means, and the ends are not specified beyond the downfall of the White establishment, so they are not subject to scrutiny. From the strictly business point of view, succumbing to political pressure in South Africa could open the door to further political pressures elsewhere. It would remove from South Africa the beneficial examples of American democratic values and American business. American business in South Africa has a value beyond its economic one precisely because it does provide a mediating link with the world's leading democracy.

Moreover, the economic contribution of American business is

good in itself. It has been said that the multinationals are the workhorses of the world: continuing the metaphor, the argument in this study is that they should be harnessed, in South Africa and elsewhere, and put to work, rather than shot in a moment of pique, or put to pasture while the socialist donkey is expected to work as hard and produce as efficiently. For over fifty years, the multinationals have enjoyed unfettered growth around the world, during which time a few of them depleted resources, exploited workers and abused the host country; while most of them contributed more to the host economy than they took out, in the form of direct investment, reinvested profits, the creation of jobs and raised standards of living, and the transfer of their technologies.

It does not matter that multinationals are motivated by enlightened long-term self interest in acting as good corporate citizens: indeed this is the best guarantee of good citizenship in an imperfect world. If in South Africa they find a ready market, raw materials and willing manpower which is good for them, then South Africa obtains from the multinationals investment and technology which is essential for economic growth in the Republic. It is a symbiotic relationship, and would continue to be under a different, better, political dispensation.

5 The Sullivan initiative

No where else can we find resistance to change so galvanized to the point of making ordinary methods of initiating change an exercise in futility. [Reverend Leon Sullivan]

These codes constitute gross forms of interference in an almost 'sacrosanct' relationship i.e. between employer and employee. In a free market economy, this relationship should be left almost entirely to those two parties — the State should not interfere — least of all foreign states . . . [Professor Nic Wiehahn]

. . . there can be no industrial peace without social and ultimately political justice. One implication of support for the codes must therefore be an unambiguous political involvement by management on the side of black labour. [Professor Mike Whisson]

Is the Sullivan initiative simply a shield for United States multinationals under fire, and are the reforms undertaken by American business in South Africa nothing but corporate camouflage? Or is there a deeper, more soundly-based managerial and moral dimension to the actions of United States companies with regard to Sullivan? In the context of this enquiry, the Sullivan initiative has considerable heuristic value in clarifying some of the complex issues surrounding American business in South Africa. Attitudes and actions towards Sullivan reveal a great deal about the various foreign and domestic actors in the drama. These attitudes and actions, and their effects, are analysed here and later in this book.

Interestingly enough (for United States official policy and American business do not always agree), the current United States administration with its policy of constructive engagements sees a common goal with American business in South Africa. To some extent, Sullivan represents a rallying point for the interests of the United States government and American corporations in South Africa. For example, in March 1984 Secretary of State George Shultz strongly urged companies which had not yet done so to sign the Sullivan principles, arguing that 'voluntary adoption of effective equal employment principles puts American firms in a strong moral position'.

The Sullivan Code was first endorsed by twelve American companies in February 1977, and comprised the first set of six principles (given later) which have been amplified from time to time. Although it concentrates on the wider social, rather than economic, role of American business in South Africa, the Sullivan initiative gives American corporations high visibility and raises pertinent questions about corporate social responsibility. It seems clear that the Reverend Sullivan initiated a sincere effort to ensure that, if the American companies remained in South Africa, they would be a force for the amelioration of the Black condition, at least in the workplace and preferably in the whole society.

History as prelude

It is instructive to read of the genesis of the Sullivan Principles, of his assumptions, hopes and fears for South Africa from Sullivan himself, but these are too long to reproduce here. Clearly, his success during the American Civil Rights Campaign has coloured his vision of what is possible in South Africa. As Whisson points out, with reference to the United States:

> The campaigns that he launched were effective because they were consistent with the free enterprise model — in order to persuade your opponent to accept your view-point it is necessary to reduce his profits (for instance by boycotts) until the terms you offer are the most profitable option open to him. Success in such campaigns turns upon one's skill as an organiser, upon the freedom one has to organise, upon the power, both numerical and economic, that one can bring to bear upon specific targets [Whisson, 1980, p.17.]

The same writer continues to say that Sullivan was a good organizer who operated in a society in which theoretically at least and in the higher courts generally, there was equality before the law and the rule of law prevailed. Although Sullivan realized that South Africa was a very different society from that in which he had worked, his initial response to it was much the same as to racist American companies at home — withdraw investments, terminate businesses and so serve notice on Pretoria that it is more profitable to change than to resist. From his position on the Board of General Motors, he endeavoured to promote withdrawal, and failed to gain a single convert in four years. He then drew up his code of principles.

Whether there are labour organisers in South Africa as competent as Sullivan is an unanswerable question as they do not have the same freedom to organise. The ethos of the government, however fudged it may have become since the fall of Vorster in 1978, remains one of White control over everything pertaining to at least 80 per cent of the country. The law is not colour blind, nor does the rule of law prevail. The ethos of business is generally strongly profit orientated, which implies that if repression of non-voters is the means of industrial peace in the short run, then repression is acceptable. American based companies have a stake in South Africa so small that the direct economic effects of withdrawal would be slight, whatever the short term effects on business confidence might be. In short, the power that Sullivan could bring to bear on South Africa was little more, and maybe no more, than that wielded by those who share his views in South Africa itself. [Whisson, 1980 p.17.]

The Sullivan principles gained support from two kinds of business organizations. There were some companies which saw in the codes a means whereby criticism at home could be muted by the arguments that:

we are committed to change; we are doing what we can within the law; we are providing employment, wages, opportunities and welfare for Blacks — which is *their* priority in a situation on 20 per cent employment.

What such companies actually do may be described, more or less fairly, as 'corporate camouflage'. In addition some companies, probably a small minority, have taken a much longer-term view of their involvement in South Africa. For them affirmative action is not a slogan to quieten critics abroad but a strategy for long-term survival.

The arguments of the affirmative action companies are that in the medium term — about ten years or so — peace in South Africa will depend upon the rate of economic growth and upon the capacity of the economy to absorb Black workers into industry. The scarcity of skilled workers and managerial staff is such that personnel will have to be recruited from Europe at great cost unless the monopoly of Whites over skilled jobs can be broken, and Blacks become accepted in managerial roles. It is therefore worth the cost of some dislocation now, and some unhappiness among White workers, to force the pace of Black advancement through affirmative action. It is cheaper to train Blacks than to import Whites, especially if the latter are coming on short contracts and will leave at the first signs of trouble.

In the longer term companies with a massive capital investment may assume that South Africa will become a Black-ruled state, and that the terms on which the transformation occurs will be affected to some extent by the performance of commerce and industry. Companies which have committed themselves to a consensual model of industrial relations, rather than a conflict model, will be contributing to an overall pattern of relationships within the country inconsistent with Marxist models and the nationalization of the means of production which tends to accompany change inspired by Marxist ideologies. Individually 'good' companies might hope to be nationalized last, if at all. Collectively 'good' industry might hope for a free market economy to commend itself to the new rulers.

This type of company does not abandon the profit motive as a basic premise of capitalist enterprise, but its vision of the future is one of an egalitarian capitalist society, a society in which the vast majority of the people, whether worker, labour aristocracy, manager, bourgeoisie, multinational capitalist or native entrepreneur, has sufficient stake in the wealth of the country to make an alternative form of political economy unattractive, particularly if the transformation to the alternative can be attained only by violence. And that, argues Whisson, is in essence the ultimate goal of Sullivan's campaign.

> Any analysis of the Principles, and the manner in which they are being implemented, must begin by recognising the assumptions upon which they are predicated, and the goals they seek to attain. It may be argued, idealistically, that big business cannot, by its very nature, promote an egalitarian social order. Some may hold that the goal of all people of goodwill and historical insight should be the expeditious attainment of a society in which all surplus value is appropriated by the representatives of the workers and redistributed in the best interests of the people as a whole for consumption or

further capital formation. . . .The Sullivan ideals, which the Principles seek to further, assume only that substantial economic and social justice is possible in sophisticated capitalist enterprise, to the material benefit of all concerned. [Whisson, 1980, p.18.]

Actions as a result of Sullivan

The analysis earlier leads one to concur with Whisson's view that the American stake in South Africa is of such a size that the direct effects of economic withdrawal would not result in the over-throw of the system. However, this book is predicated upon the assumption that it is indeed possible (about which Whisson sounds doubtful) to achieve substantial economic and social justice in a sophisticated capitalist society; and further that this is the goal towards which to strive in South Africa. Despite the fact that Sullivan may be adhered to by some companies for dubious motives, and also despite the fact that Sullivan cuts across the principles of a free-market economy, the initiative might now be seen as more of a useful example in the South African workplace than many people are prepared to admit, (although this view is supported by some of the sources which are quoted here).

The former Sullivan co-ordinator in South Africa from 1982–4, describes different phases in the evolution of the Sullivan initiative, in a speech given to Amcham in August 1984. He characterizes Phase 1 as:

Each company pursuing its own goals and objectives with a view to meeting the requirements laid down by ADL in the annual questionnaire. A 'learning experience' in which mistakes were made, lessons learnt, and little knowledge was shared. A general resentment that the Principles had been imposed from outside. A general reaction to treat the symptoms rather than the causes of the social ills in our society. A time in which in-company requirements were largely achieved and 'normal environments' were created in the workplace.

In summary then, this period from the inception of the Principles to 1982 saw a proliferation of involvement without focus on key programmes or deriving the maximum benefit from limited financial and human resources. [Crawford, Amcham Speech, Johannesburg, 1 August 1984, p.3.]

Subsequently, Task Groups were formed to tackle further expanded Sullivan principles in a more concentrated way. This initiated what Crawford characterizes as 'Phase II'. The Task Groups concluded that:

- programmes identified should address issues at a national level;
- these programmes should tackle causes and not symptoms;
- due to limited resources available amongst USA companies programmes should have a multiplier effect;
- to have impact these programmes should get priority treatment from signatory companies.

The characteristics of Phase II are summarized as follows whereby Task Groups are defined as Project Based or Information Disseminators in their mode of operation:

Task Group 1 Special Projects
Task Group 2 Information Dissemination
Task Group 3 Projects on Education
Task Group 4 Information on Training
Task Group 5 Projects on Manpower Development
Task Group 6 Projects on Health
Task Group 7 Projects on Small Business Development
Task Group 8 Information on Housing.

Through the identification of these specific programmes and projects, which have become endorsed, efforts are being made by the Task Groups to persuade signatory companies to direct some of their resources into these endorsed programmes [Crawford, 1984, pp.3–4.]

In talking about the future, the former Sullivan Co–ordinator affirmed that:

What I find intriguing is that through the embodiment of the Principles, and the subsequent endorsement of them by more than 120 USA companies, the presence of USA business in RSA has, in the minds of some, created a homogeneous fraternity of business all moving in quick, even time in the same direction. And, that this perceived spirit of common commitment will provide the strength to lobby the South African government on certain issues. This perception of a co–ordinated USA business presence has two further elements.

1. Because we operate under the umbrella of a code of Principles, which is annually evaluated by ADL, and in which the signatory companies' individual performances are publicly reported, a clear identity has been created. In my opinion this grouping together under the Sullivan code has tended to focus a lot more attention, pressure and, consequently, criticism. This spotlighting has assisted in spurring the effort on.

2. This grouping of companies is now viewed by the critics as being a sizeable pressure group which should begin to flex its collective strength to bring about fundamental change in the RSA. [Crawford, 1984, pp. 3–4.]

Clearly, there has been a 'fundamental shift in focus and emphasis' since the early days of Sullivan. The Co–ordinator expected future attention to be given to such issues as:

- influx control embracing issues such as forced removals and the absence of labour mobility;

- granting of freehold rights to Blacks;

- greater emphasis on the training of teachers to address the low quality of Black education;

- aiding Black business in gaining access to Central Business Districts;

- encouraging suppliers and vendors adhering to a code of employment practices;

- increased contact with and involvement of Blacks at all levels of our involvement.

As they tackle the tasks they have set themselves, American corporations are having a beneficial influence out of proportion to their actual economic importance. If those who favour disinvestment and divestment are persuaded to desist by evidence of tangible benefits to all South Africans, this also will help nudge South Africa's evolution in the direction of a genuine free enterprise economy.

By 1983, of the approximate 350 American companies operating in South Africa, only 147 had endorsed the Sullivan Code. These companies, however, employ over 71 per cent of the total work force employed by United States companies. Of the balance, 21 per cent work for companies over which the American parent companies do not have majority control.

The co-ordinated Sullivan Code effort started by United States companies has developed to a point where in 1983, 99 per cent of Sullivan signatories reported fully integrated facilities; 100 per cent reported equal pay for equal work with significant focus of effort on education, training, health, welfare, housing and Black entrepreneurship. The extent of the effort is measured by reported expenditure in these areas: in constant 1983 dollars it increased from $1.8 m in 1978 to $48.7 m in 1983, or, reflected in another way, from an average expenditure of $35 per employee in 1978 to $383 per employee in 1983. As Sullivan has remarked: 'many of your activities have profoundly changed the social climate in your companies, in the communities of the workers, and in South Africa generally. Let me assure you that people in the United States are becoming increasingly aware of your commitment' (Amcham, 1984, p. 11). Despite encouraging progress by American business in South Africa, there do remain problems associated with the Sullivan initiative.

Problems associated with Sullivan

The first thing that seemed immediately clear, from the early days of 1977, was that the American multinationals could not bring about the larger changes envisaged by Sullivan – and that their failure to do so would inevitably lead to increasingly stringent demands on the part of Sullivan's constituencies to take punitive measures against the corporations. The inner logic of the situation suggests that an initiative like Sullivan's – until and unless there is a radical transformation of South African society – must either become increasingly militant and powerful, using more and more severe sanctions against United States companies in the absence of real change in South Africa, or must inevitably falter and fail. On the other hand, some of the companies themselves are now showing a remarkable self-generated willingness to put the essence of the code into practice, a keenness that might well remain without Sullivan.

There is a direct analogy between the Sullivan initiative and the imposition of sanctions against South Africa: 'In the absence of readiness and ability to intervene militarily, the demand for sanctions remains the militant decoration of actual passivity' (Adam, 1971, p. 135). Unless Sullivan can mobilize enough power actually to force the multinationals to do what he would like them to do, his principles might be relegated to a position of dwindling moral suasion as time goes by. That is bound to be the fate of any form of pressure or sanction which is not backed by the ability and the will to impose an ultimate authority if the targets of pressure remain recalcitrant and noncompliant. In any case, as regards labour codes generally, the Black trade unions – wielding far greater direct power *vis–à–vis* South African business – have confronted industry in a way which relegates the era of the codes to a historical penumbra. Moreover, it may be very difficult for Sullivan and his supporters in the legislative and executive branches of government to order the multinationals to do what they want them to do in South Africa, on pain of divestment or forced disinvestment for failure to comply.

In recent years, Sullivan has urged Congress to pass legislation to make his principles mandatory 'as an absolute minimum'. He asked Americans to withdraw their money from companies which did not apply his code, and affirmed that 'my aim is not to make apartheid more comfortable but to end it'. He reported that the first stage had been the formulation of the principles and a campaign to encourage American corporations to apply them effectively. Although he stresses that his principles are having an effect and bringing about important changes in the right direction, he feels that the time has come to step up pressure on defaulters, including the threat of divestment. It is unlikely that the second–term Reagan Administration will support such moves. One indication of the administration's policies is that President Reagan appointed for his Ambassador to South Africa Mr Herman Nickel, the former Washington representative of the prestigious American business magazine *Fortune*. In June 1978 he wrote a major piece in *Fortune* entitled 'The Case for Doing Business in South Africa', in which he argued that American investment was a needed force for peaceful change in South Africa. Although it is not certain how future administrations will view measures against South Africa, it is certain that there will be continued calls for an entire range of measures – from moral suasion to outright sanctions – from a number of interested groups in the United States until there is a restructuring of South African society in favour of the Blacks.

A major reason for the increased focus on American business in South Africa is domestic American politics every election year, which might or might not imply a breather until 1988. For example, the Democratic Party's 1984 election platform went far beyond any of its predecessors in calling for tough, specific measures against South Africa, including:

(a) denying South African aircraft landing rights in the United States;

(b) banning all new loans by American business interests to both the South African government and private sectors;

(c) banning the sale of sophisticated computers and nuclear technology to South Africa;

(d) reimposing the Carter Administration's stiff controls on American exports to South Africa;

(e) banning further Krugerrand imports into the United States;

(f) exerting 'maximum pressure on South Africa to hasten the establishment of a democratic, unitary political system';

(g) 'scrupulous enforcement' of the United Nations arms embargo, including restriction on the sale of 'dual–use' items which might be diverted to military, security or nuclear ends.

This platform reflected the views of the major contenders for the Democratic nomination. Others who had an influence on the wording included Congressman Howard Wolpe's House Africa Sub-committee, the Congressional Black Caucus, Senator Edward Kennedy, and various anti–apartheid lobbying organizations.

According to the Director of the Institute for American Studies at the Rand Afrikaans University,

The divestiture campaign is centrally directed out of the offices of the

American National Council of Churches, and its Investor Responsibility Research Center plays a key role. Another co-ordinating body, the Conference on Alternative State and Local Policies, has lately become highly visible.

Other key components of the central divestment campaign are The American Committee on Africa, under the leadership of executive director Jennifer Davis, The Washington Office on Africa (a lobbying agency sponsored by churches and by the United Autoworkers Union), the Black Caucus, the lobbying group TransAfrica, The American Friends Service Committee, the African National Congress, The South West African Peoples Organization and the anti-South African group in the United States Congress under the leadership of Congressman Stephen Solarz

At least 100 other groups, including organizations such as the Peoples Front for the Liberation of Southern Africa, the Southern Africa Conference Committee, the Southern Africa Support Committee and the Women's International League for Peace and Freedom, play a core role doing much of the preparatory work during national and local campaigns. Local groups and co-ordinating committees have been established in all 50 states, and in all large cities targeted for divestment actions. Colleges are also key target areas. The aim, according to these organizations, is to send a message to the South African Government that 'apartheid is unacceptable and will not receive financial support from public funds'. [Noffke, 1984, p. 4.]

The pressure groups argue that the South African economy is vulnerable to outside pressure and that restrictions should be imposed 'until such time that significant progress has been made with the removal of discrimination at all levels and also in the direction of greater participation by all population groups in the South African political decision making process' (Democratic Party Manifesto, 1984).

Although nowhere near the top of the hierarchy of American concerns, South Africa remains an issue which will be exploited for a variety of reasons. These reasons may range from political expediency like vote-catching in election years such as 1984 and 1988, to genuine moral outrage at a racially-defined system for the allocation of resources, and even to a desire to end the free-enterprise system wherever it might be found.

However, as far as the current second-term Reagan administration is concerned, both President Reagan and Dr Crocker have acknowledged the value of American business and also the

Sullivan Code, in bringing about peaceful change in South Africa. President Reagan stated his views on South Africa when he addressed the United Nations General Assembly on 26 September 1984: 'The United States considers it a moral imperative that South Africa's racial policies evolve peacefully, but decisively toward a system compatible with basic norms of justice, liberty and human dignity' (United States Information Service, 26 September 1984). While expressing his gratitude that American companies in South Africa, by providing equal economic opportunities, are contributing to the economic advancement of the Black population, the president added 'But clearly, much more must be done.'

On the same day, Dr Crocker, American Assistant Secretary of State for African Affairs, testified before the United States Senate sub-committee on Africa, explaining major objectives of American policy toward South Africa: 'Our goals — those of the American people — can only be reached through a sustained process of peaceful, evolutionary change', he said, and added: 'The real issue, then, is not whether apartheid is good or bad, but rather what is the best means of encouraging constructive change in that country' (United States Information Service, 26 September 1984). Dr Crocker emphasized that the United States was one element in a complex regional equation: 'Our approach is to engage ourselves positively, to add our weight in support of American values, to back ideas, institutions and groups that can add a dynamic for change, to propose alternatives, to open doors and build bridges — not the reverse.'

On coercive measures, including divestiture, Dr Crocker affirmed that:

> we have not relied on bluster, threats or the actual implementation of new punitive measures toward South Africa. All evidence suggests that United States influence for change is unlikely to be increased by 'pinpricks' such as restrictions on Krugerrand sales or on landing rights for South African Airways. Such moves are more likely to become a show of impotence and to erode our influence with those we seek to persuade.

Dr Crocker said the Reagan Administration remains totally opposed to the concept of disinvestment, divestment, or trade and investment sanctions on a broader basis. He went on to say:

> 'We fail to see how waging economic warfare against the

Government and the people of South Africa can advance our goals or serve the interests of either the American people or the citizens of all races in South Africa. Not only would such moves offer a fire sale of United States assets to foreign interests, damage our commercial credibility and restrict our access to an important market; in some proposals at city and state level they raise serious constitutional issues.'

Dr Crocker added that apart from the constitutional issues involved in some proposals at city and state level, such proposals, if adopted, could sabotage much needed economic opportunity for the South African Black population, remove the positive force for change represented by the Sullivan signatory companies, and adversely affect those African states neighbouring South Africa.

The debate about American business involvement in South Africa has been raging for two decades now, both in the United States and in South Africa. It has intensified since Soweto in 1976, and there are no signs of abatement, and no agreement on goals, strategy and tactics amongst the various groups involved. Stringent anti-South African legislation is likely to be reintroduced in Congress in future and the Sullivan initiative is likely to remain a bone of contention between those who argue that it merely provides a rationale for American companies to remain, and those who see the code as producing worthwhile benefits.

The debate about Sullivan and disinvestment generally is by no means confined to America. Both management and trade unions within South Africa feel that codes — whether Sullivan, EEC or the local ones, are losing relevance. Fred Sauls, general secretary of the National Motor Assembly Workers Union said that: 'Workers were not consulted and they do not, therefore, accept that the codes represent their interests. For workers, the only acceptable agreement on employment practices is one negotiated between them and management'. It is possible that labour in South Africa, since most of its members lack any other form of political expression, could come in time to use the unions to voice demands not only for changes in the workplace, but also in the larger society, i.e. they might ask companies to play a directly political role in South Africa.

Perhaps the most difficult question which has to be settled by business in South Africa is whether it should be more active in trying to bring about changes which it wishes to see implemented. There is a strong argument that it is in its own long–term interest to do so; and another equally strong argument that the business of business is simply that — maximizing opportunities and minimizing constraints in the environment, but not actively trying to change politics and society.

In the face of these broader and more difficult issues, companies are wondering about the relevance of foreign codes in particular, given changes in South Africa like the growth in strength of the trade unions, labour legislation, guidelines initiated by the Federated Chamber of Industries and companies like Barlow Rand. Some companies have long argued that they have gone beyond measures proposed by the codes, and their usefulness on the factory floor has been spent. According to a spokesman for Chloride: 'The codes are not much more than just plain good management, and it is essential in South Africa to move faster' (Financial Mail, 13 March 1981, pp. 1047–50). A spokesman for the FCI said that 'the codes are becoming a non-story. They do not, and cannot, deal with issues in detail. It's becoming more evident that this has to be done locally'. (Financial Mail, 13 March 1981, pp. 1047–50). Mike Rosholt, the executive chairman of Barlow Rand affirmed that: 'We should be reaching the stage where foreign employment codes are replaced in South Africa by local codes. Certainly, Barlow Rand has its own which we believe goes further in certain crucial areas than either the Sullivan or the EEC codes and which are specially tailored to our own requirements.' Labour observers support this view. One said that 'the codes are tame because they cannot compel a company to do anything. A signatory could live with a set of principles for ten years and not do anything' (Financial Mail, 13 March 1981, pp. 1047–59). Moreover, it was argued, some companies were hiding behind the codes in an effort to avoid implementing real changes.

A major problem from the beginning has been the monitoring of the codes. Neither the EEC nor Sullivan have found ways of monitoring which are really effective, relying on company reports which labour observers say are remote from the shop floor. When Sullivan visited South Africa in 1980 he warned that he would keep trying to set up an effective monitoring system and that he would support disinvestment action against companies which did not comply — as indeed he did do during the Congressional hearings of 1981. However, in practical terms, all the problems inherent in effective monitoring will remain to plague the sponsors of codes, and doubtless, to plague companies which feel themselves to be under unjustified external pressure.

Recognizing that there are some positive effects on South Africa resulting from the Sullivan initiative does not imply overlooking the costs incurred by the companies and the executives involved, who would probably far rather be getting on with the job:

> As a shield against increasingly noisy criticism from political activists back home, United States companies doing business in South Africa covet the approbation of a Black Baptist minister from Philadelphia and an idealistic management consultant with the manner of a prep school headmaster. The two men operate a baffling system for grading corporate conduct in a racist society. They want the companies to battle discrimination — and they keep raising the pass-fail hurdle. Many of their corporate students are deeply unhappy, but they need passing marks to fend off wrongheaded legislation, stockholder resolutions, and assorted public relations headaches. This unlikely coalition came apart at the seams last spring but was patched back together — at least for now. [*Fortune*, 9 July 84, p. 146.]

The article shows that Sullivan is expensive not only in money — $78 million spent since inception on schools, housing and social programmes — but on scarce managerial time: the 1983 questionnaire covered fifty–five pages with 116 questions calling for both data and brief essays. In that year sixty–two companies passed including Ford, Coca-Cola, and Monsanto. Companies that failed included Carnation, Firestone, and W.R. Grace.

> The Byzantine grading system leads corporations to join in an annual scramble for what executives call 'Brownie points,' programs they think will score with Weedon. Education is rightly a key priority, since the inferior schooling provided for nonwhites is a major cause of South Africa's shortage of skilled workers. Mobil's public affairs manager in Cape Town, Pat O'Malley, 55, heads a Sullivan task force on education. He argues that companies should stop focusing on bricks and mortar — building schools wins good marks — and train more badly needed Black teachers. 'We need companies that are more interested in long–term projects than points,' he says. Most spending on education by signatories has gone to segregated schools rather than integrated ones such as St. Barnabas near Johannesburg.
>
> Weedon acknowledges some of these criticisms and says he has a 'drastic revision' of the system in mind, but Arthur D. Little's

awkward position makes that a distant prospect. Until recently, companies paid their Sullivan fees the way English lords pay tailors — as late as possible. Weedon says his firm has done hundreds of thousands of dollars of unbilled work on Sullivan. He says he's unwilling to devote more unbilled time to revising the rating system. 'This is one area where I feel mistreated,' he complains.

Strains in the system are showing up in a lot of ways. Weedon's earnest attempt to mathematically quantify and compare the ethical behaviour of a very diverse group of companies — on the face of it, an impossible mandate — is an obvious source of conflict. Twenty-seven companies that signed the Sullivan principles dropped out last year, and only five new companies have signed since. Says a spokesman for Loctite, a Connecticut adhesives manufacturer that has dropped out: 'They operate with more arm-twisting than we found comfortable. The atmosphere was counterproductive and offensive' [*Fortune*, 9 July 1984, p. 148.]

In a telling sentence the *Fortune* article says that 'the glue holding the Sullivan system together isn't their commendable results (e.g. education or job training for some 50,000 workers), but rather the growing political opposition in the United States to South African investments'. Once again, it seems clear that corporate social responsibility, if it is undertaken at all, should be carried out because it is good in itself or as part of desirable corporate strategy, and not to placate critics — because they expect more from business corporations than they can possibly achieve.

Sullivan's avowed goal is the 'dismantling of apartheid', but obviously it is not in the power of a fraction of the foreign direct investors in South Africa to bring about such change. Meanwhile, executives of American business are embroiled in a costly and complex exercise:

Virtually the only companies that show up at legislative hearings are those that, like GM, Ford, and 3M, can point to Sullivan grades in the two passing categories. According to confidential documents obtained by Fortune, 23 Sullivan–approved companies have joined Ford in a covert and nameless committee to fight disinvestment. The committee is headed by William D. Broderick, 60, director of international affairs at Ford. In one memo he writes: 'The only possible way to head off the undesirable legislation is to offer a credible, defensible alternative. The Connecticut law (which requires divestment of securities of companies that have a failing Sullivan grade) meets that standard, at least for those of us who are in categories I and II.' Broderick's proposal is fine for Ford and 61 other companies with passing Sullivan grades — but some 350 U.S. companies do business in South Africa.

Some executives of signatory companies feel that they could do without the Sullivan principles. Rod Ironside, 64, assistant managing director of GM South Africa, is one. Risking a fight with GM director Sullivan, he says: 'With all due respect, the principles have served their purpose.' The argument is that the principles have achieved the easy, measurable goals like desegregation, and that no code of fair employment practices is going to reform South Africa or block restrictive legislation in the United States.

An alternative approach, compatible with a reformed version of the Sullivan principles, is advanced by Robert Godsell, 31, labor relations consultant to Anglo American. One of the largest South African companies, Anglo American has opposed apartheid for decades. Godsell says that United States companies need to be more courageous — both in pushing for reform in South Africa and in explaining the justice of their position to United States critics.

The first fellow they might speak to is Stephen Solarz. In 1982 the Brooklyn Congressman voted to overturn the Administration's ban on participation by United States companies in the Soviet gas pipeline, on the theory that the sanctions weren't working. If Solarz's sanctions worked in South Africa, the effects would be perverse. If they discouraged United States investment they would weaken a lever for peaceful change. [*Fortune*, 9 July 1984, p. 150.]

Executives are not the only ones who are disenchanted — a fairly recent example of trade–union disenchantment with the Sullivan principles is the report of the Motor Assemblers' and Component Workers' Union of South Africa to the Ford Motor Company. The report was submitted to the company at the request of Ford, after the monitors appointed by Sullivan, Arthur D. Little, reported that Ford was making good progress. In the document presented to Ford in January 1982, Macwusa, one of the unions organizing Black workers at Ford referred to the Sullivan code as a 'toothless package of piece-meal reform that allows this cruel system of apartheid to survive'. In its document, Macwusa listed the six principles and the Union's comments on each:

Principle 1: Non–segregation of the races The union says that this has no significance to the needs of Black workers, of whom 78 per cent are employed in job categories which have no White workers. 'The system of job discrimination on the basis of race is being perpetuated in its entirety.'

Principle 2: Equal and fair employment practices for all employees The union says that practical experience at Ford shows that for a Black worker to qualify for a supervisory position he must possess an academic Junior Certificate or undergo a company-offered two–year technical course while Whites who have lower primary school education fill supervisory and even senior appointments.

Principle 3: Equal pay for equal work The union commented that 84 per cent of the workers in the lowest job categories were Black and 98.5 per cent of the workers employed in the top job category were White. Since the Black worker does not occupy job seniority equal to that of the White, the equal pay for equal work statement is simply lip service and an empty slogan.

Principle 4: Initiation of and development of training programmes for blacks Macwusa claims that 99 per cent of the Black workers are misinformed about the education and training centre at Ford. Over the past five years the company has reported only on the number of Black and White employees trained, but has failed to reveal the discriminatory amounts of money spent in training them.

Principle 5: Increasing the number of blacks in supervisory and management positions The union says that appointment of Blacks to managerial positions is simply tokenism. The company abides by the law that prohibits Black Supervision over White, and 'as such these Black managers have no decision–making power or authority in the company'.

Principle 6: Improving the quality of employees' lives outside the work environment The union says that Ford has failed to address itself to the major question of housing. Ford gave large sums of money to the Eastern Cape Administration Board for the improvement of the then Emaplangeni area, subsequently demolished to make way for the new KwaFord township. This resulted in exploitation as rents ranged between R72 and R80 and the original residents, moved by the Administration Board, now lived in Black townships in conditions of squalor. 'The new Fordville, with limited housing selling at some R45,000 each, is a window-dressing scheme aimed at promoting a Black middle class'.

Macwusa also says that substantial sums of money from the company are directed towards apartheid organizations and pro-government sports bodies. In summary, Macwusa says that the Sullivan Code 'circles around apartheid's basic structures. The

Code does not demand apartheid to be abolished, but merely to modernise and ensure its perpetuation'. It does not call for an end to passes or require companies to recognize Black and White trade unions on an equal basis regardless of registration.

The criticism of Sullivan — of both his intention and his achievements in South Africa — may not be altogether fair, but the approach of this particular union is echoed by other unions, so the perceptions of the people who are supposed most to benefit from Sullivan are not complimentary about his initiative.

A number of economists and others have said that changes needed to be made to the Sullivan principles to help them fulfil their stated objectives. Here again the question arises whether the changes suggested are the kind that can be implemented by business corporations. Principal among these is the phasing out of migrant labour, which destroys family life for millions of Black workers. An effective code would insist on the right of a Black worker to live with his family near his place of work. Allied to this is the provision of family housing for Black urban workers. The Sullivan Code should insist on the free movement of labour, on equal education for all races, on the recognition of all trade unions, and ought to insist on a timetable for changes — all measures that go well beyond the power of individual companies, and perhaps even of commerce and industry combined. The problem is that American corporations have to operate within the law, and it is difficult for them (and for other foreign and domestic companies) to fulfil Sullivan's or his critics' objectives unless the plethora of discriminatory laws are changed or unless the companies actively strive, in the political arena, to change them.

Sullivan's view is that if companies cannot be a positive force for change — which he defines as the complete end of apartheid in South Africa — then 'they have no justification for continuing their business operations in that country'. However, there is enough evidence of positive contribution — within the bounds of what is possible — to justify the continuation of American business in South Africa.

In addition to the real problems facing the entire initiative, sometimes there is intemperate hyperbole which is incorrect and counterproductive. Sullivan once told a Congressional sub-committee that 'nowhere else in the world can we find injustices and man's inhumanity to man, so thoroughly organised, and so hypocritically rationalised'. This kind of statement has a predictably counterproductive effect among some South African Whites who reason that there is a measure of things like press freedom, judicial independence, political opposition, trade union activity, academic liberty, and religious tolerance in South Africa which are non-existent in many countries. The statement invites scrutiny of Poland, Syria, China, Romania, Cuba, Saudi Arabia, Chile, Libya, Iraq, Vietnam, North Korea, Haiti, Ethiopia, Zaïre, Nicaragua, Rwanda, the Gambia, the Soviet Union and many others. In Moscow there are people permanently in psychiatric wards because they expressed reservations about the communist system. Sullivan's codes also lose some credibility because they apply to American business only in South Africa, whereas it is certain that there is American business in Asia, other parts of Africa and South America where the pay and working conditions are worse than they are in South Africa. Reason suggests that correct action flows from accurate analysis, which means neither downplaying nor exaggerating South Africa's faults, but trying to gauge them as scientifically as possible.

What Sullivan has achieved, in effect, is to provide a blueprint for action by American companies which has constantly been updated since, and to publicize it widely in order to gain widespread support. The only sanction he had against defaulters at first was moral opprobrium, presumably to be followed by loss of business. The fact that he, understandably, drew on the recent American experience of counteracting the subordination of the Blacks in the United States explains why it is that his principles — intrinsically sound as they are — do not always seem applicable to the South African situation (e.g. in not initially stressing trade unions, which Blacks certainly see as their most powerful weapon). It also explains why they are not likely to bring about the massive political and social changes that he wishes to see in South Africa. Besides the fact that they affect very few people, those employed by American firms, the problem is different.

In the United States, it was a matter of struggling for the full incorporation of a minority, the Black Americans, into the political and economic life of the country, at a time when the general ethos favoured such incorporation. On the whole, Americans did not feel that their entire political, economic and social system would be altered, and that their basic security would be threatened, if the Blacks joined in. White South Africans, on the other hand, fear just that — the complete overthrow of their carefully constructed support systems — if the large majority of Blacks in the country were to be fully incorporated with equal rights, and are therefore far more recalcitrant than were the White Americans of the 1960s. It requires vision and courage, and the will to give up substantial privileges now in favour of potential but not certain gains in the future, for White South Africans to want to give equal rights to Blacks.

The problem being greater, therefore, than the one faced in the United States, the methods need to be correspondingly more powerful to bring about the changes similar to those which resulted from the American Civil Rights campaign. Even the genuine and fullest implementation of labour codes, both foreign and indigenous, is still far from being a sufficient condition for the kinds of changes that Sullivan wishes to see take place in South Africa.

To say this is not to deny the value of the codes but to keep their potential impact in perspective: obviously they are unlikely by themselves to bring about the overthrow of the apartheid system and an equitable society in South Africa. Much more is required than that.

The general tenor of worker response to the Sullivan initiative seems to be widespread scepticism as regards the foreign employment codes. And yet the codes have been beneficial, both in concrete ways and in creating awareness amongst employers and the government of the importance of labour issues. The Wiehahn Commission, for example, specifically acknowledged the role of foreign labour codes and multinational influence in influencing South African government thinking on employment practices. Certain multinationals in key industries have been labelled as pace–setters in the development of a progressive industrial relations structure in South Africa, including Ford, Siemens, 3M, and Chloride. Many observers think that being a signatory to a code does establish criteria against which the company will be judged for its actions, or lack of them, and that over time this will lead companies in the right direction. Fred Ferreira of Ford summarizes it by saying that 'A company cannot adhere to the theory alone, and when the crunch comes, not implement the principles it has been expounding.'

Predictably, views on Sullivan range from affirmations that the principles 'have been a force for change in South Africa that has extended far beyond United States subsidiaries' (Hofmeyr of Barlow Rand) to statements that they are 'unattainable and of no significance' (Whisson of Rhodes University). The key to understanding the debate on Sullivan, and on American business involvement generally is this: as always in South Africa there is a clash between those who see some progress as being worthwhile progress, and others who view any progress as being of no significance unless it brings about revolutionary change and a South Africa reconstucted in an entirely different image.

A United States Labour Officer in South Africa said that:

'the one area in which change in South Africa appears to have been significant in recent years is in labour relations. Exterior influences such as the Sullivan Principles have contributed to the fragile momentum for change in labour relations, but one cannot claim that these influences have been the most important determining factor in the direction or pace of change. Rather, they have reinforced developments already apparent in South Africa: the desire to do away with the economic inefficiencies of apartheid, the need for a more skilled work force, recognition on the part of employers that stable living conditions for their workers may improve productivity, and the general realisation that growth depends increasingly on all segments of the population in the economic life of the country'. [Golino, 1980, pp. 14–15.]

Some Americans seem to be as keen to praise South Africans for establishing a momentum towards better industrial relations as some South Africans are to acknowledge a debt to external influences like Sullivan. Indeed, there is no need to trace precedence between them as long as they interact to form a mutually reinforcing upward spiral. A fundamental argument in this book is that influences emanating from the United States do coalesce with positive forces in South Africa, and that they reinforce each other. Sullivan is one such influence which has coalesced with indigenous economic forces to form a greater positive momentum.

The perceptions of American corporations regarding the Sullivan principles

What do the American corporations themselves think of their social role in South Africa? This question has especial poignancy since the Sullivan initiative threw into sharp relief the question of what American business should be doing in a South Africa which faces world opprobrium for its racial policies.

In the best of circumstances, asking corporations about their business practices is akin to asking poachers how they catch rabbits and pheasants; in the strategically sensitive climate of South Africa, and taking account of world criticism as well, there is an understandable reluctance for the multinationals to reveal more than is necessary because of outside pressures. In addition to doing business, the American multinationals in particular have since Sullivan been faced with a constant intrusion of pressmen, visiting American dignitaries and local consuls, various groups of people monitoring the application of the codes, academics and others, some of whom cause corporate executives to fill in endless forms and all of whom take up valuable time, which is another reason for business reluctance to become caught up in social and political issues. Perhaps the most fundamental reason for reluctance to reveal business operations is the unstated feeling that the business of business is simply that — and executives do not wish to be caught up in bitter controversies which are often outside their control.

The final and clearly stated aim of groups which pressurize foreign business in South Africa is the ending of apartheid, and even further the establishment of a Black socialist state, the achievement of which is beyond the power of the multinationals even if they wished to engage in revolution. The long–standing notion that multinationals are neutral (and therefore supportive) towards right–wing regimes, but actively aid the upsetting of left–wing regimes like that of Allende in Chile is now questionable: The multinationals are working very well indeed with socialist states the world over, and somewhat ironically socialist countries are seen by some multinationals as safer countries for investment since no unrest is tolerated by the authorities, wages are low, and incentives are generous. It is not surprising that multinational executives sometimes feel that they are damned if they do and damned if they don't, and consequently prefer to work quietly with a minimum of publicity.

In South Africa particularly there are legal reasons for business unwillingness to part with certain information. The government has sought to protect business from 'strategic intrusion' (Myers, 1980, p. 47) from abroad. Responding to a subpoena threat to De Beers Industries in 1974, the government passed the Second General Law Amendment Bill to protect South African companies against outside demands for information on their operations. The provisions of the Bill — later incorporated into the Business Protection Act of June 1978 are designed to 'restrict the enforcement in the Republic of certain foreign judgements, orders, directions, arbitration awards and letters of request; to prohibit the furnishing of information relating to business in compliance with foreign orders, directions, or letters of request; and provide for matters connected therewith'.

The Minister of Economic Affairs is authorized to permit exceptions, and allow business to supply information abroad. A private law firm in South Africa, after consultations with South Africa's Department of Commerce, said the legislation 'is not intended to prohibit or restrict the normal business information passing between a South African business and a foreign parent or affiliate', but it does, however, offer business the 'machinery to refuse to furnish the information (requested by an official body) if it does not wish to do so'.

A number of companies have cited the law as a factor limiting their ability to supply information on their activities in South Africa. In addition, the South African government has introduced a number of other laws affecting business which seek to protect what the government views as the strategic role of business in South Africa. The National Supplies Procurement Act, passed in 1970 and activated in 1977, authorizes the South African Minister of Economic Affairs to order any company operating in South Africa to manufacture and deliver any goods which the government decides are essential for national security. Should a company fail to comply with the Minister's order, he has the power to seize the goods or make use of the company's facilities to provide the goods in question. In other words, foreign firms supplying any items required for defence could be taken over if their parent firms outside the Republic ordered them to stop supplying the South African government.

The Petroleum Products Act of 1977 specifically protects the important strategic sector of oil, giving the Minister of Economic Affairs authority to regulate the purchase, sale or use of any petroleum product.

United States company officials refuse to say whether a standing agreement on sales to the government exists. Officials say that disclosures of such information is forbidden by the Official Secrets Act,

> but some say that they have been notified by the government that
> they are legally prohibited from imposing any conditions on the sale
> of oil products to creditworthy South African customers — thus they
> cannot prevent sales either to South Africa's military or police. . . .
> After the 1979 cutoff of Iranian oil, the goverment introduced legisla-
> tion that ban publication of details relating to the country's supply of
> oil [Myers, 1980, p. 48–9.]

As mentioned in a previous chapter, more than half of United
States direct investment is held by four companies, Ford, General
Motors, Mobil and Caltex Oil. Interviews were held with the motor
companies concerning their role in South Africa, but not, in view of
the particularly stringent constraints on releasing information
which govern them, with the oil companies. In addition, interviews
were held with executives of US Steel, Nashua, Citibank, IBM,
Derby and Company, Price Waterhouse and the American Chamber of Commerce in South Africa, to assess their views on the role of
their companies in South Africa. By way of comparison, discussions were also held with indigenous South African companies like
Anglo American, Barlow Rand, Anglo Vaal and Computer
Sciences to determine the similarities and differences in their perceptions of corporate responsibility in South Africa. In most cases,
attitudes and actions towards the Sullivan Principles of other
labour codes were used as criteria in the attempt to elicit information on business practices; the reason for this is simply that most
businessmen and economists are in full agreement that labour
issues will be one of the most important for the future of South
Africa, at least for the next few years. Business practices towards
labour, then, are a litmus test for corporate social responsibility in
the Republic.

It is important to note these interviews took place in what Roger
Crawford of Johnson and Johnson, who was the Sullivan Co-ordinator in South Africa from 1982 to 1984, calls 'Phase I' of the
Sullivan initiative, and that they reflect the concerns of that initial
period, as described earlier in this chapter.

As is usual in this type of research, each of the companies interviewed was asked a similar set of questions, an approach which eli-
cits not only individual executive views but also permits a comparative picture to emerge as one reads through the responses. Questions on the application of the Sullivan principles led naturally to
questions of external pressures on South Africa, of labour problems, of industrial legislation, of skilled manpower shortages, and,

in some cases, to broader political issues which affect business in South Africa. The questions themselves are omitted from the following transcripts, which summarize the executives' perceptions, as far as possible in their own words and tone, of their role in South Africa.

Evaluations of the perceptions

There are certain common threads and disagreements (a synopsis is given in the next section) running through the views and attitudes of the executives interviewed. For example, it seems clear that most companies would be willing to hire people on merit, if they could do the job, irrespective of race. South African Whites in managerial positions, pushed along by the exigencies of economic growth and the needs of commerce and industry for the efficient utilization of all South Africa's human resources, have long been impatient with some Whites' need for the cocoon of job reservation. The reason most companies started looking at their (Black) human resources in the late 1960s and early 1970s was that the long period of economic growth which South Africa had enjoyed was already then leading to a shortage of skilled manpower — a shortage which has become a severe bottleneck in the 1980s.

Equally clearly, the education of Blacks has been such that even when companies have overcome their racial attitudes and looked for qualified Black recruits, there have been very few available. Companies perforce have had to initiate education and training of their own — but it should be the public sector which is educating all South Africans to become fully productive citizens. The second-rate education offered Blacks for so long is now boomeranging on White South Africa. Companies cannot undertake to educate and train millions of Blacks and still remain competitive. Although companies have to varying degrees faced up to their social responsibilities, it ought to be a matter of national policy to prepare every South African to play a full role in the economic life of the country.

Although many firms say they were doing all sorts of things before the spotlight was placed on them by Sullivan and other codes, they tend to acknowledge, either graciously or grudgingly, that Sullivan and other codes have had a salutary effect on their thoughts and actions as regards the relationships between the employer and the employee.

At the very least, the American corporations have had some sort of demonstration effect on South African business, which can only be positive. Executives tended to believe that it was not the role of business to change the political system of the country, but were not averse to putting pressure on government when their business needs required it. On the whole they preferred quiet action to overt confrontation with the government. Most of the businessmen interviewed appeared to agree that economic growth was the answer, indeed the panacea, for South Africa's problems, without questioning closely the relationship between economic growth and political change.

A number of times the observation was made that it was easier for foreign multinationals, like the American multinationals, who generally hire far fewer and more highly qualified Blacks, to perform impressively as regards employment practices. Sullivan himself immediately picked up that Barlow Rand alone employs more Blacks than all the American companies put together. The real challenge, obviously, is for South African firms to raise their employment practices to Western standards, or a few companies will stand out like islands of privilege in a sea of backward management–worker relationships. It is in commerce and industry's own interest that there should be a well-paid work force in the country — always provided that productivity rises together with real wages.

A common feeling seems to be that the era of the codes has passed its peak, and that the serious challenge facing South African management in the coming decade is the Black trade–union movement. One work has summarized the current situation as follows:

> With a white labour force that always looked to government rather than to labour organizations to entrench its privileges, South Africa has had no real tradition of labour militancy since World War II. A lusty young black trade–union movement is now appearing on the scene however. The position of black workers is exactly the reverse of that of the whites: black workers have no means of political expression, so they are likely to use their greater bargaining power in the factories not only to voice industrial demands but also to fight their political battles... Although the South African authorities were initially hostile to the codes, recent changes in official attitude and policy as well as in law make it easier for companies to comply. A much greater problem for companies — and the authorities — is handling a labour force that promises to be both better organized

and more militant in the coming decade. Complicating the problem will be the fact that international attention is likely to be even more critical and international demands even more exacting than before.
                                         [*Business International*, 1980.]

Judging by the tenor of the interviews with key executives, it is possible that the challenge of mature labour relations will be met adequately by both foreign multinationals and South African business. This is not because business executives are superior to say, government officials, with more courage and insight, it is because business faces the sanction of the free market: firms will fail unless they solve their industrial relations problems, so there is a powerful incentive to do so. Politicians, on the other hand, face no such sanction; they can cover up failure indefinitely as long as they have enough force to overcome opposition to their policies, and maintain the approval of the narrow electoral base on which they rest. For reasons of efficiency, therefore, that is, for sound economic reasons, business is likely to be a positive force in the development of all South Africans, the raising of living standards and the amelioration of poverty. This is not to say that changes in the economy will, by themselves, automatically change the political system as many business people seem to think, but they will certainly lead to a South Africa which is better to live in for all its citizens. Changes led by business may also provide the indispensable basis for social and political change as well, both by example and by paying for the structural reforms which are necessary in the coming decades.

A synopsis of views expressed in the interviews

(a) Were the sorts of changes Sullivan wanted, actually set in motion before the advent of the Sullivan Code? GM, IBM, US Steel, Nashua and Citibank, of the United States multinationals, and Anglo-Vaal of the South African companies explicitly stated that they were taking Sullivan-like steps before 1977 for sound business reasons.

(b) Does Sullivan deserve any credit for changes? The common tenor of the replies of GM, Ford, IBM, US Steel, Nashua, Amcham and Anglo-Vaal was that Sullivan speeded things up, gave focus, gave impetus, increased awareness. Wells

Ntuli of Anglo-Vaal said 'most of us Blacks welcomed Sullivan
— we think he's done us a tremendous service. Were it not for
Sullivan, I think we probably wouldn't have a South African
code today.'

(c) What are the effects of external pressures?
     GM: 'The motivation for much of the international criticism of
     South Africa has nothing to do with the welfare of South Afri-
     cans — Black, White, Brown or Yellow.'
     Computer Sciences: 'The more (the outside world) pressurizes
     and gets results, the more they think they can continue. There
     comes a point where a nation has a backlash, feels its identity is
     being threatened, would rather fight back.'
     Anglo-Vaal: 'People who say Sullivan is counterproductive
     are to me saying that "we never wanted to do it (independent
     change) and now we are getting clever and finding ways of
     avoiding it"'.

(d) Can business change the political and economic structure?
     Ford: 'We have a total economic system which needs to be
     changed and a company can't change that.'
     Amcham: 'We can't get companies to sign something which
     directly attacks the government . . . .we understand that we
     have to lead quietly but you can't get this across to the United
     States.'
     Barlow Rand: 'The political implications (of changes in com-
     merce and industry) do not frighten me, they delight me ... if
     there are going to be pressures which lead to a better dispen-
     sation for all South Africans, I can only be pleased about it'.

(e) Does the Government cause or follow changes in business
     practice?
     Citibank: 'The Government is following rather than leading. It
     sees its mandate coming from an electorate a lot of whom are
     highly racially orientated and motivated. Where business in
     general is probably more liberal, more exposed to political and
     human social philosophies expounded elsewhere . . . the lead
     is being taken by business.'
     Derby and Company: 'In South Africa . . . the economy is work-
     ing — let the politics follow. Government will follow industry

and commerce — they can change speed but not the general direction . . .'

(f)   Has the Sullivan initiative been in any way negative?

Barlow Rand: 'While American companies here curse the day Sullivan was born, our very strong impression is that he has been a great help . . .'

IBM: 'There is a certain amount of counterproductiveness from Sullivan (time wasting, sanctions regulations, hesitation by companies as regards investment in South Africa) . . .'

Citibank: 'Some of Sullivan's statements of late appear to be becoming more militant and anti-South African than pro-Black, which we think is counterproductive.'

Computer Sciences: 'I fail to perceive any credit whatsoever, no recognition that something has changed. All stick and no carrot.'

Amcham: 'Questionnaires are a nuisance . . .'

Nashua: 'Some people are using the principles as a way of attacking South Africa.'

GM: 'I, as a South African, take exception [to the fact that Sullivan was not prepared to recognize what has already been done] . . .'

Ford: 'There are problems in the Sullivan Principles . . . for example, of quantifying [the implementation of the principles].'

(g)   How useful are codes generally and Sullivan specifically?

Citibank: 'Because we are fully dedicated to meeting the aspirations and offering the same opportunities to all employees of whatever race, creed, or colour, on a global basis, as far as Citibank is concerned I don't think that Sullivan has a hell of a lot of relevance . . .'

Anglo-American: 'At first the Sullivan code was the least impressive of the [Sullivan, EEC and SACCOLA] Codes, because it did not focus on management–worker relations. . . .'

Barlow Rand: 'In terms of general South African business morality, I think it (the impact of Sullivan and the American multinationals) has been a force for good. It has caused us to look more critically at the way we were conducting ourselves . .

IBM: 'Sullivan did give the necessary impetus — that's the best thing he's done. Whether he's had a bigger effect than that . . . nobody likes to admit that its because of Sullivan that they're doing something, but it's true.'

6

An evaluation of the effects of the American multinational corporations on South Africa

A number of conclusions emerge from a study of this nature. Although the enquiry is specific to American business in the South African situation, some of the findings might have a more general application as well. In the first place, it is clear that South Africa is highly integrated into the Western–dominated world economy, some three centuries after that early multinational, the Dutch East India Company, began the process. Although this book concentrates on the importance of direct foreign investment, trade also forms a very important link between the South African and the major western economies. In general, the same countries which have the heaviest direct investment in South Africa, tend to be the country's major trading partners as well: the United States, the United Kingdom, West Germany, and Japan. Switzerland is also a major trading partner, for technical reasons concerning the sale of gold and diamonds. The importance of the external sector cannot be overstressed. The total of all current account items was equivalent to about 61 per cent of the value of South Africa's gross domestic product in 1982. The economic research division of the Standard Bank says that in 1982 the largest supplier was West Germany (19.2 per cent of South Africa's imports), followed by the United States (19 per cent), the United Kingdom (15.6 per cent), and Japan (13.1 per cent). Major export destinations were Japan (15.7 per cent of South Africa's total exports), the United Kingdom (13.3 per cent), the United States (12.4 per cent), Switzerland (9.6 per cent), and West Germany (8 per cent).

The challenges to business, including foreign corporations, in South Africa

The starting point for any discussion of the future economic path of South Africa, therefore, must be the fact that it is locked into the larger world capitalist system. The world-recognized advertisements of the major American corporations and other multi-nationals illuminate the skylines in Johannesburg, Durban, Cape Town and other centres. These advertisements, together with the news, from time to time, that South Africa and the United States have entered into a commercial contract, reinforce the image of South Africa as politically stable and a haven for investment by the world's largest industrial power. The presence of the multination-als, moreover, suggests that South Africa is indeed part of the West, despite its ostracized status in world forums, and that it is a sophis-ticated and cosmopolitan country. It is partly for these same rea-sons that the multinationals are attacked by those who wish to see the overthrow of apartheid, which appears to gain both credibility and concrete support from the corporations. Regrettably, though, some of the attack is motivated by more than a wish to see the end of an iniquitous racial system — some of the critics are against liberal democracy and free enterprise and would replace apartheid by a socialist state and centrally planned economy if they could. The ever-present danger, therefore, is that South Africa will swing from one sort of unacceptable authoritarian system to another, or to an even worse kind of Third World totalitarianism. The burden is on all those who move for change — including the critics of multi-national corporations — to spell out what sort of changes they wish to see.

Possibly the worst disservice that apartheid has rendered to the long-term cause of a free-enterprise economy is to link the two indissolubly in the minds of millions of Blacks. The danger is that they might want to throw out the baby of free enterprise with the bathwater of apartheid. No matter that a moment's thought in-dicates that a genuine free-enterprise economy is antithetical to apartheid capitalism. No matter that Blacks will likely, and contradictorily, affirm that they want Marxism and continue in the same breath to list wants which are usually the privileges afforded to citizens in a liberal-democratic capitalist country. No matter that the masses are likely to be even less free politically and worse off economically in some sort of Afromarxist Azania. If their *per-ception* is that business is somehow to blame, it is this which will govern their preferences and actions. This gives rise to one of the most critical challenges which business has to meet, and especially foreign multinationals under fire.

It is not easy because historically business has flourished in hothouse conditions provided by organized racial discrimination.

From now on, however, business will begin to suffer, both directly in the labour and economic arena and indirectly through political upheaval, unless the factors of production are free and open to all. It is also difficult for businessmen to act because they do not realize the necessity of proving the value of their system, and they are often optimistic, not cynical. The South African business community cannot afford the luxury of believing that the value of a free economic system is self-evident. There is an overwhelming need for business to undertake the education of society as to its form and function and rewards. In this book it is strongly held that democratic free-enterprise can be applied to South Africa, and that it will function if it is given a real chance, which means educating the society, and more importantly proving to the populace through its own satisfactory experience that the free enterprise system really works by making it *genuinely* free, so that everyone has an equal chance to benefit. Social and political changes can be accommodated far more easily when there is a commonality of economic interests and a narrower band of economic differences. On the road to a liberal democratic state, business, both local and foreign, has a crucial role to play.

Commercial and industrial enterprise has created more wealth and general progress in two or three centuries than even the most sanguine of Renaissance men would have believed possible. Factors of production which might otherwise lie fallow are organized into efficient units producing goods and services for society. In an open economy, ideas, energy, enthusiasm and the courage to take risks come to fruition in business ventures which benefit both the entrepreneur and the public. Yet business is often misunderstood by the public, mistrusted by workers and maligned by analysts and thinkers — not only by Marxists, socialists and communists. Why? At least part of the explanation is that serious challenges to business are deeply embedded in our history and culture. The ancient Greeks blurred the line between thieves and merchants by making Hermes the god of both. Plato and Tertullian expressed views which found an echo among the early church fathers who believed with St John Chrysostom (347–407) that 'no Christian ought to be a merchant, and if he should wish to become one, he should be ejected from the Church of God'. A millenium later, St Thomas Aquinas (1225–74) argued that 'a good society ought but moderately to employ merchants'. It required the sundering of Christendom and the secularization of Western

Europe to create the philosophical basis on which the industrial revolution could happen and business could develop rapidly. Major intellectual and moral breakthroughs occurred when John Calvin propounded a theological apologia for the businessman, and the Physiocrats and Adam Smith developed an economic defence for the entire business system. The world has changed dramatically, but the criticism remains : in addition to the traditional clerical criticism, historians, philosophers, novelists, poets, and economists attack the profit motive, the competitive instinct, and the deployment of business power.

Nevertheless, business creates the wealth and pays the revenue on which everyone else lives, including the government, which should in its turn ensure that the role which business plays in society is clearly understood. Business should abandon its costly and bland public relations effort, the glossy magazines and the smooth media men because they cannot satisfy even sympathetic critics let alone those who believe in the (spurious) argument that the principal cause of man's exploitation of man is private ownership of the means of production. Instead, the leading businessmen in South Africa, including executives of United States and other foreign multinationals, should be prepared to engage in open and honest debate with their worst critics. Actions might change perceptions, and business must lobby the government to take the many actions required to establish a free economy in South Africa. Sadly, and more seriously, if business is grateful for an invitation to a Carlton conference, but does not succeed in persuading the government to free the economy significantly further than it has done since 1977, there might not be a private business sector in 2036 — and a mere fifty years from now should be the productive zenith of the young South Africans of today.

The question arises : but what real power has business vis-à-vis the goverment? It has much in that it disposes of more resources and expertise than any other group in South African society. It creates the wealth on which both the power of the State and the prosperity of society are based. Arguably, business can influence the government more than any other pressure group — the unions, the churches and the politically powerless Blacks. Next to the government and the army, commerce and industry are probably the most powerful sector in South Africa. The proposition is simply this : with power comes responsibility, and business must meet its challenge directly, for business reasons, to ensure its own survival and shape its own survival and shape its own future. Already business is involved in national matters like manpower development and the housing of Black employees. In return, the government should speed up the removal of discriminatory laws and practices. On the assumption that a free enterprise economy in a liberal–democratic state is what is wanted for the next generation, it is pointless to hope that it will somehow materialize without effort and a great deal of courage and vision by business leaders. The American multinationals, other foreign corporations and local business are pace–setters in many spheres of South African life. Their efforts should be supported. Yet, apart from intangibles like influence, courage and vision, business has little direct power. It has no army, no police force. It must keep within the law or go out of business.

It is now that the handful of people who guide the nation's economic wellbeing should think about the unthinkable. Perhaps one way is to visualize the desirable. If it were possible to have incorporated everyone in southern Africa into the economic mainstream by the year 2036 (remembering that 7 or 8 per cent growth per annum is required to absorb all the new job-seekers coming on to the market in South Africa, and that by the year 2000 South Africa will have to feed, clothe and educate 50 million people); if *all* citizens were free and encouraged to do the best for themselves and their families; if, indeed, all people were productive and enjoying the rewards accruing to their efforts; if the market and not the State were the major allocator of scarce resources; if most bread–and–butter issues were depoliticized; if we had a kind of giant Singapore; if the government were a kind of super–municipality not worth fighting over, then (i) would anyone care who was in government? and (ii) what could business be doing *now* to ensure such a state of affairs existing *then*?

Perhaps there are other, better, more feasible scenarios. What is clear is that, to the extent that political power determines life-chances, South Africa's vast potential of creative human energy will be dissipated in bitter political struggles, somewhat analogous to those in Algeria and Zimbabwe. The corollary to this is that it makes sense, in South Africa, to make life–chances as independent as possible of political power. If government is not reduced to the point where it is not the major factor affecting individual liberty for anyone, it will always be an irresistible temptation for one elite to seize power and to rule in favour of a particular group of people.

The jokes about holding future Carlton conferences around a card table have been over–exposed, but the underlying problem is serious indeed. In the same way as South Africa has too much big government, so also it has too much big business. Monopolies and oligopolies, though they have developed for understandable business reasons in South Africa, could negate attempts to establish genuine free enterprise by the year 2036 unless steps are taken now. The trouble is that few people *really* believe in competition. Once they have made it to the top, whether of the political or economic pyramids, then competition is something to avoid : it is those at the bottom of the pyramid who have most to gain from free entry. Can South Africa develop a society in which each child has the same chance to do as well as any other child, and also the right to enjoy greater rewards if it has the intelligence and energy and courage to produce more when it is an adult? Leftist critics say that monopolies and oligopolies are bad — which they are in some ways — but then proceed to the irrational conclusion that power should therefore be removed from the monopolies and concentrated in the hands of an even *bigger* and more *absolute* monopoly in the shape of a socialist or communist state. Critics from the left of buiness are often acute and accurate in their analysis, but when they move on to prescription they sound devoid of common sense : if too much power is concentrated in large units, the answer is surely to break them into *smaller* units.

There ought to be a creative tension between government and business, each reducing the power of the other, and both accountable in some tangible way to the entire society which they purport to serve. The ethics of both government and business need to be monitored by each other and by the public; both should take part in improved education and the removal of obstacles to advancement; both could co–operate in planning policy for the economy, for the poor, ill and elderly. Unusually enlightened behavior is essential now to establish the foundations of a peaceful twenty–first century in South Africa.

The beneficial effects of the multinational corporations

Another conclusion which emerges from this work is that too few multinational firms even attempt to make a careful assessment of how their foreign subsidiaries benefit the host countries in which they operate, and to publicize these, as well as the risks and costs to the business undertaking. Multinationals in South Africa are in a particularly difficult position: if they do not publicize their contribution to the country, the public cannot appreciate what it is; on the other hand, if they do publicize their economic success, they are accused of co-operating with racialists by critics within and outside the country. Nevertheless, their contribution to South Africa needs to be examined in the light of a number of economic criteria, as well as a few non-economic ones. In the following sections the analytical framework was suggested by a study by Bergsten *et al* (1975), but the analysis here refers specifically to South Africa.

Efficiency

The American multinationals, and other foreign business in South Africa, represent part of an economic system largely reliant on market forces to achieve an efficient allocation of scarce economic resources. To the extent that there are genuinely competitive markets, there will be an efficient economic outcome of business activity; to the extent that there are imperfections (oligopoly, cartels, licensing, government intervention), it becomes more difficult to say whether the allocation of resources is the best possible. Given the existence of imperfections, there are two opposing directions that policy can follow. The first is to destroy the markets and centralize decision-making. The second is to try to get rid of the imperfections and make the markets freer. There are welcome signs that the South African authorities are moving in the direction of greater economic freedom, but there is a long way to go: restrictions should be lifted from the labour markets especially but also from transport legislation, exchange control, tariff protection, business licensing, interest rates, price control, and agricultural production and distribution. The state still controls telecommunications, postal services, railways, television, radio, major domestic air services, harbours, electricity generation and distribution, uranium enrichment, and is dominant in the fields of iron and steel, phosphates, and oil exploration. The presence of powerful multinationals creates a stronger private sector in South Africa, and perhaps leaves less room for further government intervention. Moreover, the presence of business firms from countries with competitive economies like Germany, the United States, and Japan may have some sort of demonstration effect on both the public and private sectors in the country, leading to more competition, which in turn should lead to greater efficiency.

Growth

Growth, which will raise the total future output of the South African economy, should be a top priority of economic policy-makers. Whoever might be in power, growth is imperative to provide for the basic needs of a burgeoning population. Foreign investment and foreign trade, which contribute to growth, must be welcomed and increased if the country is not to become progressively poorer per capita owing to the rapid increase in the total, and particularly the Black, population.

Full employment

American companies and other foreign business directly employ a number of people and indirectly help to maintain their dependants; although these are a small proportion of the total potential work-force, their employment is a net gain for the country. Moreover, the presence of foreign business creates demand which in turn boosts employment in local industries. The American multinationals, coming from a country whose economic system has created 6.3 m jobs since November 1982 (unemployment has fallen from 10.7 per cent to 7.5 per cent), might influence policy–makers towards thinking about the merits of an economic dispensation which allows every individual to retain and enjoy the reward accruing to his or her efforts. If this is so, their value far outweighs their tangible economic contribution.

Income distribution

The foreign business sector, and the American subset, is too small to affect income distribution significantly within the larger economy. However, while the main benefits of foreign business might have accrued to Whites, the multinationals have contributed, to a small extent, to the emergence of a Black middle–class in South Africa (Spandau, 1978, pp. 110–78).

The quality of life

Within their limited sphere, and partly because of the Sullivan initiative, the American multinationals have raised the quality of life for their employees. The educative effect on indigenous companies might mean that American companies have indirectly improved the quality of life for people outside their employ in South Africa.

However, there is another dimension involved here, and that is the value of the goods produced locally by multinationals. Goods like electronics, cosmetics, soft drinks and cars might have a double–edged effect on the poor: on the one hand, creating relative deprivation in the minds of the deprived, but perhaps, on the other, creating the effective desire for economic advancement which is necessary for development.

The suitability or otherwise of multinational products must be seen in the socio–economic contexts in which they are consumed. South Africa is in a phase of industrialization which is beginning to integrate the country and is drawing more people into the orbit of an expanding consumer society, so consumer goods such as those produced by multinationals might play a positive psychological as well as a purely economic role. It might be that in the long run the cultural effects of the American business presence in South Africa, on facets of life such as consumption patterns, values and cultural identity will be as significant as the direct economic impact. The evidence is everywhere: some South African radio announcers try to imitate the American disc–jockey patter (while others try to sound British); students wear T–shirts with Harvard and U.C.L.A. on them; many adverts are mock–American and so on. The Coca-colanization of culture may be a less attractive by–product of the important economic gains from having foreign business but it is an exaggeration to see the influence of the multinationals as reducing the world to a company town.

Management expertise and technology

The South African business community, which is developing the resources of the country, is the richer for having access through foreign subsidiaries to international management expertise and technology. Already in a majority in 1972 (Poolman, doctoral thesis, RAU, 1972), the South African managers of foreign firms (whose proportion to foreign managers has probably grown considerably in the past decade) have developed a knowledge capital which is invaluable for the commercial and industrial progress of South Africa. Finally, the presence of foreign business leads to economic security for South Africa to some extent, through access to foreign supplies.

South Africa needs the multinationals for continuing economic growth generally, and specifically in certain key sectors of the economy. It is argued that South Africa would need the multi-nationals — for sound economic reasons — under any political dispensation which valued growth, development and business efficiency. Furthermore, the research into the attitudes and actions of the American multinationals with regard to corporate social responsibility in South Africa suggests that they have acted at least as some sort of catalyst for concern about labour practices, causing awareness of labour issues to become more widespread in South Africa; and at best they have achieved certain standards which are worth emulating in the interests of correct manpower utilization and economic efficiency. Some South African firms have equalled or surpassed the efforts of the multinationals. They have probably acted from a variety of motives, ranging from enlightened self-interest to ungracious acceptance of action forced upon them by pressures external to business or even the country.

In most discussions on the effects of multinational corporations on developing countries, detractors tend to argue as though they have limitless power to subvert national aims where there is a clash of interests, to corrupt local officials, to take more out of the country than they put in and so forth:

> In summary, talking about Third World countries and their economic relationships to multinationals, I think that MNCs add to the inequalities rather than serving to reduce them. They result in an outflow of surplus, a lack of backward linkages and Third World integration. They affect the international division of labour to the disadvantage of Third World countries, making them generally the site of poor production processes. Finally, they have an adverse effect on the environment and health of Third World people and

cause the introduction into Third World countries of inappropriate technologies. [Kaplan, 1981, pp. 22–3.]

To the extent that these criticisms are true, they are as much a reflection on the developing countries as they are on the ethics of multinationals: the argument here is that South Africa, for example, need not suffer any of these abuses at the hands of foreign corporations, but can control them to ensure mutual benefit to the country and the corporation. Moreover, even in countries which are weaker vis-à-vis the multinationals, there is often a net benefit to the country, despite abuses which might result in an unequal distribution of the benefits flowing from corporate operations in the country. The system should be improved, not dismantled.

Multinationals, capitalism and socialism: the future of South Africa

As already mentioned, some critics appear to want the capitalist system on which the multinationals are based to be dismantled:

> Too much can be said about what one multinational is guilty of and I think that in a real sense multinationals are just an expression of relations of production under capitalism where profit is the primary motive, but, since these multinationals concentrate power in fewer hands to an unprecedented degree, they similarly mean an unprecedented limitation on the rights of people to decide about more aspects of their own lives, to make democratic decisions about what they want to do, what they want to wear, what they want to drive, where they want to work and under what conditions. The multinationals, in a sense, are no more guilty than other firms in going for a profit motive but the degree of concentration of power here is quite enormous and the concentration of power in the directors of multinationals who are accountable to nobody but their shareholders who basically are interested in one thing only and that is profit. Once that system continued to exist and is maintained, and particularly once it operates on a global level as it does now and as it irretrievably will — there is no going back, there is no possibility of multinationals withdrawing into their home bases. As long as this situation continues I think it is going to be detrimental to the Third World development and to democratization. [Kaplan, 1981, pp. 29–30.]

Keynes once wrote that 'practical men, who believe themselves to be quite exempt from any intellectual influence, are usually the slaves of some defunct economist'. It is Marx who has influenced much of the criticism of the multinationals that is based on the premise that a socialist or communist economy is preferable to a capitalist economy. This assumption is questionable. Both practical examples in the world and theoretical economics indicate that it is in free enterprise systems that there is the greatest amount of human freedom — social, economic and political. It is in the countries where centrally–planned economies exist that there is the least human freedom in all these spheres. It is in Poland, Cambodia, East Germany, the Soviet Union, China where individual people have the least ability to do what they want to do. In West Germany, Italy, Britain, Canada, the United States, individuals are genuinely free to choose 'what they want to wear, what they want to drive, where they want to work and under what conditions', etc. It is only by stretching the meanings of words like 'freedom' and 'democracy' to the point where they lose all meaning that one can suggest that a socialist or communist regime as it actually exists anywhere on the globe provides more freedom for a person to achieve self–actualization to the best of his or her ability. A centrally–planned economy, unless it is subject to stringent democratic control, means just that — a small elite tells the rest what to do; and it is a contradiction in terms to speak about total government control and individual human freedom as coexisting. Yet it is exactly this type of confused economic and linguistic thinking which characterizes much of the criticism of the free enterprise system and the multinationals.

Clearly, South Africa as presently constituted is not a democracy for more than a small number of its peoples. It is far from a genuine free–enterprise, perfect–competition economy. In this book, however, it is postulated that it would be to the benefit of all South Africans if South Africa evolved towards, rather than further away from, a Western–type democracy, with a basically capitalist economy. There are a number of reasons for this preference as an ideal–type toward which to strive. Throughout its history, capitalism has shown a remarkable capacity to organize the factors of production into units whose productivity has astonished most observers including Karl Marx. Where there are free markets and genuine competition, economic signals are transmitted swiftly and accurately, and scarce resources are allocated efficiently. Free enterprise draws on the individual's natural desire for self–improvement, and rewards contribution to the economy. It is an ethically–based economic system because it allows each individual the right to choose his economic way of life, and thereby provides a sound basis for social and political freedom.

Clearly capitalism is not enough to guarantee individual liberty, but it is highly compatible with such freedom: it is stretching credibility to imagine that it is somehow accidental that the greatest personal freedom is found in the liberal capitalist countries of the globe. Similarly, it is becoming harder to accept that it is fortuitous that the societies which have the least individual liberty are those in which the means of production are owned by the state.

If capitalism does have weaknesses, such as a seeming disregard for past inequities, and for notions of current equity, and for the poorer sections of the population, then ways can be found of overcoming these *within* a basically capitalist economic structure. Education can be equalized and opened to all, together with health care. Positions in society can be filled on merit alone. While the right to earn differential rewards is maintained, some sort of cushion is provided for the weak and helpless. In other words, a case can be made for some kind of welfare capitalism, shading into socialism, particularly for a country like South Africa, with the provisos that such measures are both temporary and kept within bounds.

Moving along the continuum towards a stronger socialist/communist state presents problems. Although socialist countries like the Soviet Union, China and Eastern Europe have shown economic growth, the cost in terms of subjugation of the individual to the will of the totalitarian state has been horrifying. The guns of the Berlin Wall point inwards. The communist Kampucheans murdered nearly half of their fellow Cambodians in the worst genocide of this century. Vietnamese parents put their familites into rickety boats and would rather risk death in the South China Seas than live under their communist regime. The burden is on those who advocate a Marxist state to show why anyone should have reason to believe that a Marxist autocracy which combines political and economic power will not behave as brutally as all actual Marxist governments have done so far. It is not enough to say that a revolutionary class struggle 'might' result in a genuine democracy with civil liberties, or that man 'might' change his nature when he holds supreme power in a Marxist state. Far better evidence has to be adduced in support of a Marxist model.

Non–Marxist radicals are on stronger ground, in so far as they generally accept democracy and puzzle over ways of using the economy to benefit the people. There certainly can be dialogue between such democratic socialists and liberal capitalists because there is sufficient common ground between them. They often want the same or similar ends, but differ over the means. As regards the future of South Africa, specifically, the key questions which have to be tackled are democratization in the political sphere, and the balance between government and private sector in the economic sphere. The subtle key is democratic control, for if the government is answerable to an electorate, so too, ultimately, will be both the public and private sectors of the economy, and hence the long–term priorities for the allocation of resources in society.

Does South Africa have the pre–conditions for setting up such a democracy out of all the contending groups and beliefs? It is difficult to say, and especially difficult is to establish the real views of the majority of Blacks. Nevertheless, what is possible, and indeed a moral imperative, is to work for the kind of society which is regarded as ideal, according to stated values, assumptions and carefully marshalled evidence.

Of utmost importance for this book is the contention that the practical aspirations of most people in the world, and this would include the Black majority in South Africa, are in harmony with what the practical business community, including the foreign multinationals, wants and needs. Most people seem to want similar things: full citizenship in the country of their birth; education and health care for themselves and their children; equality before the law and freedom from arbitrary incarceration; freedom of mobility, assembly and speech; a full family life and freedom to enjoy the rewards accruing to their efforts and the security of owning property.

If it is in their interest to do so, as it seems to be in South Africa at present, business will be in favour of such a free society, and indeed the more sophisticated will push for change in terms of freedom of movement, full citizenship and property rights, better education and training, the right to take any job for which people are qualified, and freedom from arbitrary arrest (business leaders protested to the Government when trade–union leaders were detained in late 1984). A society like this is actually in business's best long-term interests, but unfortunately the less sophisticated do not always see this and require some prodding to perform a leadership role in bringing about broader change in society. Even in the workplace itself South Africa still has a spectrum of genuinely responsible companies through to cruder industrial-revolution and Dickensian firms (See: F. Sitas, 'Health and Safety Conditions in Witwatersrand Foundries, *Carnegie Conference Paper* no. 112, vol. 9, 1984).

The use of the productive powers and rational organization of society by the business community to further the material needs of all South Africans and to provide the sound material basis that a stable democracy requires has a proven compatibility with individual liberty, and what South Africa needs is an extension of the fragile liberties which exist. It is not at all obvious, as some critics of the current (unacceptable) dispensation seem to think, that South Africa will be turned into a 'democracy' by destroying such little free enterprise as exists – and the multinationals which form part of it — and substituting a socialist economy in its place.

Under a socialist rather than a capitalist oligarchy, indeed, South Africa is likely to become worse on both counts of political freedom and economic growth. There is a strong theoretical underpinning for suggesting that free enterprise is likely to produce the most economic growth and political and social freedom, ranging in time from the Physiocrats in France to Friedman in the United States; but much of the obvious (less government means more individual freedom) has been lost to the muddled idealism of Marx, and to the beneficial — big — government theories of Keynes and Galbraith, which could lead to economically stagnant welfare states if taken too far and applied for too long. The value of Marxist and Keynesian economics is, at least, debatable, but it has not been possible here to engage in a comprehensive debate. None of this denies the suffering of Blacks in South Africa under apartheid-capitalism, over whom the weight, domain and scope of power exercised by the government is far greater than it is for Whites; nor does it imply that the multinationals have not undermined elections in Chile, bribed officials in the Netherlands, and exported inappropriate technology to developing countries. It does suggest that at least as far as the multinationals and the South African economy are concerned, the faults *can* be controlled and the system improved, which is preferable to any theoretical or actual alternative available.

The way to being about democracy in South Africa is not to ruin (for example, by frightening off foreign investment through socialist economic policies) the economic base on which social and political freedom rests, but to nourish it to the point where it can cater for each South African. Even if it requires a powerful struggle for Blacks to gain what they regard as rightfully theirs in the subcontinent, it is in the interests of their own people (as Chief Buthelezi and Dr Sam Motsuenyane would agree), to create a free economic system and a genuine democracy; a revolution may or may not be justified at all if it requires civil war and violent suffering of many people to succeed, but it certainly cannot be worthwhile unless it produces significantly greater freedom and prosperity for all citizens of the country afterwards.

If a South African revolution were to produce a Black anti-capitalist oligarchy which would repress further dissent as ruthlessly as the revolution had been won, practise reverse racialism on the Whites, and entrench its own elite position at everyone else's expense, it would be a double tragedy for all South Africans — but most of all for the poorest Blacks.

Paradoxically, the position of the multinationals might be least affected after such a change, and they might remain as indispensable to a new polity as Gulf Oil and other multinationals are to Angola now. In any case, the power of the multinationals either to halt or to effect political change in South Africa is severely limited. Rugman usefully summarizes the limitations of multinational power as follows:

> One of the main criticisms of the MNE from the viewpoint of political economy is the allegation that the MNE has excessive power. It is an organization that extends the influence of the home nation (often the USA) into the host nations. Sometimes it is suggested that the MNE is a vehicle for the furtherance of American hegemony. While it is correct to note that the method of FDI (foreign direct investment) permits the MNE to spread the domain of its market to foreign nations it is only a half truth to conclude that this gives the MNE control over foreign nations. In practice, the governments of host nations remain sovereign. They may be open to influence by the MNE but it has to line up along with other pressure groups, many of which (such as protected indigenous industry and workers) may have interests at variance with the MNE . . . . the MNE is in the business of business. It is a corporation, not a political party or sovereign state in its own right. Its economic powers can be offset by the political powers of host nations, if they choose to do so. The MNE

is forced to respond to its external political and social environment. The ability of the MNE to influence its environment is constrained by its need to specialize in ongoing R and R to maintain its firm specific advantage, without which it would become a paper tiger.

As well as criticism of its political dominance over host nations the MNE is also criticized on social grounds. It is accused of fostering worldwide consumerism to the extent that American cultural and environmental values (or lack of them) are imposed on host nations. Yet a relevant basic principle of economics is that the consumers own their demand functions. While the MNE can attempt to influence host nation demand it is eventually restricted in these efforts by its role as a producer. The MNE is not the consumer. Ultimately the consumers have independence and are sovereign. If they do not really want the production of the MNE they are not forced to purchase its products.

Thus the MNE needs to be constantly aware of the risks it runs in foreign nations if it appears to become overbearing and a threat to the host nation. When the consumers of the host nation adopt an attitude hostile to the MNE there is an inevitable reaction signalled by the introduction of restrictive host nation legislation. The governments of host nations are more responsive to their indigenous electorates than to foreign firms. The nation–state is not dead. Rather the host country government is a countervailing force to the power of the MNE and is well able to protect its domain. [Rugman, 1981, pp. 161–2.]

Rugman's argument (though basically correct), is over-simplified: multinationals do have money, and money buys advertising, which in turn affects consumers' demand functions. Yach (*Carnegie Paper*, 178, vol. 14, 1984) shows how, because strong anti–smoking legislation, restricted advertising and market saturation have affected business in the developed countries, tobacco companies are turning their effective advertising campaigns to the softer targets of developing countries — thereby creating a health hazard and wastefully diverting scarce resources. This is an example of why nation–states need some counter-balancing power.

Nevertheless multinationals are not as powerful as they are made out to be by their critics because, although they do have money, they do not have an army or police force like sovereign states — and it is still, regrettably, force which is often the ultimate argument in national and world affairs. What the multinationals can do to influence events in their direction is to find receptive local forces. The problem is internal vulnerability which is exploitable; so policymakers, economists and the public in host countries need to be educated into being discriminating as regards external business if it is likely to be damaging to the country.

Anthony Sampson, who popularized the phrase 'the sovereign state' in his book on ITT, says that 'without much need for plotting, the multinationals have achieved over the last twenty years, with the opening up of world communications, a position of sudden dominance: they have found a vacuum and filled it . . . .' (Sampson, 1973, p. 282). Multinationals as a group have shown some willingness to take advantage of what Sampson calls the fragmented and confused state of the countries and communities with which they deal.

However, using a situation is not the same as bringing it about, which would require far more power. The multinationals could not have their way in China for a long time, although it was the biggest market of them all, because the internal politics of China did not allow it. Now, interestingly, the Chinese are trying to transform a centrally–planned economy into one which is more market orientated; and foreign investment and trade are being welcomed. The multinationals were thrown out of Iran, in which they had invested heavily. They are concerned about attitudes towards them in Greece, France, and Zimbabwe. The political power of a nation–state, or even of an elite within such a state, can prevail over the power of the multinationals within its own borders. The multinationals did not want UDI in Rhodesia, but were powerless to prevent it; they probably do not want the institutionalized racialism of apartheid in South Africa, (which might bring some very marginal economic benefits, but which in both the short and long term exposes them to political problems and financial risk) yet they are for all practical purposes powerless against the ruling ideology. The multinationals still meet their match in nationalism.

If their political power is limited, their economic power is greater, but even here there is confusion: the same people, trade unionists for example, who accuse multinationals of exploiting developing countries often accuse them of exporting capital and jobs from the developed world and of competing with the developed world by using cheaper labour elsewhere. The accusation amounts to saying that the corporations are in fact developing the underdeveloped country by creating there both employment opportunities and the possibility of competitive exporting!

The task of economists in South Africa and other developing countries with regard to the multinationals includes pointing out ways to detect abuses, but more positively, how to make the country the kind of centre of activity which induces multinationals to bring together an efficient combination of capital, people, and technology to produce and market most profitably. Singapore, a poor new nation facing disaster as recently as 1965, has become a developed nation with all the social benefits enjoyed by citizens of countries with sound and growing economies, by doing just that — using the multinationals to its own and to their advantage.

> Much of the technology, management talent, and private capital needed to solve the world's economic problems are controlled by MNCs. Furthermore, they have the capacity to move resources, capital and management skills as a package of productive factors, custom–tailored to the requirements of a given project . . . . It is the package effect that makes multinational companies so highly competitive. It also gives them a special capacity to transfer know–how to others in the most effective way — a learn–by–doing, on–the–job situation . . . MNC's have been a powerful force in hurdling national boundaries and restrictions, so that trade, commerce, goods, services and ideas can flow more freely around the world to the benefit of all mankind. [Freeman and Person, 1980, p. 4.]

Forcing United States (and other) multinationals to disinvest in South Africa as a temporary and drastic tactic (or even the threat of it), might seem to some to be a necessary means to a laudable end (the demise of apartheid) — but even these advocates of limited tactical disinvestment probably agree that it is an utterly ruinous policy if taken too far or carried on too long. (For anti–capitalist advocates of disinvestment, this is probably precisely what they want: a total collapse in South Africa, so that a perfect socialist/communist phoenix might arise from the ashes. Could a better society emerge from such an apocalyptic scenario? The advocates of revolutionary change have yet to construct a convincing case.)

In this book, it is suggested that hampering business and economic growth in any significant way or for any length of time will not help either to feed or liberate the Black majority; whereas increased growth can be used to spread the benefits of prosperity, and even to prompt into action (by making the costs easier to bear) the ultimate political will on the part of the powerful Whites which is required to find some sort of workable solution for the long–term future of South Africa.

7 Conclusion: the impact of the United States on South Africa

The American connection: many strands

> You cannot bring about prosperity by discouraging thrift; you cannot strengthen the weak by weakening the strong; you cannot help the wage–earner by pulling down the wage–payer; you cannot help the poor by destroying the rich; you cannot keep out of trouble by spending more than you save; you cannot build character and courage by taking away a man's initiative and independence; you cannot help men permanently by doing for them what they could and should do for themselves.
>
> [Abraham Lincoln.]

In addition to investment, trade, politics — the practical business which ties nations together — there are other significant strands which bind the United States and South Africa closer.

One of these links is the English language. Whether Zulu–speaking, Afrikaans–speaking, or holding to any other home language, many of the people who live in Southern Africa speak English as well. For many others it is their first language. The importance of the English language connection is great: since each word in a language is a shared symbol, most South Africans can share with most Americans the implicit images common to both societies. When two nations use the same words to describe the phenomena with which they are faced, there is a better chance that they will be able to reach some sort of understanding (this despite witticisms which suggest that England and America, for example, are two nations divided by a common language). There is a natural tendency towards alliance between members of communities which share a common language.

Other ties amongst the Whites of both nations include a common European ancestry. In the same way that the Whites of the United States are made up of a melting pot of people who emigrated to the New World from every country in Europe, so too is White South African society an amalgam of various European communities: indeed it is in this way a microcosm of the American experience. Whites who cross the Atlantic in either direction tend to feel at home in both countries; there is an easy familiarity which comes from a common ancestry, and the shared attitudes and values which this implies, as well as similar social and even business environments in the two nations. The arrival of the *Mayflower* on the North American coast, and of the *Drommedaris* at the tip of Africa set into motion historical processes in America and South Africa which have interesting parallels, as well as differences. The common European heritage is manifested in many different ways. When Cecil Rhodes bequeathed the Rhodes Scholarships to Oxford around the turn of the century, he included the United States in his 'most favoured' nations. When Andrew Carnegie established the Carnegie Corporation in 1911, it was in order to grant funds for 'the advancement and diffusion of knowledge and understanding among the people of the United States and of the British Dominions and colonies', which included, of course, South Africa. Despite the fact that South Africa left the British Commonwealth in 1961, the Corporation has continued making grants to the Republic. Historical ties seem to develop traditional relationships which last over time.

South African and American Blacks, too, have something in common. Although most of the American Blacks are descended from West African stock, both they and the South African Blacks share a history of living under White domination, which inevitably must create some fellow–feeling between them.

Of course all South Africans, of whatever hue, are being drawn into the general Americanization of local society. For instance, this century there has been the ubiquitous influence of American films, advertising, and products on Blacks as well as on Whites. More subtle has been the influence of music: in the blues, jazz, rock and reggae, emanating from the United States and Jamaica, the ancient rhythms of Africa have returned to this continent and have helped to increase pride in being Black on both sides of the Atlantic. When editor of the magazine *Drum* in the 1950s, Anthony Sampson, asked Blacks why they did not (at first) buy the magazine, and one responded:

> Ag, why do you dish out that stuff man? . . . Tribal music! Tribal
> history! Chiefs! We don't care about chiefs! Give us jazz and film

stars, man! We want Duke Ellington, Satchmo and hot dames! Yes, brother, anything American. You can cut out this junk about kraals and folk–tales and Basutos in blankets — forget it! You're just trying to keep us backward, that's what! Tell us what is happening right here, man, on the Reef! [Sampson, 1956, p. 20.]

Whatever the fashions in the United States, urbanized South African Blacks, together with some middle–class, mainly English–speaking White young people are quick to follow. In the 1960s, for example, following American hippies, these groups found a mutual affinity in the smoking of grass or *dagga*; the Blacks in fact had been using it for centuries before it became popularized through California (the Zulu ambulance teams carried *dagga* to give to their wounded to make the pain more bearable). South African taste in popular music changed with the trends in the United States from jazz to blues and rock, the electric acid sound, reggae, punk, and the newer sounds of the 1980s. The identification of these fashionable subcultures with what happens in the United States will undoubtedly continue.

Of more fundamental importance was the Civil Rights campaign in the United States. From early in the twentieth century and gathering force as time went on, the effects on South African Black consciousness of people like W.E. DuBois, Marcus Garvey, and later Malcolm X, Martin Luther King, the Black Panthers and other Black leaders covering a spectrum of political attitudes were important in raising pride in being Black and the determination to fight for Black's rights in White–dominated societies. Links like these have heightened Black consciousness and helped create what might turn out to be a deep affinity between South African and American Blacks. Publicity–gaining episodes like the sit–ins at the South African embassy in Washington by prominent Black Americans might increase in coming years.

These intangible and non–official connections between some people in the United States and South Africa may become increasingly important in the future, as the world becomes even more electronically connected, and as consciousness is translated into action, particularly if the people concerned reach positions of power in the United States and in South Africa. The net result might even be the further Americanization of South African society in the twenty–first century, although there are so many cross–currents that it is difficult to predict with any accuracy which of them will become dominant in future.

For example as some Blacks look outwards others look inwards. Nat Nakasa tells of being in New York and listening to the Johannesburg trumpeter, Hugh Masakela, blowing Pondo and Swazi tunes in Greenwich Village: 'I wish I could go home ... just to hear the music of the people there — the Pondos, the Zulus and the Shangaans' (Nakasa/Patel, 1975, p. 11).'

South African Blacks straddle many worlds and will need to come to terms with them all; it appears unlikely that the answer lies in either extreme of returning to tribal life — even if that were possible — or, say, taking on a factitious American personality (Sampson describes one Black Johannesburg petty criminal who modelled himself on a character in his favourite book. It was written by a Black American and described the downfall of a young gangster called 'pretty boy', whose motto was 'live fast, die young, and have a good-looking corpse').

Efforts are being made to define the new Black by artists and writers:

> ...we are going to kick and pull and push and drag literature into the form we prefer. We are going to experiment and probe and not give a damn what the critics have to say. Because we are in search of our true selves–undergoing self-discovery as a people'. [Mutloatse, 1980, p.7].

It is often necessary to go beyond economics and politics, to an assessment of the social and cultural effects of the United States on South Africa, especially as mediated by American business, in order to understand fully the importance of the American connection. For those who have lived in the latter years of the British Empire, there are many daily reminders of the imperial era in South Africa. The round red post-boxes of the Royal Mail, cars driving on the left, public (private) schools, the sound of willow on leather, the plays in the theatres, newspapers which sound as though they would be perfectly at home in Surrey or Sussex, the pubs and clubs, the flower shows, the nursery rhymes which children say— and a host of other facets of South African life, both trivial and significant, are reminders of the British legacy. Being neither Britain nor the United States, but sharing a common official language with both, South Africa has borrowed freely various aspects of both societies. In more recent years, however, influences emanating from the United States have incorporated South Africa — and indeed much of the rest of the globe — into a 'Western' lifestyle which is recognizably American-led.

American cultural influence abroad usually accompanies American business, which brings not only its tangible products, but also advertisements, (even many South African–made advertisements have a pseudo–American flavour), films and music, Time magazine, clothing fashions, computers and TV programmes and many other facets of American life into foreign countries. In time to come it may be that this cultural impact will be as significant for the future direction of South Africa as the concrete goods and services, and the social responsibility examples, provided by American business.

Another connection is that the majority of South Africans and Americans also share a common Christianity. The state in both countries professes, if not always practises, adherence to the preservation of Protestant Christian values. The Judaeo–Christian tradition forms yet another framework of common understanding.

Taken together with the concrete links of American business and United States policy, such commonality as there is in language, history, culture and religion suggests that the destinies of the two republics might be linked well into the future.

United States policy

It is useful for analytical purposes to distinguish between politics and economics, as has sometimes been done in this book. In reality nations do not have politics and economics, but a political economy, a mixed mechanism which functions to allocate resources. These may range from intangible resources like power to concrete ones like assets and share of the national income. At some point in study of this nature, the economics must be viewed together with the politics to form a realistic picture.

In the United States the political and economic systems of resource allocation are complementary and generally accepted by the members of that society. As regards American business and United States policy in South Africa, under the present administration at least, the American business community and official United States policy are working together to some extent because of a perceived harmony of interests in the Southern African sub–continent. The Secretary of State urged American

corporations to sign Sullivan; the State Department commissioned
the Schlemmer study into Black attitudes; United States officials
co-operate with the American chamber of Commerce in South
Africa. At a November 1984 United Nations debate on apartheid,
the American ambassador said that the United States was seeking
'a path to change that builds rather than destroys a better future for
all the people of Southern Africa'. This attitude is probably shared
and welcomed by American business in South Africa. However,
the credibility of United States policy is contingent upon what
happens in South Africa. Even those who cannot agree on whether
United States policy is morally based or a cynical subterfuge for
making ideological and dollar profits in Southern Africa, do agree
on one point: it is what actually happens within South Africa, and
the way that South Africa interacts with its neighbours, which
creates the opportunities and constraints within which both
American business and United States policy have to operate. In the
absence of sustained progress in a democratic direction within
South Africa, the United States will be under pressure to distance
itself, officially at any rate, from South Africa.

In the process of examining the effects of various linkages
between the United States and South Africa in this book, another
significant conclusion which emerges is that even the most
powerful nation on earth has a limited impact on the internal
dynamics of South African society: a logical deduction from this
marginality of the United States is that as South Africa evolves, the
major forces which will mould the society of the future are most
likely to be internal ones–including groups like the ANC, who,
though based abroad in exile, are South Africans. Isolating the
major forces for change requires an analysis, for the most part, of
what South Africans are doing, not Americans or anyone else.

Nevertheless, the book also suggests the conclusion that
external forces can influence the nature, direction and pace of
change in South Africa. The United States influences South Africa
towards a racially integrated democratic society, with a free
enterprise economy, and perhaps steps up the tempo of change in
this direction. Americans are a practical people who would
probably agree that 'democracy is not a system for finding the
current solution in a mathematical sense. It is a means for striking
compromises between conflicting interests of a sort that it is better
to accept half a loaf than fight a civil war for all the bread'. (Bailey,
1982, p. 155). The key to whether or not one approves of the

influences emanating from the United States, and their likely effects on South African society, depends on fundamental values regarding politics, economics, culture, religion, freedom and justice. In terms of the democratic, free–enterprise evaluative model adhered to in this book, positive American involvement with South Africa is seen as necessary and valuable, even if hampered by factors beyond the control of American business and the American state.

Although fundamental values determine whether American influences are seen as beneficial to South African society, it is more difficult to assess the actual effects of these influences. They can be identified as forces which are at work, but not easily quantified. As Francis Wilson says:

> any number of plausible hypotheses can be put forward regarding the shape of the future, ranging from fundamental change by 1984, through second–best solutions, to an entrenched racial oligarchy living off the backs of impoverished Blacks far into the next century. All one can really do, we suggest, is to try to clarify our understanding of the forces at work, to interpret some of the apparent trends, and to be ready, in the light of new facts or further insights, to modify or abandon our own particular assessment. [Wilson, in Butler and Thompson, 1975, pp. 199–200.]

Admittedly, it is easier to quantify the effects of economic relations rather than social or political influences. In his work *Power and Money* , Kindleberger notes that on a superficial level economics is simpler than politics, partly because it uses a powerful hypothesis about human activity — that human beings seek to minimize costs for a given output or to maximize output for a given cost — and partly because inputs and outputs can be measured on the single scale of money. Thus it is possible to make statements like 'foreign investment contributes 2 per cent to South Africa's growth rate of 6 per cent', and therefore to have an accurate idea of the tangible, practical value of that foreign investment to the country. In politics, however, there is no single hypothesis with the power and simplicity of economic man, and basic concepts such as power, legitimacy, sovereignty, political cohesion and so on elude measurement. Hence the difficulties of assessing the impact on political realities in South Africa of United States policy.

In recent years, there have been two administrations taking almost opposite rhetorical stances (the distance between them is much less in actuality) on South Africa: the Carter Administration offered disapprobabtion, the Reagan Administration offers cautious encouragement. However, neither approach appears to have overtly affected the ruling elite in South Africa greatly, and it seems that the power of the United States to assist in the process of change in South Africa will be limited until and unless there are substantial changes internally (such as the removal of apartheid) which the United States feels it can endorse.

In the interim it is likely that external pressures will act as a catalyst and secondary cause of change in South Africa, reinforcing internal pressures. However, the mere placing of pressure, irrespective of outcome, might serve United States policy objectives quite adequately, at least in the short run. In the long run the real problem of restructuring South Africa more equitably will have to be faced. Policy towards the Republic ought to be flexible, and the pressures variable, otherwise the effects could be contradictory even in the short term: on the one hand, accelerating the need for change, and on the other hand creating a threat to security and thereby increasing the tendency to tighter control by the White rulers of South Africa.

Yet South Africa has deeper problems within its more obvious ones. Even if apartheid were removed overnight, and if all South Africans became colour–blind and careless about ethnicity, the fundamental problems of a developing country would still have to be faced. There is a population growth rate of almost 2.3 per cent, which has serious implications for housing, feeding, schooling, medical care, infrastructure and perhaps most serious of all, jobs. There is an educational and a housing backlog which will probably last into the next century. Commerce and industry are suffering a severe bottleneck of skilled labour. These are the problems which would be encountered by any government, White or Black, capitalist or communist.

It is illogical to suggest that a genuinely free enterprise economy entails racalism and subjugation, because this has been the case in South Africa historically with 'apartheid capitalism'. In truth, South Africa has never really tried genuine free enterprise. The state has intervened strongly on behalf of the Whites; it has significantly regulated the economy and participated heavily in the economy; it has tried to impose a massive ideological blueprint on society. Land and labour are not free. Business is oligopolistic and enjoys the protection of licences and tariff barriers.

The setting up of a genuine free enterprise economy would reduce government intervention, remove the attempt to order society by ideological blueprint, free land and labour, recognize merit and not race, remove licences and tariffs and force business and individuals to compete. Indeed, such an economy, if it were established, should promote the swift deracialization of society and provide the fastest way to end the economic subjugation of the Blacks. Blacks could become the most important producers in commerce and industry, advancing through hard work and merit, and the biggest consumers, enjoying and buttressing the burgeoning productivity which often characterizes free enterprise economies.

This route to development might work perfectly well, as it has in other developing societies since the Second World War, if it is given a real chance. Business, as is shown in the next section, is contributing to the solution in a variety of ways — and this includes foreign companies like the American multinationals. What is certain is that no individual or group in South Africa will win, whatever happens politically, unless the country is developed to the point at which the needs of its citizens are met.

The major concrete American contribution to South Africa is that made by American business to economic growth through direct and indirect investment, trade, bank loans, (until September 1985 at least) technology, management expertise and so on, but the American influence is felt in a variety of other ways.

For example, more than half a century ago, as the result of a visit paid to South Africa in 1927 by the President and the Secretary of the Carnegie Corporation of New York, there was a significant American contribution to South Africa in the form of the Carnegie Commission's report on the Poor White problem. In the section on education E.G. Malherbe wrote that: 'these principles (of education) concern not only the poor Whites but our whole body politic. If the latter becomes sound and healthy the former will no longer be a problem.' Substituting Blacks for Whites the statement might be true, at least in kind if not in degree, today. The Carnegie Corporation recently funded the second Carnegie Enquiry into Poverty and Development in South Africa: this American-sponsored exercise might well have far-reaching ramifications as regards the problem of eliminating poverty in South Africa.

The influences are diverse and there are real distinctions between them: besides the philanthropic foundations, there are the

United States Government, the American media, the universities (most textbooks in business schools, for example, are American) and of course American business, which all affect South Africa. The contention here is that the influences are, on the whole, beneficial.

As the Study Commission concludes:

> Change will be a piecemeal and uneven process. United States policymakers will find tension, frustration and moral uncertainty as they deal with specific day-to-day issues while simultaneously keeping ultimate goals in focus . . . the United States can constructively assist the process of change in South Africa. There is time, but, as we have stressed, not much time. [Study Commission, 1981, pp. 455–6.]

As discussed earlier, it has taken both South Africa and the United States a relatively long time to realize, for understandable historical reasons, that it is directly with each other that they must deal (and not indirectly via, for example, London) in order to find the best mutually beneficial arrangements. The analysis in this work suggests that the United States and South Africa will find themselves increasingly thrown together, because of politics, and economic links, and that the potential beneficial effects of the United States on South Africa are considerable, if only South Africa would allow the potential to be realized.

This does not imply either that South Africa should be a subservient state or that the United States ought to display the hubris which characterized the European powers when they felt free to dispose of the destinies of the Afro–Asian world. For example, not long ago, Winston Churchill could say of the desert kingdom he carved out of Palestine for the Hashemite king exiled from Saudi Arabia that 'I created Transjordan with a stroke of a pen on a Sunday afternoon in Cairo.' Churchill is also reputed to have passed Stalin a piece of paper during a meeting in 1944 offering the Soviet ruler a 10 per cent share in Greece, 50 per cent in Yugoslavia and Hungary, 75 per cent in Bulgaria and 90 per cent in Rumania (Stalin assented with a blue tick on the paper).

Fortunately, that kind of arrogance has become less feasible in the postwar world. The United States offers a blend of incentives and punishments to smaller states, while the latter take steps to earn the incentives and reduce the punishment: how far they are prepared to go in this direction depends on their perception of the

value of American co-operation and the cost of American dis-
pleasure.

American corporations and American influence should be
valuable to the peaceful evolution of Southern Africa. The African
National Congress is now over seventy years old, and was a legal
organization during its first half–century. It was also a moderate
and non–violent organization for most of that time, politely asking
for civil and political liberties under the influence of people like the
first Black South African Nobel prizewinner Albert Luthuli. As
might be expected in the face of refusal to recognise their rights,
some Blacks slowly shifted from passive to active resistance. In the
same way as Whites minimized the support of Robert Mugabe
while they controlled the country and were shocked at his victory
in Zimbabwe, so too White South Africans might be minimizing
the support that the ANC and other groups aiming at Black
liberation have in South Africa. The real views of Blacks ought to be
a major concern for both White South Africans and foreign investors. South Africa has long appeared to be a gold–rich, stable,
Western–orientated society which offers excellent business
opportunities: what needs to be determined is whether the
appearance conforms with the reality. It is preferable to find out
whether there are strains beneath the surface, and what the
alternative viewpoints are, than to find out too late that one has
been sitting on a metaphorical San Andreas fault all along.

Regrettably, a complicating factor, both for internal South
African policy and for United States policy towards South Africa, is
that the legitimate Black struggle for ordinary citizen rights as
understood in the Western World has become confused with a
communist search for influence in Southern Africa. Chief Luthuli
stated categorically   that 'we are African nationalists, not
communists'. Since then, however, perhaps because they have had
to turn somewhere for support the ANC has come much closer to
the SACP (South African Communist Party), with which it shares a
joint revolutionary council. It now seems possible that a 'free
Azania' under an ANC–SACP government would be under Soviet
tutelage. Then South African Blacks simply might have exchanged
one set of rulers for a different set of rulers. This would be un-
fortunate for postwar history indicates that people living under a
communist dictatorship are typically neither free nor fulfilled in
their humanity.

It is now that South African liberal democrats must work powerfully towards preventing further polarization between Whites and Blacks. The task is daunting. On the one hand, liberals are weakened by their gentlemanly insistence on treating those with whom they differ as worthy and sincere adversaries, which some may be; but the problem is that others are dangerously mistaken (want the same ends as liberals but are prepared to use a high-cost means such as disinvestment to achieve them) or ruthless enemies (communists who do not even want the same ends, e.g. democracy, and who would give the liberals no chance whatsoever of living according to liberal principles if they gained power over them). On the other hand, the principled liberal stand loses ground to extremists all too easily because of what happens in South Africa: in a maelstrom of forced removals, bannings, detentions and labour unrest, and a prolonged and violent uprising, in a situation where many are poor, malnourished and ill-educated, and have no political power, the voice of quiet reason is liable to be lost.

All who value the freedom of the individual must steer a difficult course through the Scylla of White intransigence and the Charybdis of Black reaction, in order to counteract the disturbing internal dynamic of polarization in South Africa. Despite the fact that White South Africa has partially included Asians and Coloureds in the political decision-making process, and tried to make peace with erstwhile external Black opponents, there is a danger that in the absence of powerful moves towards a real democracy and a genuinely free economy, increased extremism by the Blacks and increased authoritarianism by the Whites (the former fighting more determinedly for power in South Africa and the latter holding on to power with equal determination for as long as possible) is a likely unfolding of events in South Africa.

Soon, South Africa might arrive at an historical juncture at which, because of continuing polarization, there are diminishing opportunities for those who wish to see a liberal democratic free enterprise society to actually make it work. If the opportunities are lost, it is likely that all South Africans will suffer — a kind of ordeal the essence of which was captured by Yeats:

> Turning and turning in the widening gyre
> The falcon cannot hear the falconer;

Things fall apart; the centre cannot hold;
Mere anarchy is loosed upon the world,
The blood–dimmed tide is loosed, and everywhere
The ceremony of innocence is drowned;
The best lack all conviction, while the worst
Are full of passionate intensity.

[W.B. Yeats, *The Second Coming.*]

The business community is able to help prevent further polarization, and even to redress in some measure the historical inequities between the races, for example in education; and it is pressurizing the government more strongly than ever before for reforms:

These national employers' organisations — ranging from the usually government-supporting AHI to the black Nafcoc — have never before combined forces on a statement of this nature. Never before have the private sector's demands on national issues been articulated quite like this or been as overtly political.

The memorandum spells out what business perceives as going wrong with the management of the economy — including its political dimension of control. There is an almost total repudiation of fundamental government policies: 'In the national interest they (the six organisations) are committed to an ongoing programme of legislative reform to give effect to the following goals:

— meaningful political participation for blacks;

— full participation in a private enterprise economy for all South Africans regardless of race, colour, sex or creed;

— the development of a free and independent trade union movement;

— the administration of justice as safeguarded by the courts; and

— an end to the forced removal of people.'

It is important to remember that this is the response to current conditions not of any organisation of the Left, but by concerned and moderate men comprising the most productive sector of the economy. It is nothing less than a challenge to government to change its ways before it draws down on SA universal odium, sanctions and disinvestment. It conveys a sense of urgency. [*Financial Mail*, 18th January 1985, p.35.]

The Government appears to be less able (because of its own inadequacies and the views of the White electorate which brought it to power) to facilitate a more equitable restructuring of South African society. Although there has been a breaking of ranks in the ruling Nationalist Party over the issue of power–sharing with Indians and Coloureds (leaving the great issue of the Africans untouched), the Nationalist leadership appears ready to make practical and symbolic concessions which it judges do not significantly weaken the White–ruled dispensation, while at the same time being as authoritarian as it considers necessary. Indeed, events during the 1985 period of unrest in South Africa have led to a significant bipartisan Republican and Democratic questioning in America of the policy of constructive engagement on the grounds that, far from moving towards increasing civil liberties, South Africa is becoming more authoritarian internally.

Whether accommodation between the races and a peaceful evolution of South African affairs can be achieved despite current realities is a subject too vast to be tackled here, but a legitimate question for this work is whether the United States and especially United States business can help all South Africans, under whatever conditions the country might find itself in the future. The evidence in this book suggests that the United States can help South Africa, but that this co–operation largely depends on what South Africa does: the more democratic it is, the greater the possible co–operation with the United States.

It is evident that external countries can achieve only a limited amount of internal restructuring in South Africa in the absence of active physical intervention. Two–thirds of a century ago, the first secretary of the South African National Congress, Sol Plaatje, went with a deputation of other prominent Blacks to England to plead their case (against such things as 1913 Land Act) with the British Government. Most political leaders ignored their representations, but they did manage to see Prime Minister Lloyd George, who wrote two private letters to Prime Minister Jan Smuts on their behalf — to no avail. As the century draws to a close, the lesson remains the same: outsiders, even powerful ones, have limited ability to change things. It is the internal political process which is of paramount importance.

External powers can act as catalysts in this internal process, and can also provide support in a variety of ways, as seen in this work. In addition, they may simply act as an example. The United States provides a model of an open society, whose citizens, for example, travel freely and visit the world. One of South Africa's difficulties vis-à-vis America is that few Americans visit the Republic, so there is less of a wide spectrum of better–informed American opinion on South Africa than might otherwise be the case. Of the 23 million Americans who went abroad in 1983, only a fraction of 1 per cent visited South Africa. Ordinary Americans would help establish another important linkage between the two countries if far more of them visited South Africa, thereby building slowly a wider body of better–informed opinion on South Africa within the American public.

In the same way, smaller, private American business investment, which is not subject to the political pressures faced by the large public corporations, would help South Africa develop, while at the same time avoiding the 'hassle factor' which accompanies investment by high–profile corporations. All South Africans would benefit if South Africa emulates, as far as possible, the American example of a real free enterprise, strong economy which is creating jobs. The pervasive American attitude that things actually *can* get done, and their optimism about solving problems would be useful practical characteristics for South Africans to have, given the challenges they face. The unchallenged American technological lead can help develop South Africa. The American political example of power changing hands peacefully every few years is fully worthy of emulation.

Many of the collectivist countries, by contrast, tend to be closed societies with few of the civil, judicial, religious and other customary rights of the West, like the freedom to travel. Often, they are ruled by totalitarian political systems and ill–served by inefficient industrial and agricultural production. The triumph of actual experience over dogma is slowly relegating the Marxist model to an historical irrelevance: though there have been achievements such as those in China, they have been achieved only at certain limited levels and at enormous cost to tens of millions of people. Now China itself is experimenting with a freer economy. Totalitarian communist systems which have to rely fundamentally on coercion are likely to fade over time.

In the meanwhile, the example of the United States, as the

Fig. 7.1. American involvement: proportion of major American
corporations in selected categories who do business
directly or indirectly with South Africa

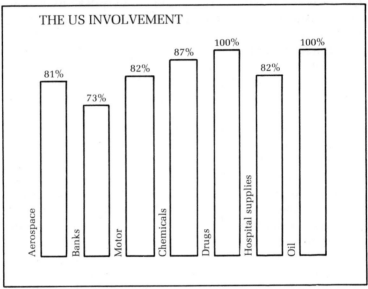

Source: *Connecticut Governor's Report on South African
Investment Policy.*

strongest democratic society in the world, can serve as a practical
guide for South Africa to some extent, though it is clearly naïve to
expect the American or British or French way to work exactly the
same in Africa: foreign models require indigenous adaptations,
and a clear recognition of time and place, to be useful elsewhere.
For its part, the United States can help nourish such fragile
structures of freedom as do exist in South Africa. However, the
United States cannot do this effectively without a strong (business)
presence in South Africa, so disinvestment, in this view, would be
counterproductive. Regrettably efforts to reduce American
corporate involvement appear to be intensifying. The threat of

divestment of stocks, or cessation of trade, with companies which do business with South Africa is potent because, as is shown in Figure 7.1, the American business involvement in South Africa includes a very high proportion of major American corporations. This 'secondary boycott' may soon become a more dramatic sanctions threat than that of withdrawal of direct investment in South Africa.

If the massive purchasing power of major organizations, like New York City, were to be precluded from dealing with any company which did business with South Africa, then some 6,000 or so United States firms might be forced to stop all business with South Africa.

American business in South Africa

The South African economy has grown remarkably in the century or so of industrialization since the discovery of diamonds and gold — and particularly since the Second World War. South African business including foreign corporations and private investors — has achieved this development, partially aided historically, and now increasingly hindered, by the State's racial apparatus.

The political and economic systems have been partly in harmony and partly in opposition to each other for some time, but the tensions between them are likely to increase. The South African economy is growing. The imperatives of growth have forced changes, notably in the labour relations sphere, which would have seemed impossible a decade ago. The racial logjam is breaking up. South African business, a term which is used to encompass the American and other multinationals as well, has contributed to the changes taking place in South Africa directly by making econonic growth possible, and indirectly, through things like example in the workplace and lobbying the Government. Without a strong economy, none of South Africa's human problems can be solved — and it is the business sector which carries most of this re-sponsibility. The workplace is at the centre of relations between the races in South Africa, and if accommodation can be reached there, there is hope for the larger racial and political spheres. Again, business has a responsibility of historical proportions to bear. As for lobbying the Government, it is clear that business regards the costs of apartheid as outweighing whatever benefits there might have been to some sectors historically. In 1984, therefore, the

Nationalist Government was astounded ('disappointed and sad') at being criticized by Afrikaner businessmen for incarcerating trade-union leaders. It was not only the Associated Chambers of Commerce (Assocom) and the Federated Chamber of Industries (FCI), but also the Afrikaanse Handelsinstituut (AHI) which publicly questioned government action against trade-union leaders after the November stay-away in the Transvaal. The business groups were concerned that detentions could endanger labour peace, and expressed willingness to cope with unrest through normal business industrial relations processes. In 1985 the Government was displeased when a group of leading South African businessmen went to talk to the ANC leadership in Zambia about their concerns for the future of South Africa. Business has urged Western business interests to join them in a reformist alliance to pave the way for talks between Blacks and Whites. The chief executive of the Associated Chambers of Commerce said that the South African business community was directly involved in seeking political structures which would broaden democracy and create a climate of confidence for negotiations: 'Business is not governing the country. It wants to make the country governable'.

These events would have been inconceivable in South Africa a few years ago. It is mainly because of economic growth, and the attendant need for skilled Blacks at all levels, the recognition that Blacks have become the biggest market, the maturing of Afrikaner capital, and pressures by the business community generally, that South Africa is beginning to approximate to a sophisticated free enterprise economy of the twentieth century.

South Africa is a society in transition, with various forces of differing degrees of strength pulling the body politic in conflicting directions. In this situation, the business community is trying to keep the economy going through the worst depression in half a century and a capital boycott; making changes in the workplace; lobbying the Government and sounding notes of practical reasonableness (for example, that the Government should look at the economic and political fundamentals of urban Black unrest) both at home and abroad in debates on South Africa. This involvement of the business community is like a stabilizing anchor to a storm-tossed South Africa, and it would be unwise of anyone — from the South African Government to proponents of disinvestment in the United States — to want to part ship and anchor.

In addition, support for the efforts of the private sector throughout this book rests on the twin foundations that

(a) economic growth is essential for the construction of a better society in South Africa; and that

(b) a real free enterprise economy, and not the apartheid mish-mash, or a socialist/communist model is in turn the best way to achieve economic growth.

If apartheid were removed and if business were allowed to create wealth in an unfetted market economy; if there was a unified educational system; if there was complete freedom of labour mobility; if the Group Areas Act and other legislation which keeps Blacks in the poor rural areas were abolished, there are sound reasons for expecting the economy to grow and for wealth to be increasingly more evenly distributed in South Africa. The business community, in general, supports these rational moves. In the long run, perhaps, the best way to compensate for the historical injustices of apartheid is to remove all distortions of market forces.

Of the alternative economic systems, post–war experiments in Scandinavian–type welfare capitalism have succeeded in dealing with poverty and unequal distribution of income, and such societies are very democratic in terms of all the criteria outlined at the beginning of this work. The problem is that, after fairly long periods of economic growth, the economies of these welfare states have tended to stagnate as the state's wealth–gathering machinery puts more and more money into less and less productive sectors. This is why, as argued earlier in this work, some sort of welfare capitalism may be a useful step on the way to a free enterprise economy — especially in a country like South Africa which has to overcome the effects of historical bias against a large section of the population — but not necessarily the best long–term economic policy.

More doctrinaire socialist and communist experiments in the twentieth century have either failed or succeeded partially — but at great human cost in freedom and dignity for limited economic benefits. At a time when Communist China, representing a quarter of mankind, is experimenting with free market forces to improve the Chinese economy, South Africa too should be capitalizing on its highly developed business community and moving further towards *real* free enterprise. The problem is that business is based on an illiberal economy. The abolition of, for example, influx control and Group Areas would be moves towards genuine free enterprise.

South Africa's commercial, industrial and agricultural productivity should be encouraged and increased for the benefit of all South Africans — and perhaps one day for the benefit of sub-Saharan Africa. Although South Africa generates most of its capital requirements internally, foreign investment is an essential addition because so much capital is needed to develop the country, particularly now that gold is no longer providing economic windfalls to counterbalance political disasters. Foreign investment should be encouraged, because economic development is as important to Buthelezi's South Africa and to Mandela's South Africa as to Botha's South Africa. South Africa needs now to be *developed* towards democracy by the world community, not isolated and destroyed by civil war.

The United States multinationals are aiding development, and largely do meet the criteria for foreign investment suggested by Bishop Tutu, who is a high-profile proponent of foreign economic pressure on South Africa:

(a) the provision of family housing at the place of work to undermine the system of migrant labour;

(b) ensuring that all their Black workers are unionized in the trade union of their choice;

(c) granting the right to their Black workers to work at the place of their choice to undermine the system of influx control;

(d) investing in Black education.

South Africa needs to be nudged by its friends in the direction of becoming a democratic state with a free economy. In his misplaced zeal (he admits dislike for the free enterprise economy and it is held here that economic freedom is the basis of all freedom), Bishop Tutu and like-minded advocates of economic pressure inadvertently might push South Africa into becoming a type of society which accords even less well with Christian principles than does the present one. Damaging the functioning private enterprise sector which includes the American multinationals is tantamount to destroying the very basis on which a free society of the future can be built certainly in the short–term and perhaps even in the longer term — and it should be seen for the destructive act that it is.

It is not within the capability of the business sector to solve some of the major national problems like the consultation/incorporation of Blacks into the political process, or the granting to Blacks of the rights to sell their labour without geographical or legal hindrance. It is within the power of business to lobby the government for reform; to train, develop and promote Blacks on merit; to foster integration in the workplace; to promote Black entrepreneurship and small business; to create more jobs by operating efficiently and growing; to advise on practical educational priorities for the development of South Africa; and to explain tirelessly, as well a show by example, how *genuine* economic freedom works in favour of ordinary citizens, rather than of established economic or political structures. The burden is formidable and the tasks unusual for business executives; but then, South Africa is an unusual society. If business is not to become a victim of the problem, it needs to become part of the solution — that is, to shape the future in a way which permits business to flourish in future.

Often what is directly good for business coincides with a greater social and political ideal. It would be unreasonable to expect business to go the extremes of either acquiescing in its own demise when threatened, or actively wielding physical force against governments which it does not find congenial; but open debate in society and overt lobbying of government on the subject of what business would like to see happen for it to prosper is not only acceptable but desirable.

If anything, business in South Africa has been on the reticent side, at least until 1985 even on the level of debate and discussion. Hermann Giliomee has stated that:

> Where businessmen with their ideology of growth and development are challenged by other ideologies or the state they are usually pusillaminous and defensive. They will lobby the state for the constraints apartheid imposes upon them but if they are rebuffed they happily accommodate policies and regimes anathema to them . . . . in South Africa they can easily accommodate apartheid. Here they can always draw succour from their belief that growth will bring about the desirable political change and that the well–tried laws of economics cannot be denied over the long run.

The difficult question which is faced by both foreign and more especially domestic business in South Africa is to what extent they ought to commit themselves to overtly political action to bring about the sorts of changes they desire — without subverting the essence of business and damaging the free enterprise system in the process.

In recent times an increasing number of businessmen and commercial and industrial bodies have voiced serious concern about the direct effects on business of government policies, and made suggestions for changes. Mike Rosholt of Barlow Rand and others have pointed out that discriminatory practices and the achievement of the full economic potential of the country are not compatible — and that there are now very few remaining government obstacles to eliminating discrimination within one's own firm, to doing sufficient training and so on. Mr Justice Steyn of the Urban Foundation has argued that business can stimulate home ownership for its employees. A secure labour force is good for business, and adequate employee housing should be undertaken for that reason alone — but it is also good for society and the country. If government policies restrict the locality of employee housing, business has every right to lobby government to change, for good business reasons.

After all, as already argued, it is primarily business which physically builds the country, and which provides most of the revenue on which government and the rest of society depends for its existence. At the least, the productive sector of society ought to have a say with regard to what sort of environment it needs in order to remain productive.

Clearly, not everyone agrees with the idea that the business sector, including the foreign multinationals, is a positive force in the right direction. For example, the Study Commission recommends stockpiling of key minerals, diversification of sources of supply and encouraging allies to do the same, assisting Black South Africans, providing economic aid for South Africa's neighbours, clearly defining American interests in Southern Africa, establishing a body to coordinate policy towards South Africa and finally limiting the expansion of American companies — all of which sounds sensible and straightforward except the last.

In opposition to the Commission's recommendations is the evidence in this book that amongst those forces available to the United States, the American multinationals are the most powerful force for peaceful development in South Africa. To curb their expansion does not make sense, except in the narrowest of political terms. The United States and other multinationals, as vital components of the business sector, reinforce the direct and indirect contributions of business to the evolution of South African affairs. The importance of the multinationals even goes beyond the value of concrete investment, of expertise in key sectors and of example of corporate social responsibility: 'the most important component of growth in a private enterprise economy is business optimism; without that, all else fails' (Natrass, 1981, p. 295). One of the most valuable contributions of the United States and other foreign corporations has been to preserve a spirit of optimism, particularly in troubled times.

Finally, the argument that the American multinationals represent a form of American imperialism is not a cogent one. As we have seen, the multinationals co-operate closely with communist and socialist states over which the United States has no power, as well as with states in which the United States does exercise considerable influence. Kindleberger expresses it as follows:

> On the whole the Marxist–Leninist interpretation of imperialism and its extension to the neo-imperialism of foreign investment after the dissolution of empires is not very convincing. To be sure, particular interests supported imperialism for reasons of private gain. But it is impossible to prove, as opposed to assert, that these interests had control of the decision-making machinery of government. They influence decisions, along with other forces; there is grave doubt that they consistently control. By the same token, it is difficult to find political controls in economic relationships between independent states. The government of the investor seeks to protect his interests. It has other concerns as well, in the preservation of peace, or the status quo, or good relations, and these are not in all times and places subsidiary to its support of the economic welfare of its citizens. This eclectic and agnostic view will not budge the True Believer who has found the answer in the simplistic economic materialist view. That cannot be helped. [Kindleberger, 1970, pp. 85–6.]

From the evaluation in this book of the American multinationals in South Africa, it is clear that there is no agreement on the significance of multinationals for the world. Judgements are strongly influenced by views of business and the market mechanism in general. In this work it is suggested that the free market produces the most rational division of international labour and the best use of global resources. The multinationals are an effective way of organizing business on a world scale. As pointed out by a number of observers (e.g. Muller, 1983, pp. 214–29), the impact of multinationals is, or at least can be, beneficial for both home and host country. In summary, as far as South Africa is concerned, the United States and other foreign multinationals have not affected noticeably the sovereignty of the state: indeed they may have lent a marginal amount of stability to the state — but not as much as their critics assert, who also do not take into account simultaneously beneficial effects on the Blacks from the activities of the multinationals.

As regards the economy, there is little doubt that the growth rate achieved by South Africa over the past century would have been impossible without foreign investment, both direct and non-direct. Despite the acknowledged value of foreign direct investment, it is obvious that multinationals benefit greatly as well. As shown in Figure A1 (in Appendix 1), the amount of dividends sent out seems relatively small, as a proportion of current capital; but the initial capital investment of the multinationals may have been small and made many years back. Nevertheless, dividends keep flowing back to the home country out of increasing profits, made in South Africa — so that in the end the multinationals can send out many times the original investment in the country. Of course the country gains as well from the reinvestment portion of profits: the task is to balance the benefits. Where multinationals are worse, in terms of economic impact, are the instances in which they block — using South Africa's own legal machinery — competition by local firms. This aspect of South Africa, which is in reality a developing country, protecting the interests of foreign capital against its own entrepreneurs, may need some rethinking. Indeed, one of the biggest problems with which South Africa has to deal is monopoly capital, both foreign and local. It is not capital *per se* which is the problem, but the lack of sufficient competition, enforced by licences and law courts and the sheer economic muscle of those firms already in a monopolistic or oligopolistic position of strength. This is not free enterprise.

Although the impact of the multinationals on the labour market is limited because they employ a relatively small proportion of the economically active population, the impact of their recruitment and employment policies has spread beyond their own businesses to affect the larger South African commercial community. The multinationals have been training and upgrading labour and thereby increasing productivity and reducing production costs. Society gains from lower prices and more competitive exports.

Finally, beyond their impact on the industrialization and urbanization of South Africa, the multinationals, and particularly the American ones, have shaped local society by their products, their promotional activities and the lifestyles they promote. The result has been the blurring of national cultural identities as South Africans move further towards an Americanization of society. How these trends are viewed depends upon the individual's assessment of the value of indigenous South African cultures as opposed to the Western cosmopolitan cultures introduced by foreign business. It is often a matter of taste over which, of course, there can be no dispute.

The most important impact of the multinationals lies in their ability to organize efficiently the factors of production so as to produce abundant quantities at low cost. As for helping some groups against others in South Africa the multinationals have a varied impact: they contribute to growth and thereby bolster the Whites, who currently control the power structure; but at the same time they strengthen the Blacks through employment, income, training, exposure to technology, confidence, and the acceptance of trade–union activities. How these multifarious effects will balance out and help to shape the future of South Africa is hard to say with any certainty, because they represent a few factors in a large and complicated equation.

The radical viewpoint is that multinationals impose economic, social, and political costs, and play an important part in per-petuating dependence and exploitation in developing countries. If the multinationals bring costs along with their benefits, there is a need for some regulation: however if regulation is too strict investment will be frightened away with a consequent reduction in prosperity. When regulation is selective and flexible, there is good reason to expect a net benefit to both business corporation and host country from the operations of the multinationals.

Certainly South Africa is sufficiently developed not to be easily exploitable by multinationals, and to reduce slowly dependence on multinationals in key sectors, emerging in time as a net beneficiary of foreign investment in every form. It is apparent that there can be no value–free assessment of the multinationals or of the capitalist business system. The facts do not speak for themselves but are open to widely divergent interpretations, particularly in South Africa, reflecting different views about the desirability of a free market economy. However, multinationals overall should not be categorized as helpers of apartheid. The theoretical neatness of the critics does not take account of the reality of these flexible and powerful organizations. Mr Oliver Tambo, President of the African National Congress, was wined and dined in New York by senior executives of corporations such as Ford, General Electric, General Motors, Citibank, Manufacturers' Hanover Trust, and Gulf Oil in 1981. He shared a safari picnic with South African business leaders in Zambia in 1985. 'Business has gone a long way towards a comprehension of Africa that goes beyond labels and stereotypes', according to Mr Wayne Fredericks, a Ford executive who was at the dinner. 'The result has been corporate actions that would have been unthinkable just three years ago.'

Although this work suggests that the influences on South Africa emanating from the United States of America are in the correct direction, it is not possible to predict with any certainty whether South Africa itself will achieve *real* democracy and *genuine* free enterprise. Nevertheless, if South Africa does evolve into an open, unfettered society of free individuals, it will be a far better country for all its citizens; and the two Republics whose historical experience is in many ways startlingly similar and yet so different, could then share common values and mutual interests in the world.

Finally, and fundamentally, it is the underlying philosophical influences emanating from the United States which are of primary importance, because the solution to the problems addressed in this book resolve themselves into philosophical as well as practical *choices*:

(a)   What kind of society should South Africa become?
(b)   On what values should it be based?
(c)   And what are acceptable means and time–scales for bringing about the transition from the current society to the preferred one?

The choices presented and defended throughout this work may be described synoptically as the evolution of South Africa towards an open democratic society with a largely unfettered economy, and that all means for bringing this about should be used short of civil war and economic destruction. There are a number of underlying reasons for these choices. John Locke articulated the notion that 'the economic community is the essential realm of creative freedom while politics is essentially a realm of regulative coercion' (Thomas, 1984, p. 155).

Clearly, this bedrock idea underlies American thinking, and is quite possibly responsible for America's economic success; and it has also, admittedly, affected the interpretation of the facts analysed in this book. This classical liberal approach lies in contrast to the Aristotlean view of politics as the embodiment of public ethics. The history of the twentieth century commends caution with regard to fine–sounding 'political' solutions. On the other hand, there are some problems associated with the *laissez–faire* societies preferred by classical liberals. Thomas (1984, p. 156) points out a number of problems with the liberal tradition. The first is that liberals assume that liberalism is not simply the product of historical cultural forces but a result of natural growth and development. 'They (liberal social arrangements) do not represent either the will of the gods or the inner purposes (teloi) of nature.' The second is that *laissez–faire* economics in its present form produced both a tremendous flow of wealth and goods side by side with poverty and misery. Thirdly, in a world of multinational corporations and centralised economic power, the free enterprise idea becomes an ideology for protecting existing economic power structures. Most liberals assume that the products of their system are sublime and those of other systems corrupt. Finally, he argues that liberals denounce governmental power but not economic power.

While there is some truth as well as exaggeration in these contentions, the conclusion in this work remains that, given a choice, a liberal ordering of society would be chosen. The weaknesses outlined above are less bad, and *can* be overcome more easily, than those of other systems. A liberal democratic society can provide cushioning for poverty, prevent the excesses of monopoly capital, promote competition, hold business accountable, consider alternatives to specific problems — all in a reasonable, practical, manner which does not damage the underlying liberal social arrangements of that society.

In South Africa, because of the need to compensate for past injustices, a truly creative mix of policies — suitable to the time and place — can be devised, to promote the transition to a more just society, while still remaining within the broad framework of a liberal democracy. If the weaknesses can be overcome, the strengths of a liberal democracy, especially the freedom and dignity of the individual in such a society, are far greater than those of the alternatives. The United States has tried, more than any society, to embody the ideas of political and economic freedom. It is somewhere here, perhaps, in the subtle realms of fundamental values and choices, that the deepest meaning of the American connection may be found for South Africa.

Postscript

Just as the evolution of South African affairs has an unwritten ending, so does the further development of multinational corporations. In South Africa and internationally, they defy simplistic categorization and raise a number of unresolved questions. Will the multinationals become conglomerates; will they mediate between the demands of business efficiency and political national control; will they form the bone–structure of a new form of world order; or will the multinationals be a source of tension in a world which adheres to the powerful appeal of nationhood? In the foreseeable future it will probably be a mixture of all of these.

In South Africa, despite everything, some multinationals are continuing to expand. For example, Dow Chemical is planning to double its investment in South Africa to R100 million by 1990. General Motors has recently reaffirmed its intention of expanding its South African investments annually. On the other hand, John Chettle of the South Africa Foundation accepts that new investors who were looking for foreign opportunities have been discouraged: 'In that respect they have already been successful. But will they succeed in driving US firms out of SA? Will they get a Bill through Congress that takes some new economic sanction against SA — a ban on Krugerrand sales, a forced reduction of fixed assets? I still doubt that' (*Financial Mail*, 1 February 1985, p. 38). As the *Financial Mail* puts it, it is not:

> the amount of money that has left SA that counts, it is the unknowable billions of dollars that never got there. The main impact of the campaign so far is that it has succeeded in putting the Administration and many large companies on the defensive.
>
> It is the fact that USA–SA trade has stagnated at $4.5 billion a year and that, while 284 US companies do business inside SA the fact remains that since 1980 fully 30 US companies have abandoned the SA market while only 11 new firms have set up operations there.
>
> It also is the fact that while the divestment movement was once confined to liberal bastions and black political enclaves, it is spreading across the country. [*Financial Mail* 1 February 85, pp. 38–9.]

As the divestment and disinvestment campaign spreads it adds to the intolerable burden of a country in which close to a quarter of the Black labour force is unemployed.

As far as foreign direct investment is concerned, South Africa represents some sort of testing–ground for the multinationals: if they can be forced out of South Africa for political reasons, they might find the number of countries with which they can do business dwindling rapidly in the future, for reasons which have nothing to do with normal investment considerations. This falling back of the multinationals would be a loss, particularly for developing countries, which lack not only substantial capital, but also the technical and managerial skills to employ capital effectively. Often, the best way of obtaining this combination of capital and skills is through the multinationals.

Heilbroner and Thurow give a useful summary of some of the possible developments concerning multinational corporations:

> To some extent they will be the international carriers of efficiency and development, especially in the high technology area for which they seem to be the most effective form of organization. But if the power of the nation–state will be challenged by those international production units, it is not likely to be humbled by them. There are many things a nation can do that a corporation cannot, including, above all, the creation of the spirit of sacrifice necessary both for good purposes such as development and for evil ones such as war. Perhaps all we can say at this stage of human development is that both national–states and huge corporations are necessary, in that they seem to be the only ways in which we can organize mankind to perform the arduous and sustained labor without which humanity itself would rapidly perish. Perhaps after the long age of capital accumulation has finally come to an end and sufficient capital is available to all people, we may be able to think seriously about dismantling the giant enterprise and the nation–state, both of which overpower the individual with their massive organized strength. However desirable that ultimate goal may be, in our time both state and corporation promise to be with us, and the tension between them will be part of the evolutionary drama of our period of history. [Heilbroner and Thurow, 1978, p. 643.]

In South Africa, the multinational workhorse can be harnessed to work for the benefit of all its citizens: to accommodate concerns about multinational power, there can be forms of agreement like production sharing and industrial lease. The main thrust of these types of agreements is that the multinationals invest not only capital, but skills and technology in the country. This would help South Africa to develop economically more swiftly that would otherwise be possible, while at the same time creating a growing local pool of technically and managerially trained South Africans for the future.

Most of the countries which are now developing rapidly are changing from traditional smoke–stack industries to high–technology ones, which depend on highly–skilled human capital and R&D facilities. Multinationals are particularly well–placed to help South Africa develop in these areas. And economic development is utterly important, primarily for the elimination of poverty: 'Wisdom is better than strength; nevertheless the poor man's wisdom is despised, and his words are not heard' (*Ecclesiastes*, 9; 16). Then, when people are no longer poor, but healthy, educated, articulate and skilled, they are far more likely to succeed in the long search for social equality and, ultimately, political liberty.

Appendix 1: South Africa's Foreign Liabilities and Foreign Assets

The South African Reserve Bank does not release information about foreign liabilities country by country because individual countries are very sensitive about their investments in South Africa. However, the Reserve Bank has undertaken a Census of Foreign Transactions, Liabilities and Assets three times, in 1958, 1973 and 1980, and has published global figures, which are given in Table A1.

Foreign liabilities

Foreign Liabilities include the following domestic assets owned by foreigners:

(a) share and other equity capital in South African organizations, including capital shares in the case of partnerships;

(b) financial and other claims on residents of South Africa, including claims on South African banking institutions and securities issued by South African authorities;

(c) South African currency notes and coin;

(d) real estate and farms, including improvements situated in South Africa;

(e) inventories and other physical assets situated in South Africa;

(f) insurance policies issued by insurance organisations resident in South Africa;

(g) leases, concessions and land or mineral rights in South Africa; and

Table A.1. Foreign liabilities of South Africa, 31 December 1980 (R m)

	EEC countries	Rest of Europe	North and South America	Africa	Asia	Oceania	International organizations	Unallocated	Total
Direct investment									
Central government and banking sector	377	16	13	24	3	—	—	—	433
Long-term	373	10	10	—	—	—	—	—	393
Short-term	4	6	3	24	3	—	—	—	40
Private sector	7,460	1,048	2,904	203	129	117	—	19	11,880
Long-term	6,316	916	2,659	106	112	114	—	7	10,230
Ordinary and other shares, nominal value	879	173	326	12	17	16	—	1	1,424
Share premium, reserves and undistributed profit	4,818	672	2,058	68	80	85	—	2	7,783
Branch and partnership balances	56	4	124	—	5	2	—	—	191
Debentures, loan stock and similar securities	67	—	28	—	—	—	—	—	95
Mortgages and long-term loans	493	67	123	25	9	11	—	4	732
Other	3	—	—	1	1	—	—	—	5
Short-term	1,144	132	245	97	17	3	—	12	1,650
Total direct investment	7,837	1,064	2,917	227	132	117	—	19	12,313
Non-direct investment									
Central government and banking sector	1,087	240	513	243	36	19	536	27	2,701
Long-term	902	197	399	4	20	—	—	18	1,540
Short-term	185	43	114	239	16	19	536	9	1,161
Public corporations and local authorities	2,759	805	412	13	162	6	—	38	4,195
Long-term	2,696	788	406	13	160	6	—	34	4,103
Short-term	63	17	6	—	2	—	—	4	92

Private sector	3,017	927	1,509	347	377	30	—	69	6,276
Long-term	2,240	828	1,020	130	169	19	—	50	4,456
Ordinary and other shares, nominal value	150	52	56	13	11	4	—	6	292
Share premium, reserves and undistributed profit	1,476	509	569	73	16	11	—	37	2,691
Debentures, loan stock and similar securities	8	2	9	3	—	—	—	1	23
Mortgages and long-term loans	576	261	383	7	140	2	—	5	1,374
Other	30	4	3	34	2	2	—	1	76
Short-term	777	99	489	217	208	11	—	19	1,820
Total non-direct investment	6,863	1,972	2,434	603	575	55	536	134	13,172
Total investment									
Central government and banking sector	1,464	256	526	267	39	19	536	27	3,134
Long-term	1,275	207	409	4	20	—	—	18	1,933
Short-term	189	49	117	263	19	19	536	9	1,201
Public corporations and local authorities	2,759	805	412	13	162	6	—	38	4,195
Long-term	2,696	788	406	13	160	6	—	34	4,103
Short-term	63	17	6	—	2	—	—	4	92
Private sector	10,477	1,975	4,413	550	506	147	—	88	18,156
Long-term	8,556	1,744	3,679	236	281	133	—	57	14,686
Ordinary and other shares, nominal value	1,029	225	382	25	28	20	—	7	1,716
Share premium, reserves and undistributed profit	6,294	1,181	2,627	141	96	96	—	39	10,474
Branch and partnership balances	56	4	124	—	5	—	—	—	191
Debentures, loan stock and similar securities	75	2	37	3	—	2	—	1	118
Mortgages and long-term loans	1,069	328	506	32	149	13	—	9	2,106
Other	33	4	3	35	3	2	—	1	81
Short-term	1,921	231	734	314	225	14	—	31	3,470
Total foreign liabilities	14,700	3,036	5,351	830	707	172	536	153	25,485

Source: South African Reserve Bank Supplement to *Quarterly Bulletin* (December 1982), pp. A-2, A.3.

(h) patents, trade marks and similar rights granted to residents of
     South Africa.

In recording and analysing foreign liabilities and assets it is
important to distinguish direct investment from other investment
because of differences in the investment decisions which give rise
to the two classes of investment. In the case of direct investment,
there exists a special relationship between the transactors, which is
associated with the potential for one entity to exercise significant
influence over another in a different country. The benefits direct
investors expect to derive from their investment are different from
those anticipated by other investors. They are in a position not only
to receive income on the capital invested, but also to derive such
other benefits as management fees, the expansion of markets or
securing sources of raw materials. In contrast, portfolio investors
are primarily motivated by such considerations as income yield,
capital appreciation, marketability, tax advantages, and safety of
principal.

It is difficult to determine the boundary between direct and non–
direct investment. According to the Balance of Payments Manual
some degree of equity ownership is almost always considered to be
associated with an effective voice in the management of an enterprise. This criterion is also mainly used in defining direct investment in South Africa, but provision is also made for other ways in
which foreigners obtain an effective say in the management of
South African enterprises.

The results of the census indicate that South Africa's foreign
liabilities amounted to R25.5 billion at the end of 1980, in
comparison with R10.4 billion at the end of 1973 and R2.7 billion at
the end of 1956. The average annual rate of increase in foreign
liabilities therefore, accelerated from 8 per cent during the period
from 1956 to 1973 to 13.5 per cent during the period from 1973 to
1980, despite the fact that South Africa had a net outflow of capital
from 1977 to 1980. This acceleration occurred in nearly all the main
classes of foreign liabilities, but was particularly evident in the case
of loan capital and share premium, reserves and undistributed
profit.

As shown in Table A2, South Africa's foreign liabilities consist
mainly of long–term liabilities. In all three of the census years these
liabilities amounted to more than 80 per cent of the total foreign
liabilities.

Table A.2. Percentage share of the main types of foreign liabilities

	At the end of		
	1956	1973	1980
Share capital	23.1	10.4	6.8
Share premium, reserves and undistributed profit	38.2	44.5	42.7
Branch and partnership balances	3.0	2.0	0.7
Debentures, loan stock and similar securities	4.4	4.2	4.1
Mortgages and long-term loans	15.1	20.6	25.7
Other long-term capital	0.4	1.1	1.3
Total long-term liabilities	84.2	82.8	81.3
Short-term liabilities	15.8	17.2	18.7
Total foreign liabilities	100.00	100.00	100.00

Source: South African Reserve Bank, *Supplement to Quarterly Bulletin*, December 1982, p. 5.

However, from the end of 1956 to the end of 1980, the share of foreign short–term liabilities rose slightly from about 16 per cent to nearly 19 per cent. The foreign long–term liabilities consisted largely of share premium, reserves and undistributed profit and mortgages and long–term loans obtained abroad. The latter category increased from 15 per cent of total foreign liabilities at the end of 1956 to nearly 26 per cent at the end of 1980. At the same time, the share capital of foreigners in South African enterprises declined from 23 per cent of foreign liabilities to just below 7 per cent, mainly because of certain exchange control rulings in South Africa as well as in other countries, a rapid rate of increase in public corporation's investment and political developments. Nevertheless, at the end of 1980 equity investments of foreigners still amounted to R13.1 billion, compared with the R12.4 billion of foreign long–term and short– term loans outstanding.

Direct investment accounted for R12.3 billion, or about 48 per cent, of total foreign liabilities at the end of 1980, compared with nearly 50 per cent at the end of 1956. The foreign direct investment consisted mainly of long–term capital and, more in particular, equity capital. The equity capital of direct investors increased from R1.0 billion at the end of 1956 to R9.8 billion at the end of 1980, or from 75 per cent of foreign direct liabilities to nearly 80 per cent.

Non–direct investment by foreigners increased at a more rapid rate than direct investment during the 1970s. As a result, the ratio of non–direct investment to total foreign liabilities, which had declined from 50 per cent at the end of 1956 to 46 per cent at the end of 1973, increased sharply to 52 per cent at the end of 1980. This increase was due to a sharp rise in the share of long–term loan capital in total foreign non–direct investment, namely from 30 per cent at the end of 1956 to 51.5 per cent at the end of 1980. The share of non–direct short–term liabilities increased from 15.5 per cent to just more than 23 per cent over the same period. These increases occured at the expense of non– direct equity investment, whose share declined from 54 per cent at the end of 1956 to 23 per cent at the end of 1980.

Foreign investment in South Africa was predominantly in the private sector, amounting to R18.2 billion at the end of 1980, or to 71 per cent of total foreign liabilities. Foreign investment in the private sector, in turn, was largely in the form of direct investment. At the end of 1980 the share of direct investment was equal to 65.5 per cent of the foreign liabilities of the private sector, which was only slightly lower than 67 per cent at the end of 1973, but considerably higher than 55 per cent at the end of 1956. However, foreign investment in the private sector declined from 86.5 per cent of total foreign liabilities at the end of 1956 to about 71 per cent at the end of 1980, whereas the shares of the central government and banking sector and public corporations and local authorities increased. In particular, the share of public corporations and local authorities rose sharply from 3 per cent to 16.5 per cent over the same period, because of a corresponding sharp increase in loans obtained abroad by these institutions.

A classification of the foreign liabilities of South Africa according to type of economic activity, shows that these liabilities were mainly concentrated in the sectors covering manufacturing; finance, insurance, real estate and business services; mining and quarrying; and wholesale and retail trade, catering and accommodation. These four sectors accounted for 80.5 per cent of the foreign liabilities at the end of 1980, in comparison with their contribution of 67 per cent to gross domestic product at current factor costs during 1980. The foreign investment in manufacturing and wholesale and retail trade, catering and accommodation was mainly in the form of direct investment, whereas direct investment was only slightly higher than non–direct investment in the sector finance, insurance, real estate and business services. Foreigners' investment in mining and quarrying consisted largely of non–direct investment, which accounted for more that 70 per cent of the foreign liabilities of this sector. Non–direct investment of foreigners was also relatively important in the sectors covering electricity, gas and water; transport, storage and communications; and community, social and personal services, owing to the relatively large share of the foreign liabilities of the public sector included in these sectors.

The EEC countries still remain the main source of foreign capital to the South African economy, but their share of foreign liabilities declined from 71 per cent at the end of 1956 to 58 per cent at the end of 1980. This decline occurred because of a corresponding sharp increase in the shares of other Western European countries and countries in North and South America. The share of Asian countries, although still relatively small, also increased sharply over this period, whereas that of African countries at first increased but then declined slightly during the 1970s.

The value of this foreign investment for South Africa, from the point of view of stabilizing the balance of payments and economic growth, is beyond dispute:

The root cause of South Africa's economic problems lies, on the broadest level, in the inability of its production process to develop sufficiently to be able to supply its industries with modern machinery and equipment. This results in South Africa having to import most of its machine requirements. From 1959 to 1974 machinery and transport equipment were the biggest imports, while their share of total imports rose from 36 percent in 1959 to 48 percent in 1972. These requirements have to be paid for by either an influx of foreign capital or by an expansion of exports.

In fact since the accession to power of the Nationalist government in 1948 foreign capital has filled this gap virtually every year. For example, in 1971 when the balance of payments deficit was just over R1,000 million, more than 80 percent of the deficit was made up by an R818 million inflow of foreign capital. Similarly in 1974, over 90 per cent of a R1,000 million deficit was compensated for by inflows of foreign capital. The Bureau of Economic Research at the University of Stellenbosch has estimated that well over R1,000 million in foreign capital will be needed annually in the near future if the levels of gold and foreign exchange reserves are to be maintained.

However there have been exceptions to this state of affairs. A net outflow of foreign capital occurred in 1957, in the years 1959 to 1964 and again in 1973 and 1977 to 1979. The predominant cause of these sudden reversals of the flow of capital has been political uncertainty. An outflow of short–term capital began in 1976 after the Soweto disturbances as it had (in 1961) after the Sharpeville crisis. The confinement of the outflow largely to short–term capital was due to the restrictions of exchange control.

The imposition of strict exchange control has also, with one notable exception, established a remarkably stable pattern of dividend remittances from subsidiaries of multinational companies and from other companies with foreign interests in South Africa. [Fig. A1] illustrates this.

Whilst the influence of the political situation can be noted in 1961 and 1976 this is not nearly as marked as is the case in respect of capital outflows. Far more marked is the impact from 1978 onwards of an announcement in 1977 by Senator Owen Horwood, the Minister of Finance, that profit remittances would in future be restricted to profits earned in any current year. This control was quickly relaxed again when it became apparent that the measure was counterproductive: companies which traditionally reinvested up to 60 percent of their profits, suddenly increased their dividends lest they got stuck. [Muller, 1983, pp. 224–5.]

Since Muller's article was written, exchange controls for foreigners were lifted, and the South African authorities reaffirmed that they would not create a 'mousetrap' economy, one which money can enter but not leave. This policy was aimed at boosting confidence and helping to ensure that foreign investment kept flowing into the country from many parts of the world:

Researchers at stockbrokers Davis Borkum Hare estimate that, following abolition of the financial rand, foreign investments worth some R2.05 billion were liquidated. This was done through the sale of some R1.35 billion in mining shares, plus the sale of non–resident holdings in companies like the Premier Group, Rennies and Metal Box; and those in unlisted companies like Vickers Engineering and Lucas Industries.

Against this, however, it can be strongly argued that abolition of exchange controls has boosted foreign confidence in South Africa. If there were major foreign doubts, the sell–off of South African investments would have been considerably greater than in fact occurred. Opportunities for a 'one–off' capital profit following abolition of the financial rand, and declines in the gold price and in

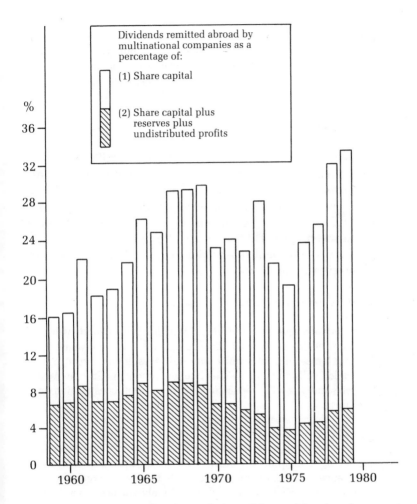

Fig. A.1. Dividends remitted abroad by multinational
companies in South Africa

Source: *South African Reserve Bank Quarterly Bulletins.*

mining dividends, certainly played a greater part in most 'sell'
decisions than politics.

Nonetheless, the build-up of foreign political pressures, and the
willingness of some foreign interests to liquidate long-standing
South African investments, suggests that the disinvestment
campaign could have a cutting edge that should not be lightly

regarded. Imported capital will continue to be vital to economic growth here in the foreseeable future. So, to counter–balance whatever political pressures may be brought about to discourage it, we need in South Africa to implement exemplary economic policies. We need to do this especially while our less acceptable social policies are being reformed. [*Financial Mail*, 17 August, 1984, p. 32.]

Foreign Assets

South Africa's foreign assets amounted to R13.3 billion at the end of 1980, in comparison with R3.4 billion at the end of 1973 and R0.8 billion at the end of 1956. The foreign assets increased at an average annual rate of 8.5 per cent from the end of 1956 to the end of 1973 and this rate of increase accelerated to nearly 21.5 per cent during the next seven years. This rapid rate of increase during the latter years was mainly brought about by a change in the valuation of the gold reserves of the country.

According to the *Financial Mail*:

In the face of recession, as the downside of the cyclical South African economy again asserts itself, local companies, large and small, are looking increasingly at acquisitions and investments abroad. SA–controlled subsidiaries are rising like mushrooms in Europe, Australasia and the US, in sectors ranging from construction to stationery.

The present spate of foreign investment flows against the currents of restrictive exchange controls, the wilting rand, and domestic despondency. The Reserve Bank, haunted by visions of capital flight, monitors every deal – and for the most part disallows remittance of funds, forcing companies to borrow offshore. Despite all this, the trend to secure subsidiaries abroad has never been stronger, and the confidence of SA companies to establish themselves in foreign lands is at an all–time high.

It is a trend that bears stern examination. The pay–off, in theory, is considerable – much–needed geographical diversification, footholds in unlimited and otherwise inaccessible markets, increased exports, and eventually a flow of dividends back to SA. But in practice the pay–off remains largely unrealised.

The economy has already paid a price, in capital losses and diverted resources, for the unbridled enthusiasm with which SA companies have launched themselves on the world. Cautions Ronnie Lubner, chief executive of Plate Glass (PGSI), one of the few local companies to profitably invest abroad: 'If this trend continues there will be a lot of strewn bodies and burnt fingers.'

SA's largest and best-managed groups have long partaken of the international pie. To a large extent, the overseas acquisitions of these giants were simply a function of their scale – domestic markets were too easily outgrown. SA's only true multinational Anglo American Corp (AAC), shook off its SA chains decades ago, establishing itself through a myriad of pyramided holding companies in global markets as diverse as finance and oil.

AAC vies with Royal Dutch Shell and Seagram of Canada as the single largest foreign investor in the US. But the true extent of AAC's holdings – channelled through Bermuda-based Minorco and UK-based Consolidated Gold Fields – almost defies analysis. 'If you want to dig up the full extent of AAC's investment in the US,' Ruth Kaplan, who researched AAC's US investments for the American Committee on Africa, told me: 'You'd better be prepared to spend years doing it.'

Anton Rupert's Rembrandt also took the international plunge in the Sixties, more surreptitiously and notably less successfully than AAC. Rembrandt now holds considerable investments abroad, mostly through its Luxembourg intermediary, Rupert Foundation Societé Anonyme. Rembrandt's excessive liquidity has probably sparked more takeover rumours on Wall Street than any other foreign company, and analysts continue to predict that a US acquisition is imminent. But, as far as overseas investments are concerned, Rembrandt's annual reports give no clue as to the past, present or future.

Barlow Rand too has been abroad for years, notably through Thos Barlow (Holdings) Ltd in the UK and Wrenn Handling Inc in the US. But the R590 m acquisition of UK industrial group J. Bibby signals the depth of Barlow's commitment to overseas growth. Barlow chief executive Mike Rosholt notes that: 'It has always been part of Barlow's long-standing strategy to acquire significant overseas business interest,' and also infers that the Bibby acquisition will be used as a springboard for further acquisitions in the UK and US.

Behind AAC, Rembrandt and Barlow stand a host of companies suddenly clamouring for their place in the sun. [*Financial Mail*, 19 October, 1984, p. 31.]

The trends with regard to both foreign liabilities and foreign assets reinforce the twin contentions in this book that South Africa is becoming ever more firmly locked in to the 'Western' capitalist economic system, and that this is good for economic growth. According to the Reserve Bank's statistics on South Africa's foreign liabilities and assets in 1956 and 1981, total foreign liabilities at end–1981 stood at R32,490 million compared with R2,746 million at the end of 1956. Total foreign assets stood at R13,460 million and R839 million at the same respective dates. Thus, over the period assets grew from 30.5 per cent to 41.4 per cent of liabilities. At the same time, between the two dates there were interesting changes in the geographical distribution of foreign assets. In 1956, of total foreign assets, 27.7 per cent were held in the EEC, 10.1 per cent in North and South America, and 30.6 per cent in Africa. By the end of 1981 the percentage of assets held in the EEC and in Africa had fallen to 21.1 per cent and 18.3 per cent respectively, while North and South American assets had risen to 23 per cent of the total. Perhaps more than anything, these figures emphasize the increasing isolation of South Africa from the rest of the continent and increasing involvement with North America.

On the liabilities side, a generally similar picture emerges. In 1956, 71.3 per cent of liabilities obtained in the EEC, 14.3 per cent in North and South America, and 2.6 per cent in Africa. By 1981, 55.1 per cent were owed to EEC countries, 23.1 per cent to North and South America, and 2.4 per cent to Africa.

Appendix 2: Businessmen advertising corporate concern

"There is a better way"

As responsible businessmen committed to South Africa and the welfare of all its people, we are deeply concerned about the current situation.

We believe that the reform process should be accelerated by:

- Abolishing statutory race discrimination wherever it exists;

- Negotiating with acknowledged black leaders about power sharing;

- Granting full South African citizenship to all our peoples;

- Restoring and entrenching the rule of law.

We reject violence as a means of achieving change and we support the politics of negotiation.

We believe that there is a better way for South Africa and we support equal opportunity, respect for the individual, freedom of enterprise and freedom of movement.

We believe in the development of the South African economy for the benefit of all of its people and we are, therefore, committed to pursuing a role of corporate social responsibility and to playing our part in transforming the structures and systems of the country towards fair participation for all.

L.G. ABRAHAMSE	Chairman	Syfrets Trust Limited
R.J. ABRAHAMSEN	Chief Executive	Nedbank Group Limited
R.D. ACKERMAN	Chairman	Pick 'n Pay Stores Limited
C.S. ADCOCK	Managing Director	Toyota S.A. Limited
PROF. G. ANDREWS	Director	Graduate School of Business Wits University

P.J. BADENHORST	Chief Executive	United Building Society
C.J. BALL	Managing Director	Barclays National Bank Limited
S.F. BARNETT	Chairman/Managing Director	Sterns Diamond Organisation Limited
J. BEARE	Chairman	Beares Limited
A. BERMAN	Joint Managing Director	Natal Consolidated Industrial Investments Limited (The Frame Group)
A.H. BLOOM	Chairman	Premier Group Holdings Limited
W.G. BOUSTRED	Chairman	Anglo American Industrial Corporation Limited
L. BOYD	Chairman	S.A. Motor Corporation Limited
I.D. BRITTAN	Chairman	Boumat Limited
D.G.S. CAMPBELL	Chairman	Frasers Consolidated Limited
P.L. CAMPBELL	Managing Director	Metal Box S.A. Limited
A. CARLEO	Managing Director	Putco Limited
T.N. CHAPMAN	Chief Executive	The Southern Life Association Limited
J. CLARKE	Managing Director	IBM S.A. (PTY) Limited
R.S. COHEN	Chairman	Amalgamated Retail Limited
T.G. COULSON	Chairman/Managing Director	Blue Circle Limited
Z.J. DE BEER	Chairman	Anglo American Properties Limited
C.S. DOS SANTOS	Managing Director	Score Food Holdings Limited
J.G. DOUGLAS	Chairman/Managing Director	S.A. General Electric Company (PTY) Limited
C. DUKE	General Manager	Abbott Laboratories (S.A.) (PTY) Limited
D.J. ENGLISH	Managing Director	Rank Xerox (PTY) Limited
A.J.F. FERGUSSON	Chairman	The Prudential Assurance Company of S.A. Limited
R. FERRIS	Managing Director	Kodak S.A. (PTY) Limited
D.T. FLETCHER	Chairman/Managing Director	Caltex Oil (S.A.) (PTY) Limited
J.A. FRANKEL	Joint Managing Director	Tiger Oats Limited
M.R. FÜRST	Managing Director	Hewlett–Packard S.A. (PTY) Limited
S.M. GOLDSTEIN	Chairman	S.M. Goldstein Limited

E.E. HART	Chairman	Whitehall Products (S.A.) (PTY) Limited
DR. W. HASSELKUS	Managing Director	BMW S.A. (PTY) Limited
H.S. HERMAN	Joint Managing Director	Pick 'n Pay Stores Limited
M. HILKOWITZ	Managing Director	Liberty Life Association of Africa Limited
J.B. HODGSON	Ch...rman	Darling & Hodgson Limited
G.W. HOOD	Managing Director	OK Bazaars (1929) Limited
J.R. HOUSTON	Managing Director	NCR Corporation of S.A. (PTY) Limited
I.J. JACOBSON	Chairman/Chief Executive	Trade & Industry Acceptance Corporation Limited
P.H. JACOBSON	Chairman	Bradlows Stores Limited
S.L. JAFFE	Chairman	Delswa Limited
A. JAFFE	Chairman	Currie Finance Corporation Limited
J.K. JOHNSON	Managing Director	Kellogg's Limited
N.I. JOWELL	Chairman	Trencor Limited
C.B. KAPLAN	Chairman	Micor Holdings Limited
J. KING	Managing Director	S.A. Associated Newspapers Limited
M. KING	Managing Director	Kirsh Trading Group Limited
D.C. KROGH	Executive Deputy Chairman	Legal & General Volkskas Assurance Limited
S. LEWIS	Chairman	Foschini Limited
P. LLOYD	Managing Director	Beer Division, S.A. Breweries Limited
S. LURIE	Joint Managing Director	Natal Consolidated Industrial Investments Limited (The Frame Group)
I. MACKENZIE	Chairman	African Finance Corporation Limited
J.A. MACKNESS	Managing Director	CNA Gallo Limited
D.M. MAHONEY	Managing Director	Control Data (PTY) Limited
D.B. McCARTAN	Chairman	Nampak Limited
P.W. McLEAN	Managing Director	The Argus Group
F.J. MEYER	Senior Vice President	The Coca–Cola Export Corporation
H.W. MILLER	Executive Chairman	The Argus Group
P.B. MOFFIT	Managing Director	S.A. Cyanamid (PTY) Limited
T. MOOLMAN	Joint Managing Director	Caxton Limited

M.N. NEWMAN	Executive Chairman	S.A. Bias Holdings Limited
G.W. NOCKER	Chief Executive Officer	Colgate–Palmolive Limited
J. OGILVIE THOMPSON	Chairman	De Beers Consolidated Mines Limited
H.F. OPPENHEIMER		
A.D. OVENSTONE	Executive Chairman	Ovenstone Investments Limited
S.R. PEIMER	Joint Managing Director	Natal Consolidated Industrial Investments Limited (The Frame Group)
B.P. RABINOWITZ	Chairman	The Property Group of S.A. Limited
G.P. RACINE	Chairman/Managing Director	Mobil Oil S.A. (PTY) Limited
G.W. RELLY	Chairman	Anglo American Corporation of S.A. Limited
M. SACHAR	Chairman	Grand Bazaars Limited
C.J. SAUNDERS	Chairman	The Tongaat Group Limited
R.J. SCHMITT	Managing Director	Nampak Tissue Division
P. SEARLE	Managing Director	Volkswagen of S.A. (PTY) Limited
A. SEARLL	Chairman	Seardel Investment Corporation Limited
M. SIMCHOWITZ	Chairman	W & A Investment Corporation Limited
E.J. SMALE	Managing Director	AECI Limited
C.A. SPALDING	Managing Director	Johnson & Johnson (PTY) Limited
A.M. SPITZ	Executive Chairman	M & S Spitz Footwear Holdings Limited
J.B. SUTHERLAND	Chairman	African Oxygen Limited
P.R.S. THOMAS	Managing Director	The Unisec Group Limited
L. VAN DER WATT	Chairman	Associated Furniture Companies Limited
G.H. WADDELL	Chairman	Johannesburg Consolidated Investment Company Limited
C.N. WEIL	Managing Director	Checkers Stores Limited
DR. A. WESSELS	Chairman	Toyota S.A. Limited
P.D. WHARTON–HOOD	Managing Director	The Prudential Assurance Company of S.A. Limited
R.A. WHITE	Managing Director	General Motors of S.A. (PTY) Limited
PROF. N. WIEHAHN	Director	Graduate School of Business Unisa

C.T. WOOD	Managing Director	Citibank Limited
P.G. WRIGHTON	Deputy Chairman	Premier Group Holdings Limited
W.S. YEOWART	Immediate Past President	ASSOCOM.

Source: South African press. September 1985

The concerns shown in this advertisement were echoed by American Chief Executives, with business interests in South Africa, a few weeks later.

Bibliography

Acton, H.B., *The Morals of Markets: an Ethical Exploration*, London, Longman in association with The Institute of Economic Affairs, 1971.

Adam, Heribert, *Modernizing Racial Domination*, Berkeley, University of California Press, 1972.

Adam, Heribert, and Giliomee, Hermann, *The Rise and Crisis of Afrikaner Power*, Cape Town, David Philip, 1979.

Aharoni, Yair, *Markets, Planning and Development: The Private and Public Sectors in Economic Development*, Ballinger Publishing Co., 1977. U.S.A.

Albernethy, David B., 'The Major Foreign Policy Positions of the Reagan Administration: Implications for United States – South African Relations', *International Affairs Bulletin*, ed. Spicer, Michael, vol. 5, no. 2, pp. 18–44, Johannesburg, South African Institute of International Affairs, 1981.

Alexander, Charles, '*Economy and Business*: Notes from the Underground', *Time*, 7 September 1981, pp. 58–61.

American Chamber of Commerce in South Africa (Amcham), *U.S. Business Involvement in South Africa*, Amcham, January 1984.

Anglo—German Foundation for the Study of Industrial Society, *Worker–owners: the Mondragon Achievement*, 1977.

Apter, David E. and Goodman, Louis Wolf, eds, *The Multinational Corporation and Social Change*, New York, Praeger Publishers, 1976.

Aron, Raymond, *The Imperial Republic: the United States and the World 1945–1973*, Engelwood Cliffs, NJ, Prentice–Hall Inc., 1974.

Arrighi, Giovanni, *The Geometry of Imperialism: the Limits of Hobson's Paradigm*, London, New Left Books, 1978.

Baldwin, David A., ed., *America in an Interdependent World — Problems of United States Foreign Policy*, New Hampshire, University Press of New England, 1976.

Barber, James, Blumenfeld, Jesmond, and Hill, Christopher, *The West and South Africa*, Chatham House Papers, 14, Royal Institute of International Affairs, London, Routledge and Kegan Paul, 1982.

Bergsten, C. Fred, and Krause, Lawrence B., *World Politics and International Economics*, Washington DC, Brookings Institution, 1975.

Berman, Harold J., ed., *Talks on American Law*, rev. ed. by Members of the Harvard Law School Faculty, Voice of America — Forum Lectures, US, 1973.

Bishton, Dr Bob, and Kaplan, Dr Dave, *Are Multinationals a Positive Factor in Developing Economies?* UCT Commerce Students' Council, SRC Press, UCT, 1981.

Bishton, R.E., *The Management Philosophies and Controls in Capital Budgeting*, doctoral thesis, University of Stellenbosch, 1979.

Boland, Lawrence A., *The Foundations of Economic Method*, London, Allen & Unwin, 1982.

Bontharone, D., Criticos, N., Grinstead, P., and, D'Aguir, L., *The Multinational Corporation — an Evaluation of the Organisational and Strategic Position of the Local Subsidiary in the Light of Host Country Influences*, Business Policy II Seminar, UCT, September 1980.

Bradlow, Edna and Frank, *Here comes the Alabama: the Career of a Confederate Raider*. Cape Town/Amsterdam, A.A. Balkema, 1958.

Brandon, Henry, *The Retreat of American Power: the Inside Story of How Kissinger Changed American Foreign Policy for Years To Come*, New York, Doubleday and Co. Inc., 1973.

Burden, Tom, Chapman, Reg, and Stead, Richard, *Business in Society: Consensus and Conflict*, London, Butterworths, 1981.

Business International S.A., *Apartheid and Business: a Business International Multiclient Study*, London, 1980.

Carnegie Commission, *The Poor White Problem in South Africa.* Report of the Carnegie Commission. Stellenbosch, Pro Ecclesia– Drukkery, 1932.

Carnoy, Martin, and Shearer, Derek, *Economic Democracy: The Challenge of the 1980's*, New York, M.E. Sharpe, Inc., 1980.

Caves, Richard E., Jones, Ronald W., *World Trade and Payments*, 3rd edn, Boston Mass., Little Brown and Co., 1981.

Chaliand, Gérard, *Revolution in the Third World: Myths and Prospects*, Brighton, Sussex, Harvester, 1977.

Clark, Senator Dick, *U.S. Corporate Interests in Africa*, Report to the Committee on Foreign Relations, United States Senate, Washington, U.S. Government Printing Office, January 1978.

Chester, Edward W., *Clash of Titans: Africa and U.S. Foreign Policy*. New York, Orbis Books, 1974.

Chown, John F., *Taxation and Multinational Enterprise*, London, Longman Group Limited, 1974.

Church, George J., '*Every Man for Himself*, and Every Woman, as Washington Tests a Retreat from Affirmative Action', *Time*, 7 September 1981, pp. 30–1.

Cooper, C.M., and Hoffman, H.K., *Developing Countries and International Markets in Industrial Technology, III. Transfer of Technology to Less-Developed Countries*, IDS–SPRU, November 1977.

Cohen, Robert V., *A Study of Some of the Factors Influencing New Foreign Investment in South Africa*, a technical report presented to the Graduate School of Business, University of Cape Town, in partial fulfilment of the requirements for the Master of Business Administration Degree.

Crick, Bernard, *Political Theory and Practice*, Harmondsworth, Middx, Allen Lane, The Penguin Press, 1971.

Davenport, T.R.H., *South Africa: a Modern History*, 2nd edn, Johannesburg, Macmillan, 1978.

Davenport, T.R.H., 'Yudelman's State Capital Symbiosis' *Social Dynamics*, vol. 9, no. 1, Centre for African Studies, University of Cape Town, 1983, pp. 95–101.

De Conde, Alexander, *A History of American Foreign Policy*, 2nd edn, New York, Charles Scribner & Sons, 1971.

De Kiewiet, C.W., *A History of South Africa: Social and Economic*, London, Oxford University Press, 1975.

Dialogue, vol. 12, no. 1, *Capitalism, Socialism, Democracy*. 1979.

Drum, The Beat of Drum, Ravan Press (Pty) Ltd., in association with *Drum* Magazine, Johannesburg 1982.

Dymsza, W.A., *MNC Business Strategy*, New York, McGraw–Hill, 1972.

Elliott, Jan Walter, *Economic Analysis for Management Decisions*, Richard D. Irwin, Inc., Illinois, January 1973.

Elliott, John, *Conflict or Co-operation?: The Growth of Industrial Democracy*, London, Kogan Page, 1978.

Elphick, Richard, 'Methodology in South African Historiography: a Defence of Idealism and Empiricism', *Social Dynamics*, a Journal of the Centre for African Studies, University of Cape Town, vol. 9 no. 1. University of Cape Town, June 1983.

Feldberg, Meyer, *American Universities: Divestment of Stock in U.S. Corporations with South African Affiliates*, Graduate

School of Business, University of Cape Town, 1978.

Feldberg, Meyer, *Interviews with Five Prominent Americans on U.S. Investment in South Africa*, Occasional Series: Paper 6, Graduate School of Business, University of Cape Town, November 1978.

First, Ruth, Steele, Jonathan, and Gurney, Christabel, *The South African Connection: Western Investment in Apartheid*, Harmondsworth, Middx, Penguin African Library, 1972.

Foreign Policy Study Foundation Inc., *South Africa: Time Running Out*, the Report of the Study Commission on US Policy Toward Southern Africa, Berkeley, University of California Press, 1981.

Frederickson, George M., *White Supremacy: a Comparative Study in American and South African History*, New York, Oxford University Press, 1981.

Freeman, Orville L., and Persen, William, 'Multinational Corporations: Hope for the Poorest Nations', *The Futurist*, December 1980, pp. 3–11.

Friedman, Milton, and Friedman, Rose, *Free to Choose: a Personal Statement*, Harmondsworth, Middx, Penguin Books, 1980.

Galbraith, J.K., *The Nature of Mass Poverty*, Cambridge, Mass., Harvard University Press, 1979.

Geldenhuys, Deon, ed., *The South African Labour Scene in the 1980's*, discussions of the Study Group on Multinational Corporations, Study Group Series No. 3, South African Institute of International Affairs, December 1980.

Gershenkron, A., *Economic Backwardness in Historical Perspective: a Book of Essays*, Cambridge, Mass., The Belknap Press of Harvard University, 1966.

Gladwin, Thomas N. and Walter, Ingo, *Multinationals Under Fire: Lessons in the Management of Conflict*, New York, John Wiley and Sons, 1980.

Golino, Frank R., *The Experience with the Implementation of the Sullivan Code and Prospects for the Future*, Enclosure 1. Johannesburg A–46, South African Institute of International Affairs, 24 June 1980.

Gordon, Kermit, ed., *Agenda for the Nation*, Washington D.C., The Brookings Institute, 1968.

Greenberg, Stanley B., *Race and State in Capitalist Development: Comparative Prospectives*, New Haven and London, Yale University Press, 1980.

Grubel, H.G., *International Economics*, Illinois, Richard D. Irwin, 1981.

Grundy, Kenneth W., 'Intermediary Power and Global Dependency: *the Case of South Africa*', *International Studies Quarterly*, vol. 20 (4), December 1976, p.553–81.

Hagen, Everett, E., *The Economics of Development*, Illinois, 3rd edn, Richard D. Irwin, Inc., 1980.

Harvey, Donald F., *Business Policy and Strategic Management.*

Hauck, David, Voorhes, Meg, and Goldberg, Glenn, *Two Decades of Debate: the Controversy over U.S. Companies in South Africa*, Washington, D.C., Investor Responsibility Research Center, 1983.

Heilbroner, Robert L., *Between Capitalism and Socialism. Essays in Political Economics*, New York, Vintage Books, 1970.

Heilbroner, Robert L., *Economic Means and Social Ends. Essays in Political Economics*, NJ, Englewood Cliffs, Prentice–Hall 1969.

Heilbroner, Robert L, and Thurow, Lester C, *The Economic Problem*, 5th ed, Englewood Cliffs, N.J., Prentice–Hall 1978.

Hero, A.O., and Barrett, J. eds, *The American People and South Africa*, Cape Town, David Philip, 1981.

Hicks, J., *Casualty in Economics*, Oxford, Basil Blackwell, 1979.

Hodgetts, Richard M., *Management: Theory, Process and Practice*, 3rd edn, CBS College Publishing, The Dryden Press, 1982.

Hutzel, John M., *Strategy Formulation in the Multinational Business Environment: a Guide to International Political Forecasting*, Institute for Business and Economic Research, School of Business, San Jose State University, California, 1974.

Idris–Soven, Ahamed, Idris–Soven, Elizabeth, and Vaughan, Mary K., ed, *The World as a Company Town: Multinational Corporations and Social Change*, The Hague, Paris, Mouton 1978.

International Affairs Bulletin, Johannesburg, vol. 3. no. 2 (September 1979), and vol. 4, nos. 1, 2 and 3. The South African Institute of International Affairs.

International Affairs Bulletin, vol. 4, no. 1, 1980,. Johannesburg, South African Institute on International Affairs.

International Affairs Bulletin, vol. 4, no. 2, 1980, Vale, Peter C.J. ed, Johannesburg, The South African Institute of International Affairs, 1980.

International Affairs Bulletin, vol. 4, no. 3, 1980. Johannesburg,

The South African Institute of International Affairs, 1980.

International Labour Office, *Multinational Enterprises and Social Policy*, Geneva, ILO Publications, 1973.

Investor Responsibility Research Center Inc., *Foreign Investment in South Africa*, Washington, DC, 1984.

Jackson, Richard A., ed., *The Multinational Corporation and Social Policy: Special Reference to General Motors in South Africa*, New York, Praeger Publishers, 1974.

Jenkins, Rhys, 'The Export Performance of Multinational Corporations in Mexican Industry' in *Trade and Poor Economies*.

Johnson, Paul, *A History of the Modern World from 1917 to the 1980s*, London, Weidenfeld and Nicolson, 1983.

Kane–Berman, John, *Apartheid and Business: an Analysis of the Rapidly Evolving Challenge facing Companies with Investments in South Africa*, a Business International Multi-client Study Prepared by Business International SA, Geneva, October 1980.

Kaplan, A., *The Conduct of Inquiry*, San Francisco, Chandler, 1964.

Kaplan, Dr. Dave (and Bishton, Dr. Bob), *Are Multinationals a Positive Factor in Developing Economies?* UCT Commerce Students' Council, SRC Press, UCT, Sept. 1981.

Keegan, Warren J., *Multinational Marketing Management*, 2nd ed, Engelwood Cliffs, N.J., Prentice–Hall, Inc., 1980.

Kheel, T., *Guide to Fair Employment Practices*, Englewood Cliffs, NJ, Prentice–Hall, 1964.

Kindleberger, Charles P., *International Economics*, 5th edn, Irwin Inc., 1973.

Kindleberger, Charles P., *Power and Money: the Politics of International Economics and the Economics of International Politics*, Macmillan Student Editions., London, Basic Books Inc. 1970.

Kitchen, Helen, and Clough, Michael, vol. II, no. 6,. Significant Issues Series, *The United States and South Africa: Realities and Red Herrings.*, Washington D.C., Centre for Strategic and International Studies, 1984.

Kitchen, Helen, *The Washington Papers/98* vol. XI, *U.S. Interests in Africa*, New York, CSIS and Praeger Publishers.

Kolakowski, Leszek, and Hampshire, Stuart, eds, *The Socialist Idea: a reappraisal*, Quartet Books, 1977.

Kumar, Krishna, and Mcleod, Maxwell G., *Multinationals from Developing Countries*, Lexington, Mass., Lexington Books, 1981.

Lansing, John B. and Morgan, James N., *Economic Survey Methods*. 5th Printing, Michigan, The Survey Research Centre of the Institute for Social Research, 1977.

Lake, Anthony, *The 'Tar Baby' Option: American Policy Toward Southern Rhodesia*, New York, Columbia University Press, 1976.

Lall, Sanjaya, *The Multinational Corporation*, London, Macmillan 1980.

Leadership, 'Disinvestment' issue, June 1985, Johannesburg.

Lee, C.H. *The Quantitative Approach to Economic History*, London, Martin Robertson, 1977.

Leatt, James, 'Corporate Responsibility and South Africa's Political Economy: Philanthropy or the Exercise of Power?' Inaugural Lecture, UCT, 17 October 1984.

Leftwich, Richard H., and Sharp, Ansel M., *Economics of Social Issues*, Texas, Business Publications, Inc., 1982. 5th Ed.

Liebhaberg, Bruno, *Industrial Relations and Multinational Corporations in Europe*, Aldershot, Gower Publishing Co. Ltd., 1980. England.

Lindblom, Charles, E., *Politics and Markets: the World's Political-Economic Systems*, New York, Basic Books, 1977.

Lindert, P.H. and Kindleberger, C.P, *International Economics*, 7th edn, Richard D. Irwin, 1982.

Lipton, Michael, *Why Poor People Stay Poor — Urban Bias in World Development*, London, Maurice Temple Smith, 1977.

Lombard, B. Urban, *Labour Market Discrimination and Human Resources Management in South Africa*, Pretoria, Educational Publishers, 1981.

Lonsdale, John, 'From Colony to Industrial State: South African historiography as seen from England' in *Social Dynamics*, vol. 9, no. 1., Centre for African Studies, University of Cape Town, 1983, pp. 67–83.

Lucas, Robert E. Jr, and Sargent, Thomas J., eds, *Rational Expectations and Econometric Practice*, London, Allen & Unwin, 1981.

Lutz, Mark A, and Lux, Kenneth, *The Challenge of Humanistic Economics*, California, The Benjamin/Cummings Publishing Co. Inc., 1979.

Mackler, Ian, *Pattern for Profit in Southern Africa*, Lexington, Mass., D.C. Heath and Co., 1972.

Masini, Jean, Ikonicoff Moises, Jedlicki, Claudio, and Lanzarotti, Mario, *Multinationals and Development in Black Africa*, Saxon House, 1979.

Mattelart, Armand, *Multinational Corporations and the Control of Culture — The Ideological Apparatuses of Imperialism*, Brighton, Sussex, Harvester; New Jersey, Humanities Press, 1982.

May, Ernest R., *'Lessons' of the Past: the Use and Misuse of History in American Foreign Policy*, New York, Oxford University Press, 1973.

McClelland, P.D. *Casual Explanation and Model Building in History, Economics and the New Economic History*, Ithaca and London, Cornell University Press, 1975.

Miles, Robert H., in collaboration with Camerson, Kim S, *Coffin Nails and Corporate Strategies*, Englewood Cliffs, NJ, Prentice-Hall, Inc., 1982.

Modern American Literature, Voice of America — Forum Lectures, Washington, 1977.

Moran, Theodore H., *Multinational Corporations and the Politics of Dependence — Copper In Chile*, Princeton, NJ, Princeton University Press, 1974.

Murray, Robin, ed., *Multinationals Beyond the Market*, Brighton, Sussex, Harvester 1981.

Mutloatse, Mothobi, ed., *Forced Landing.*, Africa South: Contemporary Writings, Johannesburg, Ravan Press, 1980.

'Multinationals: a Survey'; supplement to *Financial Mail*, Johannesburg, 27 June 1980.

Muller, Graham, 'Multinational Companies in South Africa' in Matthews, J., (ed.) *South Africa in the World Economy.*, Johannesburg, McGraw-Hill, 1983.

Myers, Desaix III, with Propp, Kenneth, Hauck, David, and Liff, David M; *U.S. Business in South Africa: the Economic, Political and Moral Issues.* Bloomington, Indiana University Press, Investor Responsibility Research Center Inc., 1980.

McPherson, Michael S., 'The Economic Prerequisite to Democracy', in *Challenge; The Magazine of Economic Affairs*, New York, M.E. Sharpe Inc., January/February 1982.

Nakasa, Nat — see Patel.

Nattrass, Jill, *The South African Economy: its Growth and*

Change, Cape Town, Oxford University Press, 1981.

Nedbank Group Economic Unit, South Africa: an Appraisal, 2nd edn, Johannesburg. The Nedbank Group Ltd., June 1983.

Negandhi, Annant R., ed., Functioning of the Multinational Corporation.' a Global Comparative Study, Pergamon, Pergamon Policy Studies, Oxford, 1980.

Newens, Stan, Ed., Third World: Change or Chaos, The Bertrand Russell Peace Foundation Ltd., for Spokesman, Nottingham, 1977.

Nöffke, Carl, 'Paper on Divestment', a Presentation to the M.M.F., South Africa, 22 November, 1984.

Nsekela, Amon, J., ed., Southern Africa Toward Economic Liberation, London, Rex Collings, 1981.

O'Dowd, M.C., Multinational Corporations in S.A. — What Are Their Options?, South Africa Foundation., Briefing Papers No. 24, Atone Press, June 1980.

O'Mahony, Patrick J., Multinationals and Human Rights, Great Britain, Mayhew–McCrimmon Ltd., 1980.

Olson, Prof. Keith W., updated this volume (originally Dr Wood Gray and Dr Richard Hofstadter), An Outline of American History, United States Information Service, 1976.

Patel, Essop, ed., The World of Nat Nakasa, Johannesburg, Ravan Press/Bateleur Press, 1975.

Penny Joshua, The Life and Adventures of Joshua Penny. Cape Town, South African Library, 1982.

Poolman, Joseph, Aspekte van die Invloed van Buitelandse Ondernemings op die Bestuur van hulle Suid–Afrikaanse Filiale. PhD thesis, University of Pretoria, 1972.

Radice, Hugo, ed., International Firms and Modern Imperialism, Harmondsworth, Middx, Penguin Modern Economic Readings, 1975.

Randall, Dudley, ed., The Black Poets, New York, Bantam Books, March 1972. (3rd Printing).

Razis, Vincent Victor, Swords or Ploughshares? Johannesburg, Ravan Press, 1980.

Razis, Vincent Victor, 'What of Business in 50 years?' and 'The Big Questions for Big Business', in Sunday Times/Business News. 1 and 8 January, 1984.

Razis, Vincent Victor, 'US Policy on South Africa', in Wilson, Francis, ed., South African Outlook, vol. 109, no. 1295, 1979.

Razis, Vic, 'A Pragmatic Look at Disinvestment', Management,

Johannesburg, September 1985, pp. 14–16.

Revel, Jean–François, *The Totalitarian Temptation*, Harmondsworth, Middx, Penguin Books, 1978.

Richman, Barry M. and Copen, Melvyn, *International Management and Economic Development*, New York, McGraw–Hill, 1972.

Ricks, David A., *International Dimensions of Corporate Finance*, Englewood Cliffs, NJ, Prentice–Hall Foundations of Finance Series, 1978.

Robock, Stefan H., Simmonds, Kenneth and Zwick, Jack, *International Business and Multinational Enterprises*, rev. edn, US Richard D. Irwin Inc., 1977.

Rodriguez, Rita M. and Carter, Eugene E, *International Financial Management*, Prentice–Hall Inc., 1976.

Rogers, Barbara, *White Wealth and Black Poverty*, Englewood Cliffs. N.J. Greenwood Press, 1976.

Rostowsky, H, ed., *Industrialisation in Two Systems: Essays in Honour of Alexander Gershenkron*. New York, John Wiley 1966.

Rothstein, Robert L., *The Weak in the World of the Strong the Developing Countries in the International System*, New York, Columbia University Press, 1977.

Roumeliotis, Panayotis V. and Golemis, Charalambos P., *Transfer Pricing and the Power of Transnational Enterprises in Greece Intra–Firm Transactions and Their Impact on Trade and Development*, at IDS/UNCTAD Seminar: 7–11 November 1977.

Rousseas, Stephen, Return of the Economic Royalists in *Challenge*. The magazine of Economic Affairs, New York, M.E. Sharpe Inc., January/February 1982, pp. 36–43.

Rugman, Alan M, ed., *New Theories of the Multinational Enterprise*, London, Croom Helm.

Rugman, Alan M., *Inside the Multinationals: the Economics of Internal Markets*, London, Croom Helm 1981.

Rugman, Alan M., Lecraw, Donald J., and Booth, Laurence D., *International Business: Firm and Environment*, New York, McGraw–Hill Series in Management, 1985.

Sampson, Anthony, 'A Venture into the New Africa', *Drum*, London, Collins, 1956.

Sampson, Anthony, *The Sovereign State: the Secret History of ITT*, London, Coronet, 1974.

Schiavo–Campo, Salvatore; and Singer, Hans W., *Perspectives of*

Economic Development, Boston, Houghton Mifflin Company, 1970.

Schmidt, Elizabeth, *Decoding Corporate Camouflage*, US Business Support for Apartheid, USA, Institute of Policy Studies, 1980.

Schrire, Robert, ed., *South Africa: Public Policy Perspectives*, Cape Town, Juta and Company Ltd., 1982.

Schumpeter, Joseph A., *History of Economic Analysis*, New York, Oxford University Press, 1954.

Siedman, Ann, *An Economics Textbook for Africa*, 3rd edn, London and New York, Methuen, 1980.

Seidman, Ann and Makgetla, Neva, *Outposts of Monopoly Capitalism — Southern Africa in the Changing Global Economy*, Connecticut, Lawrence Hill and Co.; and London, Zed Press, 1980.

Seidman, Ann and Makgetla, Neva, 'Transnational Corporate Involvement in South Africa's Military Build–up', *Journal of Southern African Affairs*, vol. IV, no. 2, April 1979.

Serfaty, Simon, 'The Historical Legacy of the Reagan Administration' in *International Affairs Bulletin*, vol. 5, no. 2, pp. 45–59, ed. Spicer, Michael, Johannesburg, South African Institute of International Affairs, 1981.

Shapiro, Edward, *Macroeconomic Analysis*, 5th ed, New York, Harcourt Brace Jovaovich, Inc., 1982.

Simpson, David, *The Political Economy of Growth, Classical Political Economy and The Modern World*, Oxford, Basil Blackwell, 1983.

Sitas, Fred, 'Health and Safety Conditions in Witwatersrand Foundries', *Carnegie Enquiry into Poverty and Development*, vol. 9, paper 112, 1984.

Social Dynamics, vol. 6, no. 1, 1980, University of Cape Town, 1980.

Solarz, Stephen, *Leadership S.A.*, Third Quarter 1984, vol. 3, no. 3, p. 114–17.

South African Institute of Race Relations, *Towards Economic and Political Justice in South Africa*, Papers and Discussions of the 50th Anniversary Conference of the SA Institute of Race Relations, Johannesburg, SA Institute of Race Relations, 1980.

S.A. Journal of Economics. vol. 51, no. 1, Pretoria, March 1983.

Spegele, Roger D., 'Deconstructing Methodological Falsificationism in International Relations', *American Political Science Review*, vol. 74, 1980, pp. 104–21.

South African Outlook — Labour Codes, vol. 109, no. 1295, Cape, Outlook Publications (Pty) Ltd., May 1979.

Spero, Joan Edelman, *The Politics of International Economic Relations*, New York, 2nd edn, St Martin's Press, 1981.

Stockwell, John, *In Search of Enemies: A.C.I.A. Story*, New York, W.W. Norton, 1978.

Stretton, Hugh, *Capitalism and Socialism and the Environment*, Cambridge, Cambridge University Press, 1976.

Sweezy, Paul M. and Bettelheim, Charles, *On the Transition to Socialism*, Monthly Review Press, 1971.

Tanter, Raymond, and Ullman, Richard H, eds, *Theory and Policy in International Relations*, written under the auspices of the Center of International Studies, Princeton University, NJ.

Terpstra, Vern, *International Marketing*, 2nd edn, USA, The Dryden Press, 1978.

Thomas, J. Mark, 'Reagan in the State of Nature' in *South African Outlook*, vol. 114, no. 1360, pp. 154–156, Cape, October 1984.

Thompson, Kenneth and Tunstall, Jeremy, eds, *Sociological Perspectives*, Harmondsworth, Middx., Penguin Education, 1973.

Thurell, Lars H., *Political Risks in International Business: Investment Behaviour of Multinational Corporations*. New York, Praeger Publishers, 1977.

TNC's in Brazil's Electrical Industry in *Trade and Poor Economies*.

Tugendhat, Christopher, *The Multinationals*, Harmondsworth, Middx., Pelican Library of Business and Management, 1978.

Turner, Richard, *The Eye of the Needle: Towards Participating Democracy in South Africa*, Johannesburg, Ravan Press, 1980.

UNCTAD, extract from *Major Issues Arising from the Transfer of Technology to Developing Countries*, New York, 1975.

United Nations Economic and Social Council, *Transnational Corporations in World Development: a Re–examination*, Commission on Transnational Corporations Fourth Session, 15–26 May 1978, Item 7 (a) of the provisional agenda. 20 March 1978.

Usher, Dan, *The Economic Prerequisite to Democracy*, Oxford, Basil Blackwell, 1981.

Vaizey, John, *Capitalism and Socialism — A History of Industrial Growth*, London, Weidenfeld and Nicholson, 1980.

Van der Merwe, Hendrik W., *Business and Race Discrimination in South Africa*, luncheon meeting of the International Relations Section of Town Hall, Los Angeles, 23 June, 1980.

Vaitsos, Constantine V., *The Attitudes and Role of Transnational Enterprises in Economic Integration Processes Among the LDC's*, London School of Economics, 14–15 October 1977.

Vaitsos, Constantine V., *Intercountry Income Distribution and Transnational Enterprises*, Oxford, Clarendon Press, 1974.

Vaitsos, Constantine V., *The Integration of Latin America with the Rest of the World in View of the Operations of Subsidiaries of TNE's, Intra–firm Transactions and Their Impact on Trade and Development*, at IDS/UNCTAD Seminar: 7–11 November 1977.

Vernon, Raymond and Wells, Louis T. Jr, *Manager in the International Economy*, 4th edn, Englewood Cliffs, NJ, Prentice Hall Inc., 1981.

Vital, David, *The Survival of Small States: Studies in Small Power/Great Power Conflict*, London, Oxford University Press, 1971.

Waltz, Kenneth N., 'The Myth of National Interdependence' in *The International Corporation*, Kindleberger Ed, Boston, Mass, MIT Press, 1970.

Wells, Sidney J., with revisions by Brassloff, E.W., *International Economics*, rev. ed, London, G Allen and Unwin Ltd., 1973.

Westcott, Gill and Wilson, Francis, eds, *Economics of Health in South Africa*, vol. I, *Perspectives on the Health System*. Johannesburg, Ravan Press, 1979.

Weston, J. Fred and Sorge, Bart W., *Guide to International Finance Management*, USA, McGraw–Hill, Inc., 1977.

Whiteley, Paul, ed., *Models of Political Economy*, London and Beverley Hills, Sage Publications, 1980.

Whisson, M.G., 'The Sullivan Principles', in *Social Dynamics* vol. 6, no. 1, 1980, UCT, 1980.

Widstrand, Carl, ed., *Multinational Firms in Africa*, Uppsala, Scandinavian Institute of African Studies, 1975.

Wiles, P.J.D., *Economic Institutions Compared*, Oxford, Basil Blackwell, 1977.

Wilson, Francis, in Butler and Thompson, *Change in Contemporary South Africa*, Berkeley, California University Press, 1975.

Wilson, Francis, *Migrant Labour in South Africa*, Johannesburg, The South African Council of Churches and Sprocas, 1972.

Wilson, Francis, and Westcott, Gill, eds, *Economics of Health in South Africa*, vol. II, *Hunger, Work and Health*. Johannesburg, Ravan Press, 1980.

Wilson, J.S.G. and Scheffer, C.F. eds, *Multinational Enterprises — Financial and Monetary Aspects*, Leiden, A.W. Sijthoff, 1974.

Wintrop, Norman, ed, *Liberal Democratic Theory and its Critics*, London, Croom Helm, 1983.

World Bank, *World Bank Annual Report 1981*, World Bank, Washington, 1981.

The World Bank, *World Development Report*, Washington 1981.

Wright, Harrison N., *The Burden of the Present, liberal–radical controversy over Southern African history*, Cape Town, David Philip, 1977, with London, Rex Collins.

Yach, Derek, 'Smoking and Poverty', *Carnegie Enquiry into Poverty and Development*, vol. 14, paper 178, 1984.

Young, Oran R., *Systems of Political Science*, Englewood Cliffs, NJ, Prentice–Hall 1968.

Yudelman, David, 'Industrialisation, Race Relations and Change in South Africa.' *African Affairs*, vol. 74, no. 294., January 1975, pp. 82–96.

Index

(Note: the word *passim* indicates that the subject so annotated is referred to in scattered passages throughout the pages indicated.)